Rediscover Your Heart

Rediscover Your Heart

Seven Keys for

Personal and

Planetary

Transformation

FRED MATSER

FINDHORN PRESS

ISBN 978-1-84409-164-5

Back cover inside flap photograph of Fred Matser
by Elizabeth Handy, reproduced with kind permission of the
photographer and which first appeared in the book,
The New Philanthropists by Charles and Elizabeth Handy
(Heinemann 2006 and now in paperback).
Photo of Deepak Chopra by Jeremiah Sullivan

Compiled and edited by Jacqueline Young
Cover and interior design by Damian Keenan
Typeset in Adobe Garamond Pro
Printed and bound in the European Union

1 2 3 4 5 6 7 8 9 10 11 12 14 13 12 11 10 09

Published by
Findhorn Press
305a The Park, Findhorn
Forres IV36 3TE
Scotland, UK

Telephone
+44 (0)1309 690 582
Fax
+44 (0)131 777 2711

info@findhornpress.com
www.findhornpress.com

Dedication

I dedicate this book to all people who are willing to experience life in its fullness and who are willing to take risks and go beyond their comfort zones to serve humanity and our beautiful planet with a caring and sharing attitude.

I also dedicate this book to my wonderful parents, children and wife whom I love dearly and for whom I also wrote this.

CONTENTS

PART I
BIOGRAPHY— 'I CHANGE'

CONTENTS

PART II –
PHILOSOPHY— 'BEING THE CHANGE'

CONTENTS

PART III –
CONTRIBUTIONS— 'VISIONS OF CHANGE'

CONTENTS

Acknowledgements

Way back in 1994, Caroline Myss suggested that I write a book about what she called "The transformation of a businessman into a pioneer in the field of spirit". Due to a combination of laziness and being too busy, I did nothing until I talked about it with my very good friend, Jacqueline Young.

I had done some writing before but never a whole book about my life experiences and ideas. I wanted to write in English because of the potential to reach more people, compared to my native, Dutch-language market. I needed help and Jackie, a British writer and author, skilful and great to work with, was just the right person.

I am grateful to Jackie for all the time, love and care that she has put into this book. I also want to thank my secretary, Michele, my former P.A., Clementine, Rola and John Nelson for their participation. I also owe special thanks to Simenon for his thoughtful work in the latter stages of the development of the first edition of the book.

I feel honoured that Mikhail Gorbachev and Deepak Chopra were willing to write the Foreword and Afterword for the book; I also thank Jane Goodall for her kind words for the book jacket. My heartfelt gratitude to you all! I really cherish your friendship.

In the latter of the book you will find uplifting contributions from some of my friends and acquaintances: to all of you who have contributed, I thank you very much!

When I first met my publisher, Thierry Bogliolo, at the Book Fair in Frankfurt, I immediately had a good feeling about him. I thank him for having the courage, with Findhorn Press, to travel with me on this journey.

I am also grateful to all my spiritual teachers for their inspiration and support. I wish to thank especially the late Professor van Praag and Glynda Yoder for their important teachings. In my previous business career I also had the support of many dedicated people of whom I would like to mention the late Mr. Blase, the late Mr. Koyck and my friends Hans Rood and Ids van der Zijpp. I also wish to express my gratitude to my former secretary Tineke, to Bert Jan and to Egon for their support in many ways.

Sincere thanks too to all those who kindly read the manuscript and shared their comments and suggestions with me: Chris, David, Diane, Dolf, Helene, Jerry, Patrick, Peter, Saskia, Pauline and Aldo and to Joanne Angel and Clare Jackson for their proof-reading.

Last, but not least, I would like wholeheartedly to thank my wife, Chris for her continuous loving support and understanding on all levels.

Most recently, following the successful launch of the book and its associated Rediscover Your Heart Awards in New York in July 2008, Jackie and I have collaborated again to compile this new UK edition of the book. The text has been extensively revised and updated and I am grateful to all those who contributed to this process with their valuable feedback after reading the first edition.

It has been a real joy to get lots of positive feedback and to hear from many people around the world how they have found the book inspiring and uplifting. This has really encouraged me and I feel grateful that the book and the awards are fulfilling their intended purpose of contributing in some small way to empowerment and inspiration.

Photo © White House Photo,
Courtesy Reagan Library, PD

Foreword

I have known Fred Matser for many years now. I first met him during my visit to the United States in May 1992. Among the thousands of people I have met during my trips abroad he stands out as a remarkable person, a true humanitarian, a man of deeds rather than words.

I have no doubt Fred could have maintained a successful career in business, continuing his family's tradition, but he chose a different path. His heart and mind reach out to disadvantaged people, particularly children, in various parts of the world. He wants to help, and he looks for ways of helping that, rather than making people dependent on more aid, empower them and provide them with the tools to be in control of their lives. I have always thought that this is the best way of fighting poverty and underdevelopment.

When Russia was going through a time of hardship after the break-up of the Soviet Union, Fred was truly a friend in need. His generous donation helped the Gorbachev Foundation to restart and complete a project that saved the lives of hundreds of children with leukaemia. He also helped my late wife Raisa to launch The Raisa Gorbachev's Club, an initiative that is still ongoing, bringing together Russian women in a search for solutions to the social problems of Russian society.

Fred's concern for the environment is genuine, forward-looking and practical. He was of great help in establishing Green Cross International, which I founded to promote awareness of environmental problems and spur people to act in the face of the global environmental crisis—the greatest challenge to mankind's future. Fred's suggestions were instrumental in launching the Legacy Project, aimed at addressing the environmental consequences of the arms race, and in drafting the Earth Charter—a set of 'commandments' for a harmonious relationship between Man and Nature.

For me, Fred represents the emerging global civil society—the widening transnational network of people who want to see globalisation with a human face. I believe that the role of such people and their organisations is extremely important and is bound to grow. In fact, I would say that both Fred and I are doing our best to make it happen.

It is necessary because the challenges of the twenty-first century are many and they are daunting. To some they seem insurmountable, a cause for despair and even panic. But that is not how it should be. Remember how our common efforts during the 1980s helped stop the nuclear arms race and end the Cold War. When it seemed to many that the momentum of confrontational politics was unstoppable, that mankind was rapidly moving toward the edge of a precipice, we did not panic. We acted—by protesting in the streets, by developing people-to-people contacts, by negotiating agreements. That is why walls fell, armies disengaged, and missiles were scrapped.

Politicians have not made good use of the opportunities created by the end of the Cold War. Enormous amounts of money are still being wasted on weapons production and trade and industrialised nations are not doing nearly enough to help the poor and the disadvantaged and to save the environment. Politics is lagging behind the rapidly evolving global processes. Without the prodding from civil society, from activists and advocates for the poor and for the environment, politicians would continue to drag their feet while the world's problems multiply—while the climate warms, while pollution increases, while the poor go hungry.

We need many more people like Fred Matser if we are to learn to live sustainably and humanely in our global world. We need millions of men and women with the vision, integrity and ability to act so that they can make a difference for hundreds of millions of others. One person setting an example can help and inspire many others. This is what Fred has been doing. He is a real leader.

Mikhail Gorbachev
Former President of the USSR
Founder and President, the Gorbachev Foundation
Chairman of the Board, Green Cross International
Nobel Peace Prize Laureate
Moscow, 2008

About Fred

There are many global citizens in the world but Fred Matser is a Universal Citizen. With Fred every man, every woman, every child has universal equal rank regardless of how the world perceives them. The famous and the unknown are treated with the same warmth, friendliness, and respect. This is the source of his charismatic approach to all things. He expresses his genuine Heart in the form of networking for good, creating caring projects for the most vulnerable, and spreading good cheer and oneness with "twinkling eyes". Those of us who know Fred know the universal respect he gives and the universal response he receives. In *Rediscover Your Heart*, the reader is privileged to information and personal history that Fred rarely discusses in person. He is truly the forerunner Citizen for a transformed world.

Glynda Yoder, friend since 1986.

One of the Billions—An Invitation

Dear Reader,

Like you, I am just one of the billions of people and life forms on this planet. At the same time, I feel a real respons-Abil-ity to cooperate with my fellow human beings to inspire and support a global transformation into a more caring and sharing society.

In my own life, I have travelled a path from modest beginnings through several surprising turns of events to positions of responsibility and leadership. I ran a property development company from a relatively young age and had some amazing paranormal experiences that changed my view of reality. During that time, I became aware of suffering in the world on many levels. I gradually became more interested in initiating and fund-ing creative approaches toward healthcare, the environment and peace building. On the way I have met many remarkable healers, humanitarians, public figures and other extraordinary individuals. The overriding themes of my work have been inspiration and empowerment through personal and planetary change.

Like many people, I have experienced personal tragedy and suffering. At the same time I have shared in abundant love and joy and have witnessed first hand how hope, inspiration and love can transform people's lives. I've also enjoyed watching the unfolding of various initiatives, including the Twinkling Eyes Club that I founded, spreading 'miles of smiles' around the globe. Through all this I learned to become more compassionate and I am still learning.

Part I of the book tells my life story and how I changed as the result of experi-ences and inspiration along the way. At the end of each chapter you will find some Reflections where I consider what I learnt on my journey. I also give the Keys for personal and planetary transformation that these experiences inspired me to formulate. You may like to use these, or the affirmations that accompany them, to reflect on your own life. In Part II I examine how we can all 'be the change' and share some guiding principles that could transform the way we live on this planet. Part III has contributions from a host of wonderful friends and acquaintances: children, women, and men; young and old; influential and renowned people and those much lesser known. All share their personal dreams for change and visions for the future.

As this book goes to print we find ourselves in the midst of an economic crisis that has not found its counterpart in this generation. Although for many of us this situation is difficult and painful, and may still become worse, it is also an opportunity to cleanse and repair dysfunctional systems and to change values that have hindered our society. These include abuse of power, financial greed and mismanagement. We now have a real chance to rethink our social and economic systems and cooperate to transform our world. We also have the opportunity to reflect on ourselves and our relationships with our families, friends and close associates.

I hope that what I have shared in this book will inspire you, dear reader, to think about these new opportunities and will encourage you on your own journey to rediscover your heart.

I invite you to turn the page and travel the journey with me.

Fred Matser,
The Netherlands, 2009

PART I

Biography - 'I Change'

"Love is in the Air—
Bring it Down to Earth"
Nina Matser

CHAPTER 1

The Shadow of War—the Birth of Peace

It was a dark, spring evening during the Second World War in the Netherlands when my parents heard a sudden, loud knock on the front door. A chill of fear went through them as they looked at each other, for the country was then under German occupation. Since my father worked secretly as part of the Dutch underground, he was always alert to the dangers of being discovered. So he quietly sprinted upstairs to a safe hideout under the floorboards. Meanwhile, my heavily pregnant mother went to answer the door fearing that a Dutch collaborator might have betrayed my father.

She worried that German soldiers might barge in to search the home and was concerned for the safety of her two children sleeping upstairs: three-year-old Bobbie, who had a serious heart problem, and two-year-old Marjoke.

Yet opening the door my mother was very relieved to see a friendly Dutch police inspector she knew called Schön. He whispered, "I've come to tell you good news. The American and Canadian soldiers are on their way. We're going to be liberated!"

I can only imagine the relief that went through my mother on hearing this. She went upstairs as quickly she could manage to share this glorious news with my father. As she did so she felt the first strong contractions that signalled my imminent birth.

I was born shortly afterwards, in the spring of 1945, in my parents' bedroom in our modest brick house in the Dutch town of Hilversum. My parents had planned to name me Paul, but as that was the name of a Dutchman who had turned collaborator, they didn't feel it to be appropriate. Instead they agreed to name me Fred. Though it would have been more typical in Holland to have been named Frederik, for some reason they liked this name, and I have been called just 'Fred' all my life. Decades later someone pointed out that, in Swedish, my name actually meant 'peace'. This seemed very apt as I was born on the cusp of war and peace.

Eleven months after my birth, tragedy struck. My brother, Bob, who was only four years old, died from an infection linked to his heart problems. I can only imagine the utter heartbreak this caused my parents. Their grief must also have been compounded over the years by the knowledge that penicillin would probably have saved Bob's life, but at that time it was not available to them.

Bob's death was not openly discussed in our family and rarely mentioned. I imagine my parents felt that by suppressing their pain and hardships they could spare their surviving children their silent suffering. It was also uncommon at that time to discuss death with children. Since I was still only a baby, I have no recollection of the event yet, on reflection, I realise that I too have had difficulty in expressing emotions in my life.

Like so many others in the post-war years my parents could not dwell on painful events. Life needed to go on and, in common with others who had survived the war, they needed to focus on rebuilding their lives and providing for their young family.

A couple of years later, in 1948, my younger brother was born and my parents decided to name him, Paul. They still liked the name, and by then their memories of the war were beginning to fade a little. In 1952 my younger sister, Anke, was born bringing our family total to six. Yet this situation was only to last to the 1960s for further tragedy lay ahead.

My father and mother in the late 1950s

Family Life

Our family life was comfortable and happy but also quite strict and frugal. My mother ran the household in a tight budget and we had few extravagances. We were only allowed margarine and jam spread very thinly on our bread and given just a few thin slices of cheese each at mealtimes. A cooked egg was a once-a-week luxury on Sundays. Baths were also only a weekly luxury and were shared. The rest of the time my brother and I had to wash in cold water from a sink in the attic. At the time we children didn't like these deprivations and used to complain about them. Now, however, I feel they were a good foundation for life as it has made me truly appreciate luxuries such as good food, hot water and showers.

Bath night for all of us children was on Saturdays before dinner. My two sisters would share the bath water first and then it would be Paul's and my turn. I used to thoroughly enjoy our baths together. We would spend ages playing with little ducks and boats and other toys and look forward to our hot dinner and the family games that would follow. Saturday nights were a kind of party night. We would have great fun playing lots of games such as Monopoly or Scrabble with my parents. These simple Saturday get-togethers are some of the happiest memories of my childhood.

My mother was always at home and was really caring. She always did her best for the family, feeding and clothing us as well as she could and instilling good manners in us. Looking back I realise she must have been suffering a lot inwardly during this time, from the pain of losing Bob, yet she did not allow her grief to get in the way of giving us the best childhood she could.

In contrast to my mother, my father was away from home much of the time and was always busy working. He was a real entrepreneur. After some formal training he went to work in an estate agency. Later he set up on his own selling and letting property as well as buying land and developing projects. During the post-war period there was a huge need for housing. The government created many incentives to stimulate the economy, including tax breaks and subsidies for the building of social housing projects. My father, who had little money of his own, made full use of these incentives to build up his business, later called Johan Matser Ltd. He was one of the very first, if not the first, major independent property developers in the Netherlands. He was a man of vision and intelligence who used his courage and creativity to build a substantial property development company.

It was always expected that Paul and I would join my father's business. However, Paul and I were very different people and we never had that much in common other than our shared love of Dinky Toys and cars when we were young. Gradually we went our separate ways and, as I set my sights on other things, the expectation was that Paul would be the one who would follow in my father's footsteps. Yet this was sadly not to be.

Lessons from my Father

As my father's business began to thrive our family's financial situation improved and we were very fortunate to be able to travel abroad. When I was about ten years old my parents took my elder sister Marjoke and me on a trip to Belgium and Germany. Later on we also went on family holidays by car to places like France, Austria, Switzerland and Italy. It was quite unusual for Dutch families to travel abroad on holiday at that time so we were very fortunate. In fact, I remember being the first child in my primary school class to go outside of the Netherlands.

I found these trips incredibly exciting with all the new sights and experiences. My siblings and I fought a lot over who would sit by the car window in order to get the best view. I vividly remember seeing the great mountains, with their lakes and snow-capped peaks, for the first time. I had never seen mountains before, since my home country, the Netherlands, is almost entirely flat. I think these trips opened my eyes to a wider world.

My father's office was initially located behind the garage at the back of our home. As the business grew, he kept adding rooms until finally there was a five-room office in our back garden. This meant that our home life was not very private since anyone visiting the office had to pass through the little alleyway between the garage and our house.

In those days it was normal to work six days a week so, even on Saturdays, there would be a constant stream of people passing by and popping in our home. My mother was always making coffee. Perhaps these experiences have helped me to get along easily with all types of people.

My father had a strong sense of responsibility for his employees. For example, he loved to share and would give spontaneous bonuses when he had a successful business venture. Frequently he invited others to share in potentially lucrative business deals. On my parents' twenty-fifth wedding anniversary my father did something unknown in those days: he created a contribution-free pension fund for all his employees.

Despite this fund taking a huge chunk of his capital, he was pleased to be able to do it. It was important for my father to create the best conditions for his employees. He took a sincere interest in their welfare, visiting them at home or in hospital if they were sick. He also made a point of employing physically disabled people and giving them equal opportunities. All of these initiatives were quite

Ready for my ski test aged eleven

rare at the time, and illustrate his innovative and philanthropic approach that also inspired me in my own life. On very hot days, he was even known to close the office and take all his employees swimming in the nearby lake! He also had a good sense of humour and loved to play practical jokes.

I remember one time in particular when I accompanied him to a meeting with the Mayor of Hilversum. When the mayor had to leave the room for a moment my father, to my amazement, produced a fake dog pooh from his pocket. Winking at me, he mischievously placed it on the pristine carpet and waited for the mayor to return. Once the mayor was re-seated my father glanced over in the direction of the dog mess and the mayor followed his gaze. On seeing the mess, he jumped up with a horrified expression and ran out of the room calling for a cleaner. Meanwhile my father picked up the fake pooh and concealed it in his pocket. When the mayor returned with a cleaner and pointed to where the mess had been on the carpet there was nothing to be seen. He looked around in confusion while the cleaner just stared at him as if he were crazy. My father just smiled and said nothing but caught my eye and we both enjoyed the private joke.

School Days

My elementary school was a ten-minute walk from our home and I went there for six years. My main memory is of being forced to write with my right hand even though I was naturally left-handed. Although I think I was an able student I was not keen on doing my homework. At that time I was easily distracted and my main passion was sports. I especially loved hockey and would go to the hockey club at every opportunity. I also really liked skiing.

As a result my schoolwork suffered and I ended up having to repeat two grades in high school in order to catch up. Eventually I became more serious about my studies. I had a friend in the same class—two years older than me—who made the same decision. We studied hard together and finally I completed school successfully with quite good grades just after I turned nineteen. My intention was to study psychology or sociology at university. I was also interested in geography and economics because I had very good teachers in both subjects. The two of them inspired me and I wanted to learn more. However, things were to turn out completely differently for me.

An Unexpected Invitation

During my teenage years my father's health started to deteriorate. He was first diagnosed with diabetes in the late 1950s and then later with Parkinson's disease (rigid type). As his condition worsened, it became hard for him to keep his balance and he had increasing difficulty speaking. Saliva would dribble from his mouth, and he often had to hold his handkerchief over it. This was not easy for him, especially in his position as the head of quite a large company. Yet despite these difficulties he carried on working. By this time his company had several subsidiaries and at any given time, depending on the workload, he was employing from 120 to 200 people.

Every night after dinner my father would go for a walk. He was very conscientious about taking this exercise because of his diabetes. One of us children always had to go with him, and it was a choice between the walk and the washing up. The washing up was preferable because it took less time. So as a result my father often had to select one of us to accompany him on his walk.

On one occasion in the spring of 1964, my father picked me to walk with him. At that time I was in the process of trying to make up my mind which subject to study at university after passing my final exams at secondary school. I was expecting him to ask me about this during the walk. However, while we were walking down a lane lined with old trees, my father turned to me and, right out of the blue, asked me to join him in the family business.

I was shocked by the invitation. It was a complete turn around for my father. Throughout my school years his one focus had been on my getting good exam results so that I could further my studies at university. Yet now he was saying, "Come into my company instead of going on to higher studies and be my successor! I cannot wait for Paul because of my deteriorating health." Paul still had another two years to go at school, and I realised that my father must have been aware of how fast his health was declining and that he might not be able to continue his work as he had hoped.

Two years previously my father's company had moved to new premises, a big villa in a nearby neighbourhood. I realised that if I was going to work there I would be around my father all the time: I would see him in the office and I would also see him at home as I was still living there at that time. It would also mean giving up my own dreams of studying and being with my friends at university and living away from home at students digs. I felt very confused and did not know how to respond to my father's request. I said that I needed to think about it for a few days before giving him an answer. What should I do? I simply did not know.

After a couple of days I made the decision to agree to my father's request. Given his failing health I did not feel that I could say "No". Yet at the same time I was reluctant to give up my own life plans. I agreed to join the business for a period of one year on the condition that, at the end of this time, I would be free to reassess my choice. This decision of course also had implications for my brother Paul. He did not appear unduly concerned as he didn't seem to have a particular interest in the business at that time, nor even later as it turned out. So, after graduating from high school, I joined my father's business at the age of nineteen.

Growing Responsibility

My father's idea was that I should get experience in each of the different departments for several months—marketing, sales, development, financial administration, design, construction etc.—so that I could get a good overall picture of the business. I started out being a receptionist. To my utter surprise, after only one week, my father gave me a desk around the corner from his in the boardroom. He said that from now on I was going to be his assistant and he wanted me to participate in all the meetings. To my further surprise, without consulting me, he began introducing me as his successor. This statement was contrary to our agreement, which was that I had the freedom to make other choices at the end of the year. On the one hand I naturally felt pride that he was appointing me as such but on the other I felt trapped.

I found the board meetings dull and uninteresting and longed for 5.30 p.m., when I would leave immediately to join my friends who were enjoying student life in Utrecht. We had many good times drinking beer, partying and having fun. Often during my first professional year, I wouldn't get to bed until early in the morning but would then have to get up a few hours later to make it to the office by 8.30 a.m. It was quite a wild life. My friends were amazed that I could party and get up early for work while they were still asleep and actually so was I! I also continued to be involved in sports. In 1966, while working at my father's business, I trained intensively for the National Dutch Ski Championships. In the end I was unable to take part because, disappointingly, I broke my thumb in a ski fall two weeks before the championship. But that same year I became involved as a board member for the Dutch National Ski Association.

My deadline of a year at the company came and went. I continued to work with my father, uncertain of the future. Twice afterwards I asked my brother if he would take my place in the company. If he accepted I would then be able to begin my academic studies. However, both times he declined. The first time was right after he left school and the second was when he dropped out of university after a year of studying law. My sisters were not considered for this role since, at that time, it was still quite rare for women to hold positions of leadership. Since there was no one in the family to take my place, this made it very difficult for me to withdraw.

Eventually, after careful consideration, I decided to stay on with the company and make a more serious commitment to my job. I took weekly evening classes in Amsterdam to become a certified estate agent, as I thought this would be useful for the business. After two years I successfully passed the exams.

In getting to know the business, one of the things that helped me most was that I was not ashamed to ask lots of questions. In those days this approach was quite unusual as business structures were much more hierarchical than they are now. It was expected that one would unquestioningly follow the advice or suggestions of more senior staff. In asking all my questions, I came to realise that many people, even those much older and more experienced than me, often did not have answers to my questions or didn't really know what they were talking about. This gave me the confidence to learn and to develop my own ideas and ways of doing things as I realised there was more than one answer to questions and no set ways of doing things

Gradually I began to like the work more and enjoyed the challenge. At the age of twenty-three I was secretary to the board, at twenty-five I was a member of the Executive Committee and at twenty-seven I was made CEO. It was pretty unusual to be given this level of responsibility at such a young age, but my father's illness necessitated it.

I am grateful to all my colleagues and co-workers for having accepted and supported me in these positions. Looking back, I can also see that I had taken different positions of responsibility from a young age: for example in school and in the sports community, and perhaps fell naturally into that kind of role. Later, while working at my father's company, I also became involved in various national and international organisations related to property development and held some leadership positions[1]. I have always been keen to share ideas and learn from others. At the time I felt proud at having been elected to these various positions and I enjoyed much of the work in which I was involved because I felt I could really make a difference. However, looking back now, I feel more honoured and grateful than proud at having been given the opportunity to perform these roles. I realise that they gave me a wide range of experience both in, and outside of, the field of property development and also taught me so much about leadership and co-operation. This helped me a lot in developing my roles in the family business over the years.

When I was in my early thirties I was asked to become a board member of a much bigger company. I declined the offer as it would have meant leaving my father's company. However this offer meant a lot to me as I felt that I was not just being seen as the son of my father, or someone who had moved up in the business by default. I felt I was being recognised for my own talents and abilities.

While working at Johan Matser Ltd., I enjoyed the creative challenge of project development. I liked to figure out how to create space and make buildings attractive, functional and able to generate their own income. This led me to develop a new project that my father had started, to rejuvenate the centre of our hometown of Hilversum. Seeking to make best use of the available space, I developed a plan for a multifunctional centre with facilities not only for shopping but also for a health club. The new construction was designed to blend in with existing buildings. Our company also went on to develop an innovative football stadium that created office space underneath the stands and doubled up parking space use—for office workers during the week and football supporters at weekends[2].

---

1. I was a founding board member of the L'Association des Promoteurs Européens des Centres Commerciaux (APECCO), an association of European shopping centre developers, and of NEPROM (Vereniging van Nederlandse Projektontwikkeling Maatschappijen—the Association of Dutch Project Development Companies *(www.neprom.nl)*, which was recognised by the Dutch government as a representative organisation for the industry.

2. For further details of these projects, see Appendix A on pages 150-153.

Throughout this work I experienced huge support from my colleagues on the board and from other members of staff and the project teams. There were also very capable people who dealt with the construction side of things which freed me up to concentrate more on the creative side. To this day I feel very grateful for all this co-operation and support which enabled me to play a part in many useful and rewarding projects.

I Want to Quit!

I ended up doing this work full time from 1964 to 1982. Looking back, I can see that my work in property development was quite rewarding. However, I also remember a lot of difficult times as well, especially in the early years up to 1972, when I worked alongside my father. The difficulties came largely from my dual roles as son and company employee and were linked to my father's health, which worsened during this time. On the one hand I was my father's junior colleague on the board. On the other I was often his carer and interpreter in meetings. As my father's speech deteriorated I was one of the few who could understand him.

I would be the one to convey his opinions and wishes during negotiations and meetings. During these times I had my own, often different or even opposing, views and opinions that I also wanted to express. So often, once I had made my father's position clear, I would then speak again, expressing my own views. This was quite awkward and we had many difficult situations because of it.

It must also have been very frustrating for my father not to be able to express himself clearly and sometimes he resorted to other means. I remember one time when we were in a meeting and my father didn't agree with what was being said by the other participants. Because he could not clearly articulate what he wanted to say, he got up and shuffled to the room next door and returned with a stick and a pair of mini boxing gloves that he kept in a special cupboard full of jokey arte-facts. He put the gloves on the end of the stick and, to the great surprise of those present, started prodding the others with it to show he was prepared to fight over the issue.

As well as acting as interpreter, my physical care of my father at work included getting his handkerchief and mopping up the saliva from his lips or helping him eat food at lunchtime. While I of course gladly helped him whenever I could, it was still not an easy situation for either of us to combine these roles. In the office my father and I sat at facing desks in the same room. Quite often we would have differences of opinion about business issues and I found these conflicts both diffi-cult and draining. I realised that my father had a wealth of experience and insight and respected his views, but I also felt it was important to be true to my own convictions. Since I was not as good at compromising as my father, our disagreements were often quite heated.

At times it all got too much and I just wanted to quit. On one occasion after a big disagreement, I was so furious that I packed my bag and decided to leave. I was too embarrassed to walk out in front of the receptionist because of my emotional state and so I simply climbed out of the ground-floor window, jumped over the fence and went home. However, even then, I could not escape since I was still living with my parents and had to face my father when he came home. I felt completely trapped because, on the one hand, I had nowhere else to go and on the other, I did not feel that I could let my father and the other office workers down by leaving.

At the age of twenty-three I decided, while I was working, to take courses in business administration at the University of Amsterdam in my free time. This satisfied some of my desire to understand economics and business at a deeper level. All in all my time of working with my father was a mixed experience. I disliked the long meetings and the disagreements, but very much enjoyed the creative side of things and all the people contact. I learned a lot!

Dealing with Dishonesty

Our company had a good reputation for its integrity and our often innovative approaches. As pioneers in energy efficiency we were one of the first developers in the early seventies to build houses with a very high level of thermal insulation. We also won several awards in the field of design. While working in this field, I met many wonderful, good and honest people, but I also witnessed first hand the less attractive sides of the business and those who chose to take a dishonest path. The property development industry in the Netherlands did not have a very good reputation at the time, and there were many stories of corruption and bribery. In my working life in the industry I was exposed to this shady side several times and have always found it disturbing. One example of this was in the late 1970s, when I invited a contractor to visit my home to give an estimate for an extension to my house.

I had known this man, who was quite a bit older than me, for many years as he had done work for our company on several occasions. He had a solid reputation. I trusted him and knew his work was good and his prices fair, which was why I chose to invite him to give me an estimate. At the time he was negotiating a big contract to build houses with the technical department of our company.

To my surprise, when he came to give the estimate, he implied that if he was to get the contract for the housing project he could 'lose' the total cost for my own home extension within it. In other words, if he got the job with the company, I would get my home extension for free. I was appalled, especially as we had known each other for a long time and I thought he knew that I ran an honest business, and that each time he had been chosen to work for our company simply on merit. I told him directly that I would not be involved in such a deal.

Such offers or 'opportunities' can come up repeatedly in business life and many people may find them tempting. However, right from the outset, I made a decision that I would not accept them. That was because I chose, and choose now, to work with integrity, openness and honesty. I knew that this would have business consequences, and as a result of this stance our company certainly missed a number of both major and lesser business opportunities. I firmly believed that in place of these corrupt deals other genuine opportunities would come our way—which in fact they did. I feel it is simpler just to be honest and to be able to sleep with a clear conscience at night.

I expected the same stance from our employees and told them that if they were ever offered bribes they must inform me. One day one of them told me he had been offered a cut-price kitchen from one of our sub-contractors. I then asked around and discovered that several of our employees in charge of giving out contracts had already had such discounted kitchens installed! I did not sack them over this lapse, but made very sure that the practice was stopped and should not be repeated.

When I think about corruption, I feel lucky that I have never found myself in such challenging circumstances that might have compelled me to accept such offers. On the one hand, I do not feel that such behaviour is in my nature—it really goes against the grain of my personal beliefs. Yet, on the other hand, if my situation was different and I, or one of my children, were in dire straits, how can I know how I would act or react? I don't think anyone can ever say they will never behave in a particular way unless they are put to the test.

My Brother Paul

My younger brother Paul loved music, especially Latin American, and was keen on hi-fi sound systems and other sound equipment. As my father's health deteriorated, he felt that he wanted to help Paul settle in some sort of business as he had by then stopped studying at university. Knowing of Paul's love for music, my father had the idea of purchasing a music and electrical goods store for Paul to run.

The store sold radios, records, televisions, and some household appliances such as washing machines and fridges. On top of the store was an apartment for Paul to live in. Paul took on the job, but without huge enthusiasm. He was only in his very early twenties and was responsible for managing the large store with about twenty employees. The business was not doing very well and was losing money. It seemed like it was too much for Paul, although he appeared not to be unhappy.

On the 4th of August 1970 we received some dreadful news—a work colleague of Paul's called me in the morning saying that Paul hadn't turned up for work. He and another colleague had gone to Paul's apartment and, not getting a reply, they had gone in to look for him. They were horrified to find Paul dead. This news was the most dreadful shock for all our family. I had spoken to Paul on the phone just the evening before and he had seemed fine. It was so hard to understand what had happened. Yet our shock was about to become even worse as it soon became apparent that Paul had taken his own life. Nothing had prepared our family for this; we had no idea that he was even contemplating such action and we could not understand why he had done it.

In those days suicide was considered a taboo subject so the family, including me at the time, chose to hide the true details of Paul's death from most people. People were told that he had died from a heart problem, just like the earlier death of my brother Bob. Paul's suicide was rarely discussed openly thereafter, either in the family or outside of it. To this day we do not know why Paul took his own life and I still find it difficult to talk about because it is such a painful subject. However, gradually I felt that it was not right to hide the truth anymore, and so over the years I began to share what had happened with a few trusted friends. Nowadays suicide is more openly discussed but Paul's death remains a very sensitive subject for me and is still a source of great sadness.

At the time I was desperate to understand what had happened and to know why Paul had taken this action. I tried really hard to discover the reason, talking to people who had known him at the time, and trying to understand what he had been thinking and feeling—for he had left no note or explanation. I continued this for some time, but I never found any real answers.

However in March 2003, when I was in Spain with a group of friends, we happened to be put in touch with a well-known Peruvian medium living there. I had little experience of mediums and know that their activities and claims are sometimes controversial. Yet I also knew that they claimed to be able to communicate with those who have died and who may wish to pass on messages to their loved ones.

We went to meet the medium and, while we were together, she went into a trance and proceeded to give messages to everyone in the group by a process that has been described as channelling[3]. At a certain point she came to me and to my great surprise said, "Your brother is coming through. He is saying that he loves you very much and is in a good place now. He is saying that he had difficulties at first but now everything is fine."

I was amazed by these words since I had never met this woman before and none of us had spoken to her beforehand. I had travelled from a different country and I had not shared the story of my brother with any other members of the group. So I do not believe that she had any prior knowledge about me or my life; yet she was able to deliver such a personal and particularly relevant message to me.

I had no idea how to explain this phenomenon I realise that it can be easy to fake such messages by getting prior knowledge about a person and then pretending to obtain messages from the 'other side'. However, I could not see how this could have happened here. In any case it was wonderful to receive such an affirmative message, and it did give me more peace of mind about my brother Paul. Despite the sadness that I still feel about him I like to think that, in the words of the medium, he is indeed "in a good place" now.

Learning about Love

During my teenage years and early twenties, I had several girlfriends. I went through the experiences that most teenagers do—adjusting to my hormonal changes, overcoming shyness, falling in and out of love. Sometimes these experiences were disturbing to my rational mind but they opened up another side of life for me; that of deep emotions and feelings. It was an exploration for me in every sense of the word!

One time in 1972, when I was in Amsterdam for the day, I bumped into a friend, Ineke van den Oever, whom I had not seen for many years. Immediately I thought "Wow, what an attractive, original young lady! How could I have forgotten about her?" We went for a coffee and tried to arrange to meet again but several times we had to cancel. After a few months we finally had dinner together and immediately became very close. In fact, we stayed together from that day on! After some time I proposed and, in 1973 we got married and went on to

---

3. 'Channelling' in this context is defined as the reception of information by paranormal means. Mediums are said to be able to receive information via ESP (extra-sensory perception). I have read that this may be: auditory, where the medium hears voices internally giving them information; visual, where they 'see' images in their mind's eye; or kinaesthetic, where they experience a sensation, e.g. a smell or a sense of touch or a temperature change. Channelling is said to involve direct contact with another entity, sometimes described as an angel, a being from another planet or a disembodied spirit of some kind that communicates directly with the person or actually 'takes over' the person temporarily. In the latter case, the person apparently goes into trance beforehand and remembers little or nothing of what has been communicated during the channelling.

have three much-loved children: Nina (born 1974), Saskia (born 1976) and Lyke (born 1980).

In the beginning we had a good marriage and our future seemed bright. At the same time I felt quite a lot of stress from the burden of my responsibilities at work and at home. I used to work very hard and long hours. I went jogging long distances six days a week and I used to smoke and drink a bit to relieve tension. I developed these habits particularly in the latter years of my father's life as his condition deteriorated and, although not excessive in any way, I believe they were part of my way of coping.

Over time I became more interested in health and fitness and stress management. Today I no longer smoke, drink only very moderately and have found meditation to be a more effective method for stress relief. Yet at that time stress was a part of my life and it increased as my father's health declined even further.

Losing My Father

By 1977 my father's condition had deteriorated so much that my mother, even with a team of visiting nurses, could no longer care for him at home. We made the difficult decision to admit him to a hospital for round-the-clock care. It was just two kilometres from our home and the family was able to visit regularly.

I visited my father frequently but on the evening of the 6th of May 1977 something special happened that left a deep impression that remains with me to this day. We were alone in the room, and I was sitting at my father's bedside with my arm touching his, when he suddenly looked into my eyes and weakly, but purposefully, squeezed my arm while maintaining eye contact. In that moment, as our eyes met, I felt a deep connection between us, a kind of exchange of energy. I felt that my father was making a gesture toward me.

It was as if he wanted to share his being and heartfelt values with me. Our communication felt like one of those primitive rites of passage where the older, wise man passes on the mantle to his son. I felt that there was a kind of understanding between us and that he was saying that everything was OK and that he loved me. It was a very precious moment that is hard to put into words, but I remember leaving the hospital feeling deeply touched.

The hospital called our home early the next morning to say that my father had passed away at around 7.00 a.m. This dramatic news made me think about the previous evening even more. Had my father sensed he was about to die? Had he made that gesture knowing that it would be our final communication? Perhaps that is why that moment has made such a lasting impression on me.

Thinking about my father, one of the overriding memories of those who knew him would probably be his kindness. He had real compassion for anyone who was sick, and I can recall many stories of his acts of kindness for sick people, both in his company and neighbourhood and farther afield. If he learned of a particular need, he would try to respond to it. For example, he provided funding for the treatment of eye problems in Africa and also helped provide clean water in Bihar, India after reading about a terrible drought there in 1970. My father arranged for a Caterpillar digger to be shipped to Bihar for drilling the wells.

A Dutch magazine ran a feature on this project but my father insisted that his name was not disclosed and it only included a photo that showed a back view of him. He did not want any fuss and preferred that his donations were not acknowledged publicly. Several years ago I heard that, after thirty years, the drill was still active and has provided thousands of people with access to water.

After his death the family wanted to honour my father and his compassionate nature. We remembered him being particularly struck by a television programme about lepers. We decided to donate money to a leprosy project in Colombia that was in desperate need after their fund money had been embezzled. We provided funds for a new building where the leprosy victims could be treated.

This building was named The Johan Hospital, after my father. But this was not the only legacy of my father. There was much I found inspirational in his behaviour and attitude to life. As well as his good humour and compassion, my father also bore the discomfort and frustration of his failing health with great dignity. He never complained either about his diabetes or Parkinson's disease, which increasingly limited his scope for action. He never looked for sympathy or played the victim. I also learned from his attitude to work and money. Although he was a successful businessman, he was not attached to them. He enjoyed the process of making money and loved to play the game, but was not interested in accumulating wealth.

His passing also made me reflect on deeper issues—What happens after life? What or who is God?, and all the other questions that I normally did not spend much time considering. I had been to Sunday school but more as a duty than out of any genuine interest. I had no sense of what God really meant to me in my daily life. Yet these early reflections on the occasion of my father's death were to sow the seeds for a whole new chapter in my life.

Stepping Down

I was thirty-two when my father died. His death reminded me of the promise that I had made to myself when I finally made the commitment to stay in the family business twelve years before. At that time I had resolved that once I reached my thirties I would take a break and go and metaphorically 'sit on the top of a mountain', symbolic to me of quietness and distance, and contemplate my future. I planned to review my life and give myself the chance to decide whether I wanted to continue in the business or to do something different.

What became clear was that I no longer wanted to continue as CEO of Johan Matser Ltd. Two years after my father's death, in 1979, I started to look seriously for a successor. I thought that I had found the right candidate, but unfortunately, after two years, he left. I resumed the position again knowing that my life needed to head in another direction. In 1982 I found a suitable CEO, which allowed me to take more of a back seat. However, at board level I still retained ultimate responsibility for the company.

By this time I had spent eighteen years of my life working for the company; I had joined at the age of nineteen, been made CEO at twenty-seven and at the age of thirty-seven I was finally able to step down. New horizons beckoned and some seeds of interest for my new life had already been sown.

Chapter Reflections

After writing each chapter for Part I of this book I reflected on some of the lessons that I had learnt from the experiences described. These reflections appear as shaded boxes at the end of each chapter and they led me to create seven Keys that I believe can be helpful in 'rediscovering our hearts'.

The Keys are important to my life and philosophy and I hope that they may also be useful to you, dear reader. Both the Keys, and the affirmations that accompany them, can be used to explore and reflect on your own life experiences, if you wish. I hope they may also be useful as tools for personal and global transformation.

Reflections

Trusting in the Guiding Hand of the Divine

Reflecting back on this part of my life, of family, business and responsibilities, I came to see that many times things did not go the way that I had planned or expected. Yet I sensed that there was always a meaning or 'purpose' in the way that things turned out.

It seemed to me as if there was an unseen, 'guiding' hand that was creating opportunities for learning and personal and spiritual growth that would later create shifts in the course of my life. So, although my plans for participating further in sport or going to university were frustrated, I realise that taking the position as my father's successor also taught me a lot. I was able to develop business skills and to learn to deal with the material world while also recognising the value of hard work, philanthropy and compassion, as demonstrated by my father. I can see how strongly the ideas of social responsibility and wholesome family values were part of my early conditioning.

Yet I was also increasingly challenged to look into my own heart and to listen to it. I realise now that this paved the way for the spiritual experiences that were to come later and my desire to implement spiritual principles in a practical way.

At this stage in my life I had no clear idea of 'God', 'soul' or 'spirit', but I already felt a sense of the 'Divine' that was in essence completely free of religion, dogma or names. I have never become a member of any religious group, although I later met many wonderful and inspiring spiritual teachers. In my current understanding God encompasses all creation in all its dimensions, including ourselves. I believe we can each experience some of God's creation through our five senses; for example, inhaling a sweet rose, seeing the smile of a new born baby or listening to music. We can also experience God in the more subtle dimensions if we are truly open to them. Having this sense of the Divine inspired me to go on a journey of personal discovery of my own heart and to seek answers for the deeper questions in life such as:

- What have we come here to experience?
- What is the purpose of our existence?
- What can we do about our world?
- And what does this mean for you and me personally?

This journey has been, and is, a gradual process where I fall flat on my face many times a day, pick myself up, and remind myself that everything has a purpose. I am aware that with my free will I can make choices and decisions in my daily life, yet I have also learned to trust and surrender to the idea of there being a 'higher purpose' behind everything that comes our way.

This led me to formulate my first key principle:

KEY 1
We can trust in the guiding hand of the Divine.

AFFIRMATION
I trust that everything has a Divine purpose from
which it is possible to learn and grow.

CHAPTER 2

Going Beyond

In 1980 I attended the Young Presidents' Organisation (YPO annual conference) in Madrid, with my wife Ineke. The YPO, an organisation of young business leaders, arranges high-powered events in different countries each year. Usually the programme included well-known speakers, and that year Uri Geller, the controversial psychic, was due to address the conference. At that time I was still quite conventional and only had a small interest in the paranormal, but the programme sounded intriguing.

Before coming to the Conference we were invited to bring broken watches and clocks with us to the session with Uri Geller, and several of my colleagues had decided to do so. On the Monday afternoon gathering, 1,300 people from all over the world sat together for the session with him. At a certain point during his presentation he asked people who had watches and clocks that didn't work to bring them up to the stage and place them on a chair. So many people approached the stage that many had to be turned away. Geller surveyed the pile of broken timepieces and then invited the whole audience to say loudly three times, "We want these clocks to work, work, work". The owners were then invited back on stage to collect their watches and clocks and, to my great surprise, two-thirds reported that their timepieces were now working!

Geller then said to the audience, "I had to disappoint some of you because there was not enough space on the chair for all of your watches and clocks, but please check these items in your pockets and see if they are now working." To my further surprise more people then also reported that their timepieces were now functioning. I was particularly flabbergasted by this whole display because two friends sitting next to me had broken timepieces that had been on the stage and that were now working. I had checked these items before my friends took them on stage and could find no way to get them working. I felt stunned as I was a person who liked to think things could be explained rationally, and yet here I was being confronted with a reality that appeared inexplicable.

A Mind-Bending Experience

Later on I witnessed Geller demonstrating spoon-bending and the levitation of a heavy person on stage. I am, of course, aware that such phenomena can simply be tricks or illusions, but a further amazing thing happened, which convinced me of the authenticity of these phenomena. The following day, during the lunch break, a group of us were talking about what we had witnessed with Geller when, to my utter surprise, someone challenged me to see if I could get members of our group together to see if we could perform this demonstration of levitation ourselves. I have no idea why the person picked me, but I decided to try it. A heavy person volunteered and I tried to repeat Geller's procedure, as we had witnessed it, in order to levitate him.

We began by sitting the man on a chair. I then stood by his left shoulder and invited three other people to stand with me around him; one was behind his right shoulder and the other two next to each of his knees. I then asked each person to place two fingers under part of the man's body—I and one other person placed our fingers under his armpits and the other two placed their fingers under his bent knees. We then tried to lift the man off the chair but could not move him at all as he was too heavy. I then repeated the procedure that I had seen Uri Geller use the day before. I placed my right hand over the top of the man's head and invited each of the other participants, clockwise, to place their right hands over mine without actually touching. Then we did the same with our left hands. All the participants' hands were now over each other. I then invited everyone to remove their hands one by one in an anti-clockwise fashion. We then tried to lift the man again and to our amazement we found that we could lift him to the height of our shoulders with ease! I had been open-minded about doing the levitation but had had no expectation whatsoever of it working. I was amazed that it worked and having experienced it myself, I was convinced the phenomenon was real, although I still had no rational explanation.

That evening we were in a restaurant for dinner, when someone who had been present during the lunch break spontaneously asked me to try and repeat the levitation. This time we were in the presence of the Archbishop of Madrid and a different group of us tried to do it. Again the levitation worked, to everyone's surprise. I, too—again—felt amazed and yet I was also aware that the procedure somehow felt easy and natural although I didn't know why.

The Tesla Transmitter

Another speaker at the conference, Dr. Andrija Puharich, a scientist and paranormal investigator, lent further credibility to these events. Puharich was convinced of Geller's powers and had previously arranged for Geller to be investigated at Stanford Research Institute (SRI) in the USA[4]. He had also written a sympathetic biography of Geller[5]. At the conference, Puharich described various scientific tests that had been conducted on Geller and some of his own experiences of Geller's 'powers'. I found this part of his presentation quite convincing but was surprised by comments he made about the work of Nikola Tesla[6]. Puharich had been researching one of Tesla's devices, the Tesla Transmitter. This was a magnetic-wave generator and Puharich had been startled to find that altering the frequencies emitted by the generator could make people quite agitated and ill. He was convinced that the Soviets had developed one of these transmitters near Vladivostok in the eastern part of the former USSR, and that they were testing it as a weapon. He was therefore making it his mission to inform the public at large about this perceived danger.

As an example of this, Puharich told of a time when a large group of people in Vancouver reportedly all suddenly experienced headaches and felt compelled to leave their workplaces. No explanation had ever been found for this strange phenomenon. Puharich had discovered from radio amateurs in the area that their reception had been disturbed at exactly the same time. Since the Tesla Transmitter used the same type of radio wavelength, Puharich had concluded that this was evidence that the Soviets were testing the device and that it had caused the disturbance. However, no proof exists that this was the case.

It must be remembered that this was at a time when the Cold War[7] between the USA and the Soviet Union was at its height, and many Westerners regarded the Soviets as very secretive and a great threat. Various accounts exist of both the Soviets and the CIA investigating ways of using paranormal and other such phenomena as weapons against each other. In fact, Uri Geller himself has subsequently publicly claimed that the CIA tested his powers to see how he could be useful to them. Obviously, this was not particularly comfortable information, but what I took from Dr. Puharich's talk was the evidence from his scientific investigation of Geller. It seemed to me a good idea that research scientists were making serious efforts to investigate such phenomena.

A further strange thing happened when we returned to the Netherlands after the conference. My wife Ineke and I came home from an evening with friends

4. This research was written up in the journal, Nature, October 18, 1974, Vol. 251, page 559.

5. Puharich, Andrija (1974) *Uri: Original and Authorised Biography of Uri Geller, the Man Who Baffles the Scientists,* W.H. Allen/Virgin Books.

6. Nikola Tesla (1856-1943) was an inventor, engineer and physicist now regarded by many as a genius and the father of 20th century technology.

7. The 'Cold War' was so called because it involved no actual armed combat, or 'hot war' but was the escalating of hostilities and the nuclear arms race between the U.S.A. and the U.S.S.R. It started in 1947, following the end of the Second World War, and ended with the dissolution of the U.S.S.R in December 1991.

and when I tried to use my key to open the front door I couldn't get it to go into the keyhole. This was the same key that I had had in my pocket during the conference, and when I examined it I found that it was clearly bent! Ineke suggested that I must have bent it by trying to force it in the lock. However, this would have required a great deal of force, as the key was made from a strong metal, yet there were no signs of force on the key itself. In the end we had to use a different key to enter the house. This had never happened before and I have no rational explanation for how this happened.

A further strange thing happened when we returned to the Netherlands after the conference. My wife Ineke and I came home from an evening with friends and when I tried to use my key to open the front door I couldn't get it to go into the keyhole. This was the same key that I had had in my pocket during the conference, and when I examined it I found that it was clearly bent! Ineke suggested that I must have bent it by trying to force it in the lock. However, this would have required a great deal of force, as the key was made from a strong metal, yet there were no signs of force on the key itself. In the end we had to use a different key to enter the house. This had never happened before and I have no rational explanation for how this happened.

Shifts in Perception

The experiences I had at the conference triggered a real shift in my perceptions of life, myself and the world around me. I was a man who had previously thought he could explain everything using his rational mind, but now I was being confronted with a reality that was inexplicable and intangible. I could find no reference point in my existing mental framework to place these experiences. I still have no full explanation for them. I have since witnessed many other similar phenomena, often together with others, which are also inexplicable and yet apparently real.

I know that there are skilled conjurors who can perform similar feats, and that certain demonstrations of so-called paranormal phenomena can be faked. I am also aware that Geller himself is controversial and has been accused by some of trickery. Yet, looking back I regard that conference as one of the turning points in my life. From the day of the conference onward my world view started to change. However, my wife did not share my growing interest in such phenomena and this contributed to a growing rift between us.

New experiences followed. At the same conference in Madrid, I met Greta Woodrew, a known and respected speaker in our YPO conference circles. In her talks, Greta made predictions about imminent changes to our planet, including earthquakes in California, and these were taken seriously by conference members. Some of them even decided to move their homes or offices in the light of what she had said. At that time I also took some of her predictions quite seriously. I was concerned about the safety of our family, as the Netherlands was thought to be at risk of flooding. After lengthy discussions with Ineke, we decided to explore the possibility of moving to Australia and, in 1982, went there as a family to have a closer look. Our trip to Australia was a great experience and we enjoyed the country very much, but we felt too far away from our roots to consider emigrating there.

Everything Falls into Place

On our flight back to the Netherlands, we flew over Switzerland, as we had a stopover in Zurich. As I looked down from the plane over the spectacular, snowy mountain panorama I felt a strong feeling of affection for the country, remembering all the happy times I'd had there in the past. Memories resurfaced about wonderful winter holidays and an old wish of mine to maybe live there one day. At the same moment I remembered a dream from my youth that one day I would love to volunteer with the Red Cross. I recalled that the World headquarters of the Federation of Red Cross and Red Crescent Societies were in Geneva, Switzerland.

As these thoughts were going round in my mind, I had an extraordinary sensation of everything coming together and suddenly making sense. For no apparent reason,and without any conscious planning, I suddenly 'knew' intuitively that we were going to live in Switzerland and I was going to volunteer for the Red Cross! Having stepped down as CEO of our company a space had been created in my life for something new to come in. Suddenly it seemed as if this was to be it!

Obviously, I needed to discuss this idea in detail with Ineke and to consider with her the implications for our family as a whole. Yet in that instant everything seemed to fall into place. I could see, in retrospect, that going to Australia and talking about the possibility of living there had helped my family to prepare mentally to move elsewhere. For a European Switzerland also seemed to be a relatively 'safe' and appropriate place for the family to be—high up in the Alps, compared to the low-lying Netherlands—and also much less remote and foreign than Australia. It was also only a little more than an hour's flight away from the Netherlands, making commuting much more possible.

It was one thing for these thoughts and feelings to come together in a moment of apparent clarity but it was quite another for this to actually become a reality. I wondered how I could get in touch with the Red Cross and what sort of work

I could offer to do. In fact, I didn't need to worry, as everything just slotted in, almost effortlessly. Many people have experienced how, when something 'feels' right, everything just seems to flow in a miraculous way. Well, that is exactly what happened to me at this time, as everything was resolved with extraordinary speed, and in remarkable ways, after my return to the Netherlands.

The first thing I had to do was make contact with the Red Cross to see if there was a useful way in which I could volunteer my services. I got an introduction to the Secretary-General, Hans Hoegh, and within a week I met him in Geneva. Hans told me that the Red Cross wanted to start a worldwide programme to combat child death and sickness due to dehydration caused by diarrhoea. At that time almost five million children under the age of five were dying from this every year. Yet most of these deaths could be prevented by the simple administration of oral re-hydration therapy (ORT)[8].

ORT is a cheap, easy and highly effective intervention that requires only salts and glucose dissolved in a particular ratio in preferably clean water and then given to the infant by spoon or baby bottle. Anyone can administer the therapy and no hospitalisation is required. Hans wanted to launch this programme at the General Assembly of the Federation of Red Cross and Red Crescent Societies in 1983, where Jim Grant, the Secretary General of UNICEF, was drawing attention to this issue in his keynote speech. He asked me if I would head up the programme and make it happen.

I spent a week considering all the ramifications of this offer, and discussing it with my wife, and then decided to accept. I agreed to volunteer the majority of my working time toward the programme, while still maintaining my supervisory commitment to the family business in the Netherlands. I would report directly to the Secretary General's office, but I would do my own fundraising for the programme outside of the organisation and would take full responsibility for it. I chose this route because I did not want the programme to become bogged down in the bureaucracy of a large organisation. This was also Hans' view. In October 1983 the programme was duly launched and I was appointed its Executive Chairman. Within a very short space of time everything had been arranged and I now knew what I was to be doing.

---

8. The first successful clinical trials of ORT were conducted by the Cholera Research Laboratory in Dhaka, India in 1968 and this therapy has been described as "potentially the most important medical discovery of the 20th century" (The Lancet, 1978). It involves administration of a balanced solution of sodium chloride, sodium bicarbonate, potassium chloride and glucose in powder form and dissolved in water. A home-made alternative is 1 litre of water mixed with 8 teaspoons of sugar and 1 tablespoon of table salt with half a banana or ½ cup of orange juice for added potassium. For more information on ORT, see: *www.rehydrate.org*.

Representing San Marino

I immediately started work by putting a team together to implement the programme. However, I needed a permit to live with my young family in Switzerland, which was difficult to get. I had called a friend, an advisor in the Netherlands, to ask how I might obtain a Swiss residency permit and he had promised to look into it. He later called me back with some extraordinary news; he had learned that the special representative for the Republic of San Marino to the United Nations in Geneva was looking for a deputy and that I might be able to apply for the position.

San Marino is one of the smallest countries in the world and, at that time, only had around 23,000 inhabitants. It is completely surrounded by Italy and is located close to Rimini on the Adriatic Coast. At this time the appointed representative for San Marino needed a deputy who would be competent for the job, but who did not necessarily have to come from the country itself. I realised that this post would not only offer a unique opportunity to get to know the people and the country of San Marino but it would also give me the right to live in Switzerland. This would mean that I could do my volunteer work with the Red Cross and live in Geneva with my family.

To be offered this opportunity seemed an amazing coincidence. I therefore applied for the position and was fortunate to be chosen from the various applicants. The position involved sometimes representing the people of San Marino at the United Nations, which enabled me to gain experience of how the UN operated—something that was to prove very useful in my later work with international organisations.

My family (l to r Nina, Saskia, Fred, Lyke and Ineke) when we lived in Switzerland

Following my appointment I was granted a residency permit and, in August 1984, when my children were aged ten, eight and four, our family moved to Geneva. We rented a house in the suburbs and often went skiing together at weekends in the winter and hiking in the mountains in the summer. My children attended an international school, which stimulated their wider view of the world, although most of the students there were from quite privileged families.

In many ways we had a wonderful time living there but in other ways it was not easy for my family, especially my wife. She would be left alone to cope on the four days each month that I had to return to the Netherlands to supervise my property development business. The first time that this happened was only a few days after we had moved to Geneva, which was particularly difficult for my wife. I remember very well how it was raining on the day that she took me to the airport and I saw her crying as I left. I felt very bad about this and was also aware that my daughters missed their Dutch friends, especially in the early days of living there.

I felt responsible if they were unhappy since it was I who had uprooted them to Geneva, so that I could fulfil my dream. So the transition was not an entirely easy one for my family and, in hindsight, I think that I was not sensitive enough to their feelings. However, I also felt that volunteering for the Red Cross was something that I really had to do and I genuinely wanted my family, whom I loved deeply, to be close by. I felt very fortunate that they supported me in my choice, even though they had no special interest in the work that I was doing. I also thought that an internationally-oriented education for my children would always be an asset in their lives.

A Transcendental Experience

While I was living in Switzerland, I decided to try to take some preventative measures against developing diabetes. I had been warned by a specialist in the Netherlands that my blood sugar levels were a little abnormal and I did not want to develop full-blown diabetes like my father. A trusted friend recommended an American therapist to me who specialised in dealing with health problems using natural methods. I decided to consult him to see what he could recommend.

The therapist advised me to follow a detox programme that included drinking lots of water, eating a vegetarian diet, bathing and therapeutic massage. I endeavoured to follow all his advice and also had several massage sessions, which I found very relaxing and helpful. During one of these massage sessions, in which background music was played to aid relaxation, I had a rather extraordinary experience.

As I was lying there in a relaxed state I gradually became aware of the song that was playing in the background—'We Are the World'. At first I was just listening to the song as music but, as I listened, I began to experience a heightened sense of awareness and a state of being that was new to me. I began to hear the song in a new way and the meaning of the words seemed to enter my whole being. I felt light, calm and comfortable and as I allowed the feeling in my state of consciousness seemed to expand. In this state I also had an unusual clarity and suddenly got a strong sense that a friend of mine had suffered a skiing accident on the slopes nearby. I got a clear image of my injured friend arriving at the very place where I was, asking for medical help. I took a deep breath, as this image was rather disturbing. I relaxed again and, as I returned to normal awareness, I tried not to think any more about this.

After my treatment was over however, I felt prompted to go over to the door and open it and there I found my friend standing in front of me! She had just arrived there and explained that she had fallen while skiing and hurt her shoulder or collarbone, just as in the image that I had seen. Although this was quite remarkable, in a way I was not even surprised to see her as I had already 'seen' her accident and arrival beforehand. Yet this was still quite a strange phenomenon and a novel experience for me at the time. Later I learned that this kind of experience is called precognition—a direct knowledge or perception of the future, apparently obtained through extrasensory means. I wondered how easy it might be to access this awareness when in a very relaxed state of mind.

Some months later I had another healing session with the therapist. This time I was relaxing in a chair on my own after the massage and was sitting with my eyes closed. All of a sudden, in this deeply relaxed state I again had an extraordinary experience. It started as a feeling of a deep sense of peace which then developed into an overwhelming feeling of pure bliss that seemed to have no beginning or end. I felt that I was actually a part of an Infinite Oneness beyond time and space. In this state I had multi-dimensional, multi-directional experiences of colours, which I can only describe in a basic way as something like an incredible kaleidoscope. At a profound level I also felt totally and unconditionally loved for the first time in my life.

During this experience, wherever I allowed my attention to go, I was immediately there. It could be in front of me, within me, behind me, beyond me, all at the same time. Each time I was there instantaneously. My skin no longer felt like a border between my surroundings and myself, as I became one with all that was around me. In a way it felt like my 'self' was imploding and exploding within a bath of tranquillity and yet the 'me' was not there at all. The whole experience seemed to go on and on as if transcending eons of time, though looking at my watch afterwards I realised it had lasted a mere few seconds.

Although this experience was quite extraordinary, it was also very real—in fact it felt more 'real' than any normal life experience—and at all times I had total clarity. I was fully aware of my surroundings before, during and after the experience. I was relaxed throughout and felt no fear; I simply surrendered to the experience. After a time I came back into my normal conscious awareness but I felt different and knew that this had been a life-changing experience. I felt that, through experiencing this unconditional love, bliss and eternity, I had actually experienced the presence of the Divine.

Talking to others since, I have learned that many people have had these moments and indeed I have also subsequently experienced others. I regard these experiences as important for they seem to teach us that beyond the world of our five senses lies an infinite reality that can encompasses dimensions beyond the known.

Distant Healing

Following this experience, my horizons began to broaden. I met some truly remarkable individuals who inspired me in my new quest for greater understanding. Amongst these were some extraordinary and gifted healers whose abilities confound modern medical explanation. One was the very modest and unassuming Dutch lady, Nannie Veerman, daughter of the famous healer and paranormal psychometrist, Gerard Croiset[9].

In 1988 I was present when she demonstrated the healing work that she did every Saturday with five people with significant physical challenges. These people were all able to make only very limited, rigid and uncontrolled movements due to their disabilities but once a week, in this healing session, they achieved complete relaxation. Nannie talked to them lovingly and sweetly in a quiet voice for a few moments and then stood back and started to move her hands. To my amazement, the bodies of all the people whom she was healing gradually stopped going into spasm and their limbs started to move smoothly and freely under the influence of her healing power. It was remarkable to see this with my own eyes. What was even more amazing was that she then left the room and was able to repeat the same phenomenon through the wall from the next room. This effect lasted around half an hour while she continued to send her healing energy. Sadly, after she stopped the healing and withdrew her focus, the people's spasms gradually started to return.

Witnessing this incredible and moving healing effect made me question the relationship between physical healing and love. How was this effect possible? Was

---

9.   Gerard Croiset (1905-1980) was able to tell information about the life history of a person by holding an object that belonged to them, a gift known as psychometry. He became famous for his co-operation with the Dutch police in helping to solve cases using this gift. His work was researched by the famous Dutch parapsychologist, Professor Ten Haeff.

there some healing force that Nannie, with her loving heart and consciousness, could access and somehow pass on to these people? Or did her energy and love somehow enable them to access this healing force themselves via her consciousness? Or was it both?

Nannie always modestly claimed that the energy of the people in the room helped her to heal her patients. You could certainly feel an atmosphere of love in the room, and all the people who she worked with were more relaxed and happy afterwards. Nannie has co-operated several times with scientists investigating her abilities. She was once filmed by a Japanese TV company that showed clear effects of her distance healing in the Netherlands on some people in Japan. As with so many healers, her abilities defied rational explanation and remain controversial. Yet I was deeply touched by her quiet, humble and loving approach and the astonishing results she seemed able to produce.

Some people might argue that the healing effects which she obtained were merely down to the phenomenon of 'placebo' — that is her treatment had no actual effects and simply her patients' belief that she was doing them good enabled them to relax and feel better. Yet this raises the question as to what placebo really is? If the mind can decide that a particular treatment method, or substance, is going to work and a beneficial effect is obtained, then does the mind become the healer?

E. Fuller Torrey's well-known book, *Mind Game: Witch Doctors and Psychiatrists*, suggests that, while psychiatry may work with Westerners, the application of other approaches may work better in different cultures. So healing may also be culture-specific and related to people's expectation and belief systems. As Westerners, we may believe in pills and pharmaceuticals, whereas indigenous peoples may believe in totems and chants and other forms of healing. Belief systems may also change over time. For example Europeans believed in the efficacy of herbs for many hundreds of years but then this belief was replaced with faith in allopathic medicine. More recently many people are turning away from orthodox approaches and embracing ancient herbal traditions once more.

In the late 1980s, as I reached the end of my thirties, I decided to pursue my interest in the phenomenon of placebo and study it in more depth. It was difficult at first, having not studied academically for so long, but I soon found that I really enjoyed delving into the complex matters surrounding this issue. I read contributions on this subject from a variety of authors and found that there were many different explanations of the placebo effect.

In the end I concluded that the phenomenon of placebo can be harnessed as a powerful healing force if people replace the stress, anxiety, and fear that surround illness with a strong belief in inner peace, recovery and the healing power of love.

Thus at a deeper level, I believe our concept of placebo basically reflects how we experience the world around us. If we are willing to go beyond our ordinary self-limiting beliefs and expand our consciousness, we may be able to open ourselves up to unlimited healing possibilities.

Experiencing the Infinite

These ideas became even clearer to me one Sunday in the late 1980s when I experienced this sense of limitlessness and infinite healing potential myself. I had already had one experience of infinite bliss when in a very relaxed state after a therapeutic massage in Switzerland. Now I was to have another, for me life-changing, experience.

I was at a concert in Amsterdam and, before the music started, was sitting, idly thinking about how the next day was going to be a Monday. It was not a great feeling and I reflected how much nicer Friday nights are, with the prospect of a weekend of leisure ahead, rather than a week of work. As I gazed around the concert hall I wondered how many other people might be having the same thoughts and feelings. As the orchestra started playing I was still a bit distracted by these thoughts. However, as I listened to the music, I gradually relaxed and felt calmer. Then, suddenly, I had the most incredible experience.

All thoughts disappeared and in that moment I suddenly found myself totally at one with the music. It was as if the music entered into me and I actually became one with the music. It was a quite extraordinary, all-consuming sensation that is hard to put into words but it felt like an experience without beginning or end. On the one hand, part of my consciousness was fully aware of being in the concert hall and yet another aspect of my consciousness was completely 'somewhere else'. I can only describe it as experiencing the Infinite—timeless, formless Divine Consciousness, the great, creative source of the universe, itself. The experience seemed to go on and on and on, although in our normal time frame it perhaps only lasted a few seconds. This was just like the previous experience that I had in Switzerland: I was fully aware yet totally free from thought.

Suddenly, however, a thought jumped into my mind, "Why me?" and in that moment it instantly became Sunday afternoon again and I found myself back in the hall just listening to the music. It was as if a great, radiant light had been switched off the moment I began to question the experience. This reminded me of the well-known Dutch saying, "Doubt is the devil's pillow", which means that doubts can destroy Divine and magical moments.

In that moment of altered consciousness in the concert hall, I experienced a profound feeling of love that felt unconditional. This experience served to awaken in me an inner knowledge of the presence of a great creative and healing force that is, for me, an expression of the Divine. I wonder if healers like Nannie Veerman, and ultimately each one of us, can somehow learn to access this force at will. The experience has stayed with me and it triggered further changes in me as a person

Reflections

Going Beyond our Belief Systems and Opening to the Infinite

Reflecting on these experiences I see this was a time when my life began to open up in all sorts of unexpected ways and I began to realise that my conventional belief system did not hold all the answers. My transcendental experiences in Switzerland and in the concert hall in Amsterdam were inexplicable and profound. They triggered a pivotal shift in my consciousness, opening me to a world beyond the five senses and the intellect. In those moments I felt no limitations and the sense of expanding beyond my human 'self' was both effortless and timeless. These experiences stimulated my curiosity about spirituality and healing and opened me up to new learning and discoveries.

I did not 'seek out' these experiences—both occurred spontaneously when I was in a relaxed state and were perhaps partially triggered by the music I was listening to. I have learned since that many people have such experiences and I do believe that they are accessible to anyone. I have also found myself that it becomes gradually easier to 'tune in' so that such experiences occur more readily. However, I also feel that it is important to approach them in a spirit of openness, humility and respect rather than with an egotistical or grasping attitude.

For me, such experiences can be life-transforming; they give us an opportunity to go beyond our beliefs, intellect and usual frames of reference to directly experience what I call 'the Infinite'.

This led me to my second Key:

KEY 2
We can free our minds to explore new horizons.

AFFIRMATION
I can go beyond my conventional belief systems
and open up to infinite possibilities.

CHAPTER 3

Embracing Humanity

The transcendental experiences that I have described in the last chapter expanded my consciousness and gave me new insights and understandings. Meanwhile my work with the Red Cross and other humanitarian organisations tested me in new ways and also taught me many things. Gradually my sense of how I might best serve humanity began to deepen. It was a process that took time and involved much trial and error. I had to go on my own inner journey and rediscover my heart.

Working with the Red Cross

During my work for the Red Cross I visited several countries, especially those in Africa and South America. I had never been to any of these places before and felt very privileged to be introduced to the different peoples of the world and to learn more about their way of life. Nowadays people travel more widely and television and the internet have brought these cultures right into Western homes. However, at that time, this was not the case and I was excited by the novel sights, sounds and experiences that I encountered.

For example, I vividly remember my first visit to Egypt where we stayed in a very basic, rather dirty hotel and I was surprised to be woken at four in the morning by loud prayers from the nearby mosque. This was my first time in a Muslim country, and I had never heard such prayers at full volume before. The sight of prayer mats and prayer corners in every public place also amazed me. I have an especially strong visual image of the huge, central station in Cairo where we went that morning to catch a train out to Alexandria, where we were to be working. The high ceilings of the station let through great shafts of sunlight, which were full of particles of dirt and dust. One of these illuminated a corner of the station where a large number of men were on their knees making their morning prostrations and prayers. It was an incredible and memorable sight, and so different to the Western train stations to which I was accustomed.

Another thing that made a deep impression on me during these visits was the assault on the senses of real poverty. Like most people I had read about poverty in newspapers and seen images of it in photos and on television, but this is sanitised and removed from one personally. I had also, of course, seen poverty in the West and had witnessed intense poverty while visiting the Dutch colony of Surinam[10] in South America, in 1968 with my parents. Yet nothing prepared me for this type of deprivation. It is not only the sight of it, with appalling living conditions, lack of proper food and clothing, but also the smell that assaults your senses. There is the inescapable smell of rot, decay, and filth, which stays with you.

At first my experience of these sights and smells was so overpowering and unpleasant that my instinct was to want to escape from it. Yet I could not. I was acutely aware that, although I myself could soon go back to my normal, comfortable existence in the West, these people had no such choice to escape from poverty. What changed everything for me was having direct contact with the people and looking into each other's eyes. As our eyes met, I would feel myself reflected back and felt inextricably connected to the other person and their suffering. In a way, I no longer felt any separation between us but felt linked by our common humanity. This strengthened my sense of wanting to be with these people and to support them in meeting their needs. These impressions from nearly twenty-five years ago have remained with me and were the start of my realisation that we are all one human family.

Danger

On some of these visits we encountered quite threatening situations. For example, in one African country, we were warned by colleagues not to make any public criticism of the ruling President, as secret police and spies were placed everywhere and there was a risk of being taken off and killed. In a South American country I also stayed in a hotel room where, I found out later, a government minister had been murdered just a few days earlier.

We also had quite a number of hair-raising and dramatic moments when travelling. On one occasion in Columbia we had to fly from Bogota to Almería in a small prop plane. The outward-bound early morning flight went without incident and we had dramatic views of Bogota located high up on a plateau. However, on the return journey we encountered some extremely bad weather and a lightning storm.

The plane was going up and down, and I was worried about hitting the plateau on which Bogota stood, as visibility was so poor—the flight attendant told us how two planes had already been lost that year, from crashing into it. To make matters worse, two chickens, which had been on the lap of a lady passenger, became so frightened that they were squawking and flying about in the plane, adding to my

---

10. Surinam, also spelled Suriname, gained independence from the Netherlands on November 25th 1975.

sense of unease. Eventually, to our great relief, the plane managed to land safely, but we were the very last plane to do so that evening as Bogota airport was then closed because the weather was so bad.

I have had three or four scary and rather dangerous situations like this on planes during my life. In each case, I've noticed that my first reaction is the natural one of tension, anxiety and fright. But at a certain point I've realised I can't do anything about the situation and am simply in God's hands. At that point I have just let go and put my full trust in God and my fear dissolves.

Smiling Faces in Surinam

I think that part of the inspiration for my work with the Red Cross may have been my early experiences when I visited Surinam in South America with my father. This was the first country that I visited outside Europe and the trip was a complete eye-opener for me. My father had decided to visit this, at the time, Dutch colony, after hearing that there was a great need for social housing and good opportunities for development projects. He put together a proposal for 2,500 new, low-cost homes to be built in the capital of Paramaribo and I accompanied him on the trip in my capacity as a newly appointed board member. However, my main memory is of the deep impressions that the people and the country made on me.

I was amazed at the mix of people living there, which included Creoles (African origin), Chinese and Hindus (from India) alongside the local people, each with their own culture, traditions, food and so on. I had never seen such a melting pot of peoples and I really liked it. I loved all the liveliness, music, singing, the colourful markets and great food and also the cheerful, open-heartedness of the people who were always smiling.

From the Western perspective their happiness was somewhat perplexing, since they lived in very poor conditions. Their homes were often shabby and none had the luxury of air-conditioning against the intense heat, which you found in some of the houses in the more affluent areas. Streets and buildings were in bad repair, with poor sanitation. Everywhere there were little children playing in the mud and dirt on the roads and putting their dirty hands in their mouths. I thought of all the hand washing back at home and wondered what germs and diseases they might be contracting. Yet I was most impressed by their bright eyes, beaming smiles and happy faces.

This showed me clearly that it is not just material possessions that bring happiness and that you cannot simply judge what may be good for a particular group of people by Western standards. For example, these people may have had a poorer standard of living, but they seemed much happier and less stressed than the average Westerner. This is not to ignore the very real problems that they faced, such as disease and high infant mortality. Yet this is not the whole picture and the bare statistics can sometimes hide the simple quality of life that can elude us in the West.

So how can we judge which population is actually better off? I thought about this often during my years with the Red Cross, and afterwards, when touched by the simple joy and happiness of local people even in the face of quite adverse conditions.

In Surinam itself, this was a time of innocence; it was a developing country that has since sadly been overshadowed by the drugs trade. Everywhere we went we encountered warm-hearted, welcoming people and we developed close friendships with several local people that lasted for many years.

'Child Alive' Saves Lives

During the 1980s, while working as a volunteer for the Red Cross, I visited various African and South American countries to discuss and arrange the implementation of the oral re-hydration programmes. In many places there were no official records of births and deaths and mortality rates, so we made the decision to focus on actual implementation of the Oral Re-hydration Therapy (ORT) 'Child Alive' programme and to monitor progress and overall impact as a secondary goal wherever possible. We knew that setting up a monitoring system could swallow up large amounts of funding costs and yet the figures could still be unreliable. With limited funding, our primary focus had to be on saving lives and on empowering the people who had a desperate health care need.

In the three years that I had the privilege of coordinating the programme, we got it operational in more than eighteen countries. The programme also promoted breast-feeding and birth spacing—encouraging longer intervals between pregnancies—which research shows leads to healthier children.

Since that time the programme has expanded to many more countries worldwide, and it is estimated that millions of children's lives have been saved by ORT. In 1983 five million children under the age of five died due to dehydration and nowadays this number has halved. At the UNICEF Fortieth Anniversary Celebration in 1986, our 'Child Alive' team was given the Maurice Pate Memorial Award for the successful implementation of the ORT programme[11]. This was an enormous honour but most important of all, of course, was the fact that this programme has saved countless young lives.

Our 'Child Alive' team at the Red Cross

A New Beginning

After three years of running the programme and two years of living in Geneva we, as a family, decided in 1986 that it was time to return to the Netherlands[12]. The Child Alive programme was now well established and I felt my work with the Red Cross was done. I also felt that, at this stage, our company back in the Netherlands needed greater input from me than I had been able to provide. In addition, my work with the Red Cross had stimulated my interest in health care. I had seen from Child Alive how simple, cheap and effective remedies could have a huge effect on people's health. The ORT programme also showed how health issues were interconnected—dehydration, for example, affects the immune system. Meanwhile the transcendental experiences that I had also gave me a sense of wholeness, which I felt could somehow be applied to health as well.

---

11. See report in the UN chronicle, August 1986.

12. The decision to return to the Netherlands meant that I also had to step down from my position as the representative for San Marino. I had really valued the experiences that I had in holding this post and felt most grateful to the people of San Marino, whom I had represented, for their support and trust.

I was greatly helped in my exploration of new approaches to health and life in general by an inspiring professor of parapsychology at Utrecht University, Henri van Praag. The stimulating talks that I had with him confirmed the validity of my idea about healing involving a holistic process. He encouraged me to develop my ideas about health and give them concrete shape. From this emerged a growing sense of the value of integrated health care, bringing together the different disciplines of orthodox and complementary medicine and even so-called 'paranormal' healing.

1989: The New Stream Health Centre

The first fruits of my increasing interest in health led me to explore the idea of setting up an integrated health centre in my home country in 1986. At the time, our property development company had a building available, a former modern art museum that had 9,000 square feet of usable space and also a good parking facility. I set up a working group with various health professionals and we brainstormed ideas for transforming it into an integrated health care centre. The concept of integrated medicine barely existed in the Netherlands at that time and when this centre opened in 1989, it became the first major integrated health centre in the country.

A start-up team of medical and complementary medical specialists and people with other administrative and business skills was created to establish and run the new centre. Wilbert Linnemans and Albert Barelds, with their backgrounds in research and social health care respectively, were the centre's managers. Daan van Balen, a psychotherapist specialising in facilitating groups, Jacqueline Young, a British health practitioner who had already been involved in setting up an integrated health centre in the UK, and Iet Dalewijk, an occupational therapist, were also part of the team.

As part of the brainstorming process we also considered and visited other integrated centres that were newly established in Europe. This included a visit to London where we visited Dr Patrick Pietroni's pioneering Marylebone Health Centre, which was sited in the crypt of a church and combined orthodox medicine with various complementary therapies, including acupuncture, homeopathy, osteopathy and counselling. We also visited the renowned Hale Clinic, which housed over sixty orthodox and complementary practitioners, and where one of the team, Jacqueline Young, was practising at the time. In the end we came up with a multi-level concept incorporating orthodox and complementary practitioners and a 'paranormal' healer working side by side, an educational facility for health and self-development training and a research facility to investigate integrated medicine.

We set about creating the space and systems and recruiting the right people to make this vision a reality. Professor van Praag introduced me to a network of people who could help. The renowned organic architect, Ton Alberts, agreed to redesign the building's interior in his unique style. He used all natural materials and incorporated wonderful flowing lines avoiding right angles and sharp corners, creating a very therapeutic and healing internal environment.

We also used paint and furnishings of soft pastel pinks and blues and great care was taken to make the building 'healthy'. For example, at considerable extra expense, all electrical fields, from light switches etc., were insulated so that staff and patients would be unaffected by them. We even had a Faraday cage, which shields all electro-magnetic waves, built into the walls of one room[13]. I used to go and sit there sometimes as I felt a wonderful sense of peace and calm without being subject to any kind of electrical interference.

A team of practitioners including orthodox medical doctors, complementary medicine practitioners (such as acupuncturists and bodywork therapists), psychotherapists and a paranormal healer were assembled. The upper floor of the building was designated as the clinical facility with the treatment rooms, meditation rooms and the research room. The lower floor, designated as the education centre, had a lecture space for up to 120 people plus five rooms for smaller seminars and meetings.

A further key concept was developing a holistic approach to health care that involved co-operation between practitioners from different disciplines and the patients themselves. We took great care to select highly qualified, experienced and reputable practitioners who were really interested in exploring new ways of working together and of empowering patients to make their own healthy choices. Our aim was to go beyond the 'them' and 'us' situation that was developing between orthodox and complementary medical health professionals at that time.

We wanted to open up the field to dialogue, investigation and research, to explore the best ways of facilitating co-operation and to determine the most appropriate types of health care for different conditions. Accordingly, the centre was named 'The New Stream' to represent these pioneering concepts and inspired by the stream that used to flow nearby.

I agreed to finance the building's initial set-up and running costs, with the aim being that the centre would be self-financing within five years. We established a charitable foundation for this purpose, as the intention was not to profit from the enterprise but rather to contribute to the promotion of new models of health care. The centre attained a measure of success, carrying out 5,000 to 6,000

---

13. This was also quite pioneering, as electrical sensitivity was virtually unknown at this time but has since become more recognised as a source of illness in certain sensitive individuals.

treatments per year, hosting a range of innovative educational events, stimulating some research and perhaps inspiring others to develop their own new ways of working. However, there were also various problems and I feel many important lessons were learned from its creation, including the following:

1. We did not have enough support for the idea from the general public. In a sense, the centre was ahead of its time, and we experienced quite a lot of mistrust and even some downright opposition. I particularly remember that we invited all the local family physicians to our opening and yet only one, out of more than thirty invited, came to find out more about what we were attempting. It seems they were stuck in their own belief systems and not willing to be open-minded about a different approach.

2. At that time most treatments in our centre were not covered by health insurance. This meant that the majority of treatments had to be funded privately by our clients, which was not a popular concept in the Netherlands at that time. Even with the subsidy we provided, many people said they liked the idea of the therapies but could not afford to have them.

3. Team building amongst the practitioners didn't work as well as we had hoped. Although we tried various group activities: regular team meetings and consultations and so on, time schedules, different interests, and perhaps conflicting egos, sometimes got in the way of real integration.

4. Not everyone really shared the vision of the centre in practice. Some were content to just 'do their own thing' or may have been more interested in furthering their own individual aims.

5. I was also involved in various other initiatives and so could not focus as much attention as I would have liked on The New Stream, although I trusted the management team to take responsibility for maintaining the project.

6. Providing extensive support funding may not have encouraged those in charge to take enough responsibility for the financial running and sustainability of the project. In fact, The New Stream did not succeed in becoming self-financing and was supported by one of my foundations until 1998. Since then it has continued to operate but on a smaller scale. The clinic space is now leased independently to a commercial health organisation while the education centre is leased separately to a media company.

I learned a lot from this experience. The New Stream project was aimed at empowering people, and it led me to set up initiatives based on this principle, such as the Start Fund[14]. For Start Fund projects, our Foundation provides the initial 'seed-funding'; the remainder has to be obtained, or generated, by the project initiators themselves. They also have to have their own committed team of people who are dedicated to seeing the project through.

The experience also made me learn about patience, and I realised that I must have the wisdom to sometimes give time to philanthropic initiatives and take more care in applying the same standards that I would in my normal property and project development business. For example: doing extensive information gathering; absorbing the information before making a decision rather than being too spontaneous; and having proper job descriptions, goal statements and agreements.

On reflection I realised that, although I had always followed these in my regular business, I had mistakenly let some of them fall by the wayside with The New Stream, thinking they were implicitly understood. Though I asked the management team to put these practices into effect, I didn't check that they had done so. Perhaps I was too trusting or should have monitored things more closely. All the people involved were very nice and skilled in their own way but also lacked certain business skills that I feel I could have contributed.

Overall I believe The New Stream did succeed in contributing to the development of integrated medicine in the Netherlands. It also helped many people therapeutically and educationally and may have been an inspiration or catalyst for some other health ventures. However, I also feel that in some ways it was ahead of its time and that if some of the lessons described above had been learned and tackled effectively, it might have been a greater success and had the opportunity to continue in its original form to this day.

Romanian Orphans

Towards the end of 1989, after the fall of the Ceausescu regime[15] , I started to hear the horrendous news stories that began to appear about conditions in Romania and, in particular, the sickness and suffering of orphaned and abandoned children there. I learned that despite food shortages and poor conditions, Ceausescu had been determined to increase the population of the country.

---

14. See page 66 for more details on the Start Fund.

15. After the popular revolution, Ceauşescu and his wife were forced to flee and were later captured and executed on December 25, 1989.

He had apparently pressured women into becoming pregnant, using various inducements and punishments[16], to try and ensure that each woman produced up to four children As a result of this policy, tens of thousands of children were dumped in state institutions because their families could not, or would not, care for them or because they were orphaned Others were abandoned because they were handicapped.

To make matters worse, thousands were infected with the AIDS virus. It is said that this came about because of repeated blood transfusions with reused, infected needles and contaminated blood that was used to 'build up' the children. It has even been alleged that children may have been deliberately infected as part of a gruesome government experiment[17].

I spoke to one of The New Stream managers, Albert Barelds, who was also a trained social worker, about how these children might best be supported. It was very difficult to get accurate information about the extent of the problem, since Romanian government agencies were in disarray following the revolution. I therefore asked Albert to visit Romania to get first-hand information and to investigate how it might be possible to contribute toward improving conditions. Albert flew to Bucharest in March 1990 and visited a major hospital there. He was very shocked by what he found and I am grateful to him for writing the following account of his visit for this book:

> I will never forget the hospitals in central Bucharest with small
> babies and toddlers lying in dirty, metal cribs with no loving care
> or attention and absolutely no stimulation around them. No toys,
> no colour—only dirty white walls in dark wards. Very few nurs-
> ing and medical staff were available, and they were either afraid to
> touch the children or disinterested, as many were orphans and/or
> from a gypsy background and therefore discriminated against.
> When I visited a few of the orphanages around Bucharest, I realised
> that the situation was so much worse than we had envisaged.

---

16. These included higher taxes for childless couples, banning of divorce and sex education and financial incentives for having more children. As a result, the Romanian population almost doubled in the 1980s.

17. This story was carried in the Romanian daily newspaper, *Evenimentul Zilei* — 'The Day's Event'—after the alleged discovery that all children tested were found to be infected with an identical AIDS virus strain, something that is apparently exceptionally unlikely as many different strains exist. It has been alleged that a foreign pharmaceutical company paid for the children to be experimented on in order to investigate the AIDS virus and that the government may have believed that, since the children were all orphaned or abandoned, there would be no comeback. This claim has not been substantiated but many believe this to be the appalling truth.

Hundreds of children, from babies to early teens, were kept in poor buildings with hardly any trained staff to monitor them, let alone care for them. I cried when I saw the conditions that these children had to live under: no care plans, no schooling, no sport, no mental or emotional stimulation, no support and hardly any food, while control was achieved through physical punishment and enforced isolation. When in poor health, the children were given blood transfusions rather than a proper diet and medication! Needles were used over and over again, obviously increasing the rate of infection. During my few days in Bucharest I was also told by senior health department staff that the situation I had observed was serious, but nothing compared to what was happening in many orphanages in rural Romania. I realised that the future for these children was very, very bleak.

It was decided that we could best help by focusing aid at a specific institution, preferably outside of Bucharest, since most of the foreign aid was initially being concentrated in and around Bucharest itself. Albert, therefore, made a second visit to Romania in June 1990, and this time visited country orphanages and regional hospitals in Galati and Constanza. In Galati, he found even more harrowing conditions:

The scenes I saw were horrific and should not have been possible as they were so inhumane. Groups of children without any clothing were left to sit in their own excrement in dark rooms with no ventilation. Physically and mentally disabled children were kept in metal cribs, and had become injured and disfigured through their longstanding confinement.

Children were kept in an outside area not fit for a dog, and the only attention I saw any of the children get was punishment. The smells in some of the rooms made me physically sick and made me want to turn around and run away. Yet of course I could not. I had made up my mind, in the first of the many orphanages that I visited, that the very least I could do for the children was to share a few moments with them and let them know that someone cared. These visits left mental scars that were very hard to live with for many months after my return.

Following Albert's report from this visit, it was decided that we would focus our aid on the Galati Hospital since it was of a size appropriate to what we might be able to deal with from the Netherlands. We connected with a few dedicated and enthusiastic construction workers from Amsterdam who were willing to go to Romania during their summer holidays in order to build toilets and washing facilities, install heating and so on. We were also able to provide toys, clothes, food and other provisions. This raised the spirits of the children and staff enormously, and the child mortality dropped dramatically from around twenty per year to less than six per year. We continued to provide support until it was possible for maintenance of the institution to be taken over by a Dutch Christian organisation.

Today the situation in Romania is much better, since various aid organisations have improved conditions in many orphanages and other institutions. There is also now increased access to retroviral drugs for children infected with AIDS and some decrease in the total number of children in these institutions. However, the need for aid and support is still very great, as tens of thousands of children remain abandoned in such institutions with very little hope for the future. I have since personally witnessed similar conditions in other countries, notably the Ukraine, where the Fred Foundation has been extensively involved in a number of projects[18] for several years now.

---

18. See Part III, Contributions 4, 6, 16, 20 and 32.

Reflections

Embracing Humanity

In various experiences I have found that I needed to go beyond my own belief systems while at the same time remaining true to myself and trusting my heart. I realised that it is important to use not only my mind and intellect but also my heart and intuition.

Looking into the eyes of fellow human beings makes me feel connected with them and reminds me that we are all part of one human family. Approaching the suffering of others with compassion and open-heartedness has shown me the common humanity that links us all. I have also learned how sometimes the simplest of interventions such as clean water, hand washing or even just a smile can have a really profound effect.

In working with the Red Cross I thought a lot about the relationship between the so-called developed and under-developed worlds and came to think of our society as 'en-veloped', that is, restricted by over-complicated systems and structures that can weaken rather than empower us. I also became more aware of the importance of approaching others within their own context and with patience and respect for their culture and social systems, rather than rushing in and imposing Western values and belief systems or exporting our own stress.

This also made me think about the difference between emotions and feelings—a concept that I explore in more detail in Part II. It seemed to me that the people I met in the developing world's rural areas were often more able to 'go with the flow' in their lives and were more in touch with their feelings. I began to explore the idea that reconnecting with our deeper feelings may be a key step in rediscovering our hearts, connecting with the Infinite and becoming able to enter more deeply into the service of humanity.

This led me to my third Key:

KEY 3
We can rediscover our hearts and serve humanity.

AFFIRMATION
By expanding my consciousness I can integrate my mind
and heart and serve humanity compassionately.

CHAPTER 4

Change and Empowerment

As I changed I started to think more about fears and empowerment. Did our fears hold us back from changing, I wondered, and how could we best empower ourselves and each other? A turning point in my thinking came in autumn 1985, while still living in Geneva, when I first heard audiotapes by Dr Gerald G. Jampolsky. Jerry, as he likes to be called, is an American psychiatrist who developed a psycho-social-spiritual approach to health known as Attitudinal Healing. The central theme of the tapes was taken from his best-selling first book, *Love is Letting Go of Fear*.

What I understood from Jerry was that our innate nature is loving but this love can be blocked by our fears. Listening to the tapes, I was able to understand this concept at a profound level and this brought about a dramatic breakthrough in my thinking. I began to realise how, even unconsciously, many of my attitudes and actions were influenced by internal fears.

I reflected particularly on the reactions, of myself and others, to all the predictions of impending doom and imminent cataclysms that were rife in the 1980s. In Chapter 2 I mentioned the prediction I was given at a conference about a cataclysm due to occur in 1984. Thankfully this failed to materialise yet various other doom-laden predictions continued to circulate. I realised that these predictions created a climate of anxiety, without the underlying fears being really addressed. One situation that I encountered, before I had learnt the principle that love is letting go of fear, demonstrated this powerfully.

Freeing Myself from Fear: Work in Progress

The American woman who had given me the prediction at the conference decided, with her husband, to act on the 'psychic messages she had received. Along with others who had heard these predictions of an imminent world cataclysm, they decided to move to a so-called 'safe' mountain area in the USA. They planned to build a house, including two small apartments and a healing facility there. I had come to know both her and her husband quite well by this time, and she invited me, and a business friend of mine, to join in the venture. We agreed to finance a substantial part of the project and in return we were each to be assigned a small flat that was part of the property. This would be available for use by our families but could be used by this lady and her family at other times.

In due course the property was completed and one evening my friend and I, and our then wives, were invited to visit the complex for the first time and to have dinner together. In the course of the evening, to my shock, the woman who claimed to be psychic proceeded to have a major argument with her husband. The disagreement continued for some time in front of everyone and we were all rather disturbed by it.

All of a sudden, in the midst of all the discord, I had a powerful moment of clarity. I suddenly saw this person and her husband in a different light from the 'spiritual' people that I had perceived them to be. Instead I saw that they appeared to be full of fear. I also realised that I was actually supporting that fear by being involved in the project. At the same moment I understood how much of my action in supporting the venture had been precipitated by my own fears about the future and the wish to protect my family if a cataclysm did occur. Then I remembered Jerry Jampolsky's words, "Love is letting go of fear" and reflected how, even though I thought I had embraced this concept, I was in fact still allowing myself to be guided by my own fear.

In that moment I resolved to let my fear go and I knew I wanted no part of the venture anymore. Shortly afterwards my wife and I left, and I have had no contact with the woman or her family since. In the material sense this was quite a lesson for me since I had made a financial investment in the property. However, I viewed this as a great lesson from God and simply walked away from it.

Reflecting back now on this event and the 'messages', which were so prevalent at that time, but which failed to materialise as predicted I realise that I did allow myself to be influenced by them to some extent. I can see that they created some fear and anxiety in me and that I partly allowed myself to believe that those people somehow had greater access to information than I did. This was because some of them did really appear to be psychically gifted. Yet I also realised that this did not make them infallible on all issues. Nor did it prevent some of them from using their 'knowledge' to manipulate others for their own personal advantage.

I now feel that I was misguided and that it is much more important to trust firmly in my own inner guidance and to focus on loving rather than on fear. On reflection I realised that the profound, personal spiritual experiences that I have been fortunate to have all occurred at times when I was able to let go of fear, relax, completely surrender and trust in my connection with the Infinite. So I believe that by letting go of fear we are more able to connect with the loving power of the Infinite and allow it to work through us.

Of course, it is also possible that some of the cataclysmic 'messages' were genuine and that maybe the disasters alluded to were averted by people's conscious prayers, or by other means, as has indeed been claimed by some. It is impossible to know for sure.

Meeting Jerry and Diane

During the period in which I was volunteering with the Red Cross, I went to a conference in Colorado organised by the late singer/songwriter John Denver, and Thomas Crum[19]. Held in 1986 the conference was called 'Choices for the Future' and Jerry Jampolsky and his partner Diane Cirincione[20] were due to be speakers. Having been impressed by their audiotapes I was hoping that I would have a chance to meet them there. In the event I actually missed their talk through a mishap and was disappointed to only very briefly have the chance to say "hello" to them both at the end of it.

Coincidentally, however, on my return flight I found myself standing behind Diane at the airport check-in. We got talking and decided to sit together on the flight where we talked at length. Through Diane I was introduced properly to Jerry soon after and, finding how much we had in common, we have all become lifelong friends. My close connection with Jerry and Diane also later led me to establish an Attitudinal Healing Centre[21] in the Netherlands. Having seen the wonderful benefits of this kind of work, I wanted it to be available to people in my own country too.

Empowerment in Health

Through Jerry Jampolsky I was introduced to a remarkable woman, Caroline Myss. Caroline is a pioneer in the field of medical intuition—the ability to intuitively profile a patient's physical/psychological/emotional and family history, using (in her case) only the name and age of a patient and their permission. In this way underlying conditions may be brought to light and healed. Years of research in medical intuition led Caroline to explore more deeply the dynamics of healing. Investigating the underlying reasons why people can sabotage their healing

---

19. Tom Crum is a speaker and workshop leader specialising in conflict resolution and stress management and the author, with John Denver, of the book *The Magic of Conflict: Turning a Life of Work into a Work of Art* (Pocket books, 1999).

20. Dr. Cirincione is a clinical psychologist and international lecturer. She has co-authored a number of books with Dr. Jampolsky as well as being an author in her own right.

With Diane Cirincione and Jerry Jampolsky in the early 1990s

processes, Caroline identified a syndrome she calls 'woundology'. This is charac-terised by a person's reliance on the power of illness for manipulation of his or her world, as opposed to attaining an independent, empowered state of health.

Caroline gave me some useful insights into my own life process and it was her encouragement that led me to write this book. She visited the Netherlands on lecture tours with Dr. Norman Shealey, an American doctor specialising in inte-grated medicine who used her diagnostic skills with his patients. I became friends with her and we later re-met several times, including at Findhorn[22] in Scotland, when we were both speaking at a conference there.

---

21. Dr. Jerry Jampolsky founded the International Centre for Attitudinal Healing now located in Sausalito, California in 1975. Today there are over 130 independent Centres for Attitudinal Healing in 29 countries on five continents, offering free support services to families who are suffering from the effects of chronic or catastrophic illness, loss and grief.

22. *www.findhorn.org.*

Peace Child

One example of empowerment that I have found inspiring is the Peace Child initiative. Peace Child grew out of the music and lyrics of *Alpha Omega*, written by David Gordon[23], and *The Peace Book*, written by Bernard Benson—a children's book about how children helped to bring peace to the world. Gordon became interested in using his music to promote peace and in incorporating Benson's text. He recruited theatre director David Woollcombe, who, with his wife Rosey Simonds, produced a performance based on their synthesis of the two works, known as *Peace Child*.

David and Rosey went on to establish Peace Child as an organisation that aimed to facilitate conflict resolution in different countries through working with children and young people on performances of the musical. In each country, the children rewrite the musical according to their own experiences of violence and conflict. Performances have taken place in many countries, including the former Soviet Union, Central America, Cyprus, the former Yugoslavia, India, Israel and Northern Ireland.

I first met David in about 1985 and became involved in supporting the Peace Child initiative, for example by offering space in our office for their European base. David and Rosey are two wonderful, warm-hearted and genuine people who have worked selflessly to put children first. They believe in the natural intelligence of children and always asked for their opinions in developing the Peace Child initiative.

In 1986 this initiative brought the first Soviet children to the USA on a youth exchange programme. It involved a joint Soviet—American production of the Peace Child musical and toured to twelve American cities. The following year the Peace Child group made a return visit to the Soviet Union and my family and I also joined it. At this time the Cold War between the Soviet Union and the USA was still going on and the Berlin Wall remained intact as a stark reminder of the separation of our different parts of the world.

The children performed the musical in various parts of the Soviet Union and, during these travels, we had the opportunity to meet and talk with many Soviet children and their parents and carers. I found these meetings really inspiring and was impressed how grim faces on the cold streets gave way to warm welcomes in homes. I felt that the musical really played a part in finding a sense of common humanity between all of us and in bridging the culture gap.

The process of these children coming together, which I found very moving, was in sharp contrast to the world of adult conflict that we often saw on TV. I also later learned that when the then President of the Soviet Union, Mikhail

Gorbachev, and American President, Ronald Reagan, met for their historic peace talks in Iceland, they were actually shown the video of the Peace Child musical performed by Soviet and American children.

Soviet—American Citizens' Summit 1988

Because of my involvement with Peace Child and our visit to the USSR, David Woollcombe kindly invited me, in 1988, to the first Soviet—American Citizens' Summit in Washington, DC. I went there with my wife Ineke and, along with David and his wife Rosey, we were some of the very few non-American or Soviet participants.

At this summit businessmen and women, writers, musicians, artists and military people were all brought together. President Gorbachev himself was not present, but the delegates included his foreign policy advisor, Rustem Kairov. It was amazing to talk with and listen to all these people since Westerners and Soviets had rarely had this kind of contact before. That Soviet citizens from all these walks of life were willing to communicate and exchange ideas with us, despite the background of the Cold War, was, to me, very encouraging and enriching. This experience inspired me to explore ways in which I might be involved in providing aid in the Soviet Union.

Aid to Moscow and Yeltsin's Take Over

A few years later, Jim Garrison[24], a very energetic and spiritual man and a long-time bridge-builder between the USA and the Soviet Union, told me how conditions in Moscow hospitals were quite bad. He was planning to fly medical supplies out there and invited me to participate. I saw this as a good opportunity to offer aid and accepted.

A huge Russian Antonov plane, the largest type of aircraft in the world, was hired from the Soviet Union for this purpose. It left San Francisco for Moscow in December 1991 loaded with medical supplies plus a delegation of twenty, in-

23. Best known for launching the career of his brother Steve, as the 1960s pop star, Cat Stevens (now Yusuf Islam).

24. President of the Gorbachev Foundation U.S.A., and President and Chairman of the State of the World Forum *www.worldforum.org* and the new Wisdom University. I was introduced to him by Jerry Jampolsky.

cluding Jerry Jampolsky. I boarded the plane in Copenhagen, where it stopped for refuelling. I remember well its vast size and all of us simply seated in the hold amongst the aid parcels (for there were no comfortable seats as in a passenger airliner). On arrival it took seventy trucks to unload all the many aid packages.

Once in Moscow we had meetings with various people to discuss how we could most usefully offer aid. These included three meetings with the then Minister of Foreign Affairs, Eduard Schevernadze[25]. At a certain point we were also invited to the Kremlin to meet with one of President Gorbachev's chief advisors at the time, Mr. Alexander Jacovlev. The atmosphere was quite tense, and you could feel that the Soviet Empire was beginning to crumble. At the same time it was so impressive to be standing in the heart of the Kremlin, which I had previously only seen on TV. The USSR at that time was a super power with by far the biggest land surface in the world. I also remember this visit as one of the most dramatic and impressive times in my life, for it turned out that we were in Moscow at the time of Yeltsin's final manoeuvring to take over which would lead to President Gorbachev's resignation and ultimately the end of the USSR[26]. We were due for our final meeting with Schevernadze at the very moment that this actually occurred. We had first met him in his ministry soon after our arrival and I noticed he was wearing a rather sombre tie that day. As a spontaneous gesture before leaving, I presented him with the colourful tie that I was wearing and he good-humouredly accepted it. On the fourth day of our visit he was due to receive us in another building but arrived thirty minutes late in a rather flustered state. He told us that he had been unable to get into his own office as Yeltsin's men had taken over.

He stayed for our farewell reception and then left to find out what was happening. It was only in retrospect that we realised at what a momentous point in history we had been in the Soviet Union—at the very point of collapse of the Soviet Empire which, until then, had always been seen as the greatest threat to Western security. As we watched events unfold over the next few days, we started to think about all the implications of this dramatic change of power. I, like many others, felt real concern about what would happen to all of Russia's

---

25. Schevernadze was Foreign Minister under Gorbachev at this time and later joined Yeltsin after his take over in 1991. He eventually became the President of Georgia.

26. A coup by disaffected politburo members opposed to the pace of President Mikhail Gorbachev's reforms took place from 19 to 21 August 1991. It failed and Gorbachev was subsequently reinstated. However support had already shifted to Boris Yeltsin who assumed power following the dissolution of the USSR and Gorbachev's resignation in December 1991

Schevernadze accepting my colourful tie

nuclear scientists and researchers. If they lost their jobs because of the end of the Cold War, their expertise might go to other countries seen as unfriendly to the West, such as Libya, which was regarded as quite a threat at that time. I wondered if the West might pre-empt this by providing funding and initiatives enabling such specialists to use their knowledge on peaceful projects such as power generation.

I did not know it then but some months later I was to meet Gorbachev himself, soon after he had stepped down from his leadership post, and had the opportunity to discuss these concerns directly with him. Some years later, in 2005, I learned from a high-ranking American civil servant, that several hundred million dollars of government money was indeed allocated over time to facilitate the job transitions of these Soviet scientists from the nuclear war industry. It is reassuring to know that this issue was addressed as nuclear armament continues to be a significant global concern.

Meeting President Gorbachev

After standing down as President of the Soviet Union Gorbachev was still much in demand on the world stage and was busy establishing his Gorbachev Foundation (The International Foundation for Socio-economic and Political Studies)[27] and the Green Cross International. I felt honoured when I had an opportunity to meet this impressive man.

The occasion was a breakfast meeting hosted by the former US Secretary of State, Henry Kissinger[28] to which I was kindly invited by Jim Garrison. I had just struck up a conversation with Henry Kissinger and we happened to be standing near to the door when Mr. Gorbachev appeared. The two of them greeted each other and Kissinger then introduced me to Mr. Gorbachev as "my Dutch friend". It seemed funny to be introduced by Kissinger as his 'friend' even though I had only just met him.

After the breakfast I joined a meeting between Mr. Gorbachev, his assistant/translator Pavel Palachenko, Jim Garrison, and five American academics. The discussion centred on offering academic scholarships in the USA to Russian students. While this sounded worthwhile it seemed to me to assume that an education abroad was a priority.

During the discussions I shared the view I had gained while working for the Federation of Red Cross and Red Crescent Societies: namely that it was important to actually visit a country and listen to the people's needs rather than just impose Western value systems on them. Gorbachev must have liked this comment for, at the end of the meeting, he said he would like to talk more about this with me. He invited me to arrange a time for us to discuss this further in Moscow.

I felt honoured to have this invitation and looked forward to our conversations together. I made my visit to Moscow for this purpose in 1992 and was interested to see how Moscow had changed since my last visit. One of the biggest differences was the appearance of the first Western-style hotels and office buildings.

As part of this visit I was taken to a children's unit in a local hospital and to other places supported by the Gorbachev Foundation. This particular hospital urgently needed a bone marrow transplant unit, which would have been the only one of its kind in Russia for children with leukaemia. However with the dissolution of the USSR, State funding for the unit had been lost and the project

---

27. See: *www.gorbachevfoundation.org*. It is a non-governmental, non-profit think tank analysing social, political and economic trends in Russia and the world while promoting democratic, moral and humanistic values.

28. Kissinger was Assistant to the President for National Security Affairs from 1969 to 1975 and Secretary of State from 1973 to 1977.

Mr Gorbachev singing Russian songs at our home on a visit to the Netherlands

was now at a standstill. The newly established Russian government did not feel obliged to honour the funding commitments of the previous Soviet regime so Gorbachev, and his wife, Raisa, were working to try to get the project restarted.

Moved by the children's plight, and sharing the Gorbachevs' concern for these children, I came up with a plan for matched funding that I proposed to Gorbachev later that day. We agreed that we would both personally commit 25% of the necessary funds for the project (Mr. Gorbachev donated his share from monies that he received from his lecture tour in America) and on this basis, we would ask the Russian Government to fund the remaining 50%. The government did subsequently agree to provide their share and to guarantee the provision of ongoing treatment and maintenance costs. In this way we created what was perhaps the first public-private partnership in Russia.

After securing the funding I was able to arrange for the original German contractor to honour the old building contract without a price increase. Development got underway and the unit became a reality. Since then it has been able to treat successfully many children afflicted with leukaemia. A year later we helped set up residential units for parents of the sick children in a building close to the hospital. This was really needed, as many parents could not afford to keep travelling from their homes, often a journey of several days, and the children were deprived of family contact while they were ill.

Mr. Gorbachev made a deep impression on me. He made quick decisions involving a lot of his personal money and influence to help with this, and other, humanitarian causes. I felt that he and his late wife, Raisa, whom I met several times as well, both had a genuine, heartfelt interest in people, especially those in need. I really appreciated the trust he put in me to execute this plan.

I made several return trips to Moscow to discuss various projects with Mr. Gorbachev. My family were also honoured to have both him and his wife as guests for dinner at our home during a visit they made to the Netherlands. We had a wonderful evening together which even involved Mr Gorbachev treating us to a rendition of Russian folk songs!

Later I established a Dutch foundation to raise support and funding for other socio-medical projects in the former Soviet Union under the management of the Gorbachev Foundation. There is still a great need for more medical, housing and food aid there.

State of the World Forum

Through Jim Garrison I became involved with the State of the World Forum. He flew in from the USA one day and we brainstormed together about his ideas for setting up a new world forum to debate important issues such as nuclear disarmament and to create vehicles for global change. He set up the first State of the Word Forum in 1995[29], and these forums ran to the end of the decade, bringing together a network of leaders and other committed individuals and groups dedicated to global change.

I attended the first State of the World Forum and felt it was a great initiative; it enabled representatives from many fields, in many countries, to come together and debate planetary issues from different perspectives and in a harmonious rather than confrontational way. There was a fantastic cross-fertilisation of ideas at the Forum, and we all came away inspired and with many new ideas for change.

However I also noticed that women and indigenous people were quite under-represented at the Forum. Having discussed this with Jim, I organised a preliminary meeting with ten or so people from around the world to discuss how this representation could be increased at the next Forum. These included:

---

29. *www.worldforum.org.* This is a non-profit organisation bringing together a world network of leaders to discuss and act upon the issues of global concern.

Phil Lane, a native American Indian from Canada; Domenica Ghidei, a Somalian refugee living in the Netherlands; Suthida (later Phil Lane's wife), from Thailand; a native American woman who was a United States government representative in charge of education funding for indigenous people; Prince Alfred von Liechtenstein (whom I had met at a conference in the U.S.A.) and his Chinese partner at that time, Ewai, who has since sadly passed away. The ideas from this group helped to bring about a better representation for women and a more prominent role for indigenous people at the State of the World Forum the following year.

At one of the later Forums that I attended I also particularly remember the impressive conduct of the delegate, Thich Naht Hanh[30], at a lunch where he was the guest of honour. All the conference members who had come to see him sat at tables and were served a three-course meal. However Thich Naht Hanh simply sat on the stage, slowly and quietly peeled an orange, ate it bit by bit and then left. I was stunned and ate very little, noting how clearly he had demonstrated that 'actions speak louder than words'.

This also led me to think about the food provision at the Forums. I felt it was important that we should consider where the food came from, how it was purchased and its environmental impact. I was also keen to support the food being all organic and self-service. I felt that if the Forums could encourage participants to think about food with greater consciousness, this would be more in line with the topics being discussed and would enable us to 'practise what we preached'.

Food purchasing is for me an example of our culture's excesses, for we tend to constantly buy more without asking ourselves if we really need it. Studies have suggested that in the West we throw away around 40% of the food that we buy, either as leftovers or as food past its sell-by date. By any standards this is an appalling waste, especially considering the countless numbers of people in the world who go hungry every day.

The Start Fund

Following the State of the World Forum, I became involved in a new project that brought together many different strands of my experiences, along with my increasing understanding of the importance of empowerment. The trigger was the matched funding principle for the bone marrow transplant unit in Moscow that worked so well. It inspired me to establish a new fund in the Netherlands in 1996 under the auspices of the Fred Foundation, to provide empowerment through seed funding. It was originally called the CIE Fund—Care for the

In-vironment (Health) and the Environment[31]—but, for simplicity, has since been renamed as the Start Fund, highlighting its provision of seed funding to kick-start projects.

The aim of the Fund was to stimulate self-reliance and to provide individuals, or groups, with financial support for inspiring projects in the fields of both health care (for which I coined the term 'in-vironment') and/or the environment. The 'seed' money awarded by the Fund is typically between 20 to 50% of total project costs, on a sliding scale in relation to the total cost of the project, which must be below 100,000 euros (around £88,000 at the time of going to press). As part of the conditions of funding, applicants must raise the remaining project costs from other sources within nine months. I see the Start Fund's role as that of kindling fires, that is we provide the initial funding to support people who have inspiring ideas and the skills to implement them, while they must 'fan this kindling into a fire' by committing to obtain the matched funding from elsewhere and make the project a reality. This system has worked well and the Fund has now successfully supported more than two hundred projects.

One example is support for Bahia Street, a non-profit organisation based in the city of Salvador, in the north east of Brazil (*www.bahiastreet.org*). It focuses on breaking cycles of poverty, inequality and violence by providing high quality educational opportunities for economically-impoverished young women and girls in Brazil. It also provides social and emotional support for these girls and their families and mobilises professionals and institutions within the local community to support educational and health activities. Our Fund has been pleased to support some of their initiatives under the inspiring and dedicated leadership of their International Director, Dr. Margaret Willson.

Other supported projects include a women's development project in Russia, various projects in the Ukraine and a kindergarten in Rwanda, to name but a few. These projects are based on the principle of small-scale support—modest amounts of money used to good effect locally—showing how well this type of funding can work, even in the poorest areas. The CIE/Start Fund projects have been genuinely inspiring to witness and they support my dream of facilitating the empowerment of people.

---

30. The Vietnamese Buddhist monk, peace and human rights activist, poet and author.

31. For more details on the CIE fund, now named the Start Fund, please see: *www.fredfoundation.org.*

Reflections

Global Change and Empowerment

One of the principal things that I learnt through my experiences during this period was how fear can block both love and empowerment. I realised that the people I came into contact with, who were dedicated to service and who inspired me, typically had the courage to go beyond fear and doubt. This enabled them to spark changes within themselves and also locally, nationally or even globally.

For me empowerment means taking responsibility for our own lives rather than giving our power away to others. It also involves supporting others in making their own choices.

This led me to my fourth Key:

KEY 4
We can empower ourselves.

AFFIRMATION
*I choose to free myself from fear
to allow changes within and without.
In supporting myself and others in this process
we can together develop a caring
and sharing society.*

CHAPTER 5

Wholeness and Integration

Living our daily, urban lives in the developed world I think it is easy to forget about wholeness and our connection with nature and with each other. We can forget that we are one human family and living together, with all other beings, on a planet with fragile ecosystems that are interdependent. In my own life nature has always played an important part and I believe there are many lessons we can learn from her about harmony and balance.

Love of Nature

I developed a love of the outdoors from a young age on forest walks with my grandfather. Early on some Sunday mornings, he would turn up at our front door on his morning walk and ask if I'd like to come with him. We would walk into the forest, mostly in companionable silence, just listening to the sounds of the birds.

My awareness of the beauty and power of nature has grown throughout my life and travels. In particular I have always loved the Alps; I feel so good in the snow and I love the crisp, clean environment high up in these mountains.

I was also deeply impressed when I first visited the USA as a young man in 1971 and experienced the incredible vastness of the Painted Desert in Northern Arizona. When standing on the high plateaus it was possible to have an unobstructed view in all directions. This gave me a sense of complete freedom, while still being bound physically to the earth.

I also found the Grand Canyon and the Petrified Forest National Park particularly dramatic and so different to the Alps that I was familiar with. I especially remember the view one day when we were walking along the plains in the Petrified Forest area. On one side of me I could see clouds with a rainbow and rain showers creating 'rain rays' yet, looking to the other side, I could see sunshine and bright sunbeams dancing in changing patterns as they touched different parts of the landscape. It was spectacular and unforgettable.

In the late 1970s and early 1980s I spent a lot of time outdoors as I was jogging long distances regularly. Yet at that time I was so preoccupied with the exercise that I didn't really notice the environment around me much. I just remember thinking, "When I retire I'd like to spend more time enjoying nature."

In the early stages of our marriage, my wife and I used to go for a walk with our children each Sunday. I used to really enjoy these excursions into the countryside, but after a while my wife didn't like going so much anymore and as the children became older they, like most adolescents, preferred other pastimes such as hanging out with their friends. As a result our nature walks became less and less frequent.

I have observed that our culture tends to respect man-made things more than anything from nature. In general, people are more likely to be excited by the 'miracle' of the latest hi-tech gadget than the miracle of a flower developing from a seed. Yet for me mere gravity and the fact that our feet and toes, which are such a small part of our total body surface area, ensure our connection to the earth and maintain our balance is also a miracle in itself. Perhaps we cut ourselves off from our inner nature and over-emphasise our mental capacity and this means we may become numb to many of our feelings and cut off from nature.

Much later in life, through my 'paranormal' experiences, I feel that I was given an insight into nature at a deeper level. These experiences showed me that the Infinite could be experienced in nature—reflected in its diversity and beauty, such as in a beautiful flower or leaf. Our own perception of nature's beauty is, for me, another aspect of this divinity; that is we can use our consciousness to appreciate nature as 'Divine energy' in action and to experience a sense of wonderment.

The more I became aware of nature the more I felt at one with her and increasingly appreciated not only her beauty but also her great importance to the planet and its future. I felt that nature has no voice or vote and no official ambassadors despite being our universal 'mother' and of vital significance to us all. So I became increasingly involved in supporting and establishing environmental charitable projects.

Some of these have been aimed at increasing awareness of environmental issues; for example, the Foundation for Environmental Awareness, founded in 1989. It created and supported several projects, including an environmentally-themed musical, with teaching materials and audiotapes that went to many schools in the Netherlands (see page 218). It also encouraged recycling and other environmentally-friendly activities. Other projects/sponsorships enabled children, young people and adults to actually experience nature—often for the first time.

An example of one of these sponsorship activities was Robert Swan's Inspire Antarctic Expeditions[32], which take young people, teachers, businessmen and businesswomen on an amazing adventure into the Antarctic. They can experience the awesome magnificence of the iceberg landscape, learn about the fragile

---

32. Robert Swan O.B.E., is the first man to walk to both the North and South poles. He has since dedicated his life to ensuring the preservation of Antarctica—the world's last great wilderness. He was a keynote speaker at the Rio de Janeiro Earth Summit. His ice-strengthened vessel, 2041, is named after the year in which the review of the Environmental Protocol of the Antarctic Treaty will begin. See: *www.2041.com.*

ecosystem of the area, and also participate in environmental clean-up operations. These are necessary because, sadly, even in this wilderness area there are tons of rubbish that have been left behind by early explorers, research expeditions and so on. Robert's expeditions have so far removed over 1,000 tons of rusting metal debris and rubbish from the area and more are planned. I got to know Robert and the Fred Foundation sponsored one of his expeditions.

I was also part of the start-up team for a group that organises leadership training in wild and natural environments. Leaders from the business community are brought into nature in order for them to reconnect with their inner nature through experiencing the outer natural world. The aim is that this will inspire them to consider the natural world more in their policy-making and business decisions. An executive I know who went on one of these group wildlife experiences in South Africa came back and told me it had profoundly changed his life. His previous approach to work had been based mainly on competition without much consideration of the effect on nature. Now he has made a shift and nature has become a greater priority in his decision- making process.

Meeting Jane

Someone who, for me is truly connected with nature, is the renowned primatologist and anthropologist, Jane Goodall[33]. I first encountered her at the 1995 State of the World Forum in San Francisco, USA and was very impressed with her well-informed and sincere lecture. I really felt that she was someone who 'walks her talk'. Over time we became close friends and in June 1997 I went with a group of people from the State of the World Forum to visit her research facility in the Gombe National Park in Tanzania. It is here that Jane did most of her ground-breaking research on primates, and it has become the most long-lasting wildlife research project in the world; it will be fifty years old in 2010.

Jane is particularly known for naming the chimpanzees she studied. When she originally submitted details of her research to Prof. Robert Hind at Cambridge University, he told her that each chimpanzee must be numbered. Jane, however, insisted on using the names and eventually he accepted this. This seemingly trivial point was pivotal in helping scientists to see that animals are not just 'cases' but have identities and personalities, too. She did a lot of important work to demonstrate how individual each chimpanzee's personality is and to illustrate novel aspects of their behaviour that had not previously been understood.

33. Founder of the Jane Goodall Institute (*www.janegoodall.org*) and a UN Messenger for Peace.

Fred the Chimpanzee

Earlier in 1997 Jane had done me the honour of naming a chimpanzee after me. During our stay in Gombe we tried to find him in the forest but had been unsuccessful. She had told me that he was ill and I had been prepared for this if I saw him.

Shortly before we were due to leave to go back to the town of Kigoma (a two-hour boat ride away) one of the local research guides came rushing down to our boat calling out, "I have seen Fred!" So I left the others who were gathering on the beach near the boat and went back into the forest with the guide. There I was

Fred the chimp with his mother behind him (partly obscured)

lucky enough to see Fred for the first time. He was just a young chimpanzee and indeed looked in poor health. At one point our eyes actually met—it was a very special moment for me.

Soon after we departed on the boat and in Kigoma we enjoyed visiting a sustainable vegetable gardening project and several schools. I treasured the memories of all my experiences in Gombe and Kigoma, during my return journey home.

More than a month later, once back in the Netherlands, I became seriously ill with a high fever and was taken to hospital. Strangely, around the same time that I became ill, Fred the chimpanzee died. Jane later told me that she did not dare tell me about Fred's fate until I recovered as she believes in the meaning of coincidences and, knowing how sick I was, she did not want to influence my state of health at that time. In fact I had developed a serious form of malaria and I write about this experience elsewhere in the book (see page 93)

Later I helped found the Jane Goodall Institute in the Netherlands with its 'Roots and Shoots' programme. Jane is now over seventy years young and still very active and busy setting up Roots and Shoots groups all over the world. The aim of this innovative programme is to inspire young people of all ages around the globe to take action in their communities to help people, animals and the environment that we all share.

Jane has a family home in the UK but returns to Tanzania at least twice a year. She travels throughout the year giving talks about Jane Goodall Institute projects, including Roots and Shoots, and how we can all make a difference with our actions every day. She was also appointed a UN Messenger for Peace by the former UN Secretary-General, Kofi Annan and re-appointed in 2007 by his successor UN Secretary-General, Ban Ki-Moon.

Respect and Compassion for Life

Jane has done much to highlight the need to preserve animal habitats in the wild as well as to argue against abuse of animals in science, captivity, films and so on while also working on conservation endeavours at a community level. I agree with her approach and strongly believe that all animals should be treated with compassion and respect. Such an approach could transform our farming systems, improve the well-being of animals and benefit humans in the process.

For example, I once read a report by a farmer who said that when he played classical music to his cows, their milk yields went up and their rate of infections went down. I was also interested to read about some work done by Prof. Popp, back in the 1980s, on light emissions known as photons. These photons can be measured and, as part of his work, he investigated the photon emissions from different foods. Apparently he found that organic, free-range eggs showed twice as much vitality as battery hens' eggs.

This suggests to me that the hens with better living conditions produced eggs with greater 'life force'. I have come to believe that food that has been given careful attention during preparation, and which has been cooked with love, is probably more 'nutritious' than food that has been mass-produced without any love or awareness. If food is eaten with conscious gratitude for where it has come from, how it has made it to our plate and all the good it is doing us, the effect might be even greater. Perhaps one day it may be possible to validate and measure this effect and the 'vitality' of food might even be included on labels.

We can also see this principle of awareness, respect and love in a wider context applied to all life, in whatever form it takes. For we are not separate from nature but are a part of her and we are governed by the same natural laws and sharing the same planet as all the other earthly expressions of life. It is this sense of connectedness that I felt so deeply during the 'paranormal' experiences that I have had.

Yet I was to find myself tested to the limit on this very issue of wholeness from quite a different direction—within my own family.

My Family: Wholeness and Separation

I was present at the births of all three of my daughters and regard their births as amongst the most important events in my life. My own father did not pay that much attention to his children as he was always working and I missed having many experiences with him. For this reason, and simply because I wanted to, I decided to spend as much time with my children as possible.

I have always really enjoyed the time spent with my daughters and, when they were young, this included great fun that we had playing games and making up bedtime stories. One series of stories that I invented for them was the adventures of some characters that I called Tom, Tim and Tanneke. They loved to hear stories of all the things these three got up to and we were very surprised when, years later, I happened to come across a children's book with these same three names as the title.

Sadly, however, my dream of a happy family came to an end. Plans for how Ineke and I would grow together and support one another were not fulfilled. Communication became more difficult. The love and beauty that we once shared faded away and frustration and irritation came in their place. It was very painful to see how our three children were affected by their parents' dysfunctional relationship. Of course, I fully accept my part of the responsibility for the failing marriage.

We went through an excruciating time of separation and finally divorce. I have chosen not to go into more detail here as, in my view, it would not serve a purpose. The process itself has already been harmful enough for all involved. In November 1996 we reached a settlement. I could go on with my life and our children were relieved of the pain of this transition period. More than ten years later, their mother and I now have an amicable relationship and are able to function as parents to our three wonderful, adult daughters.

As a result of my own experiences, I can empathise a lot with the pain that fathers, and their children, go through in divorces and separations. I am especially aware of how precious the time with your children becomes once you are no longer in the family home. I was fortunate to be able to get a place to live very nearby and to have work that enabled me to be flexible with my time. This meant that I was able to fit in around my children's schedule to quite an extent so this did not become a big issue.

However, I was also very aware of how precious contact time could be 'lost' if one or other of the children nipped back home to get something they wanted and sometimes did not return for some time. I realised how lucky I was to still have lots of 'quality time' with each of my daughters both together and individually but I still hugely missed being part of their everyday lives at home.

I feel so grateful that I have always been in regular contact with all of my daughters and that we have continued to share lots of good times together.

Integrating Male and Female

I had long been aware that as a man I found it difficult to express my feelings. My life in business had strengthened my intellect and analytical ability. It developed my skills in coordinating and the side of me that was dynamic, active and good at putting ideas into practice. However useful these traditionally 'male' qualities were, they were not fully in balance with the other side of me: the part that was more receptive, more in touch with my feelings, more involved in caring and sharing. I was aware how difficult it can be for men, including me, to embrace this 'female' side. Yet I believe that these 'male' and 'female' sides exist in both men and women and are both equally important.

As I reflected on this in the late 1980s, it became clear to me that the chaos in the world was due to an imbalance of 'male power'—a domination of intellectual, competitive and aggressive qualities—at the expense of 'female power'—reflected in greater cooperation, caring and sharing. I felt it was important to somehow help to redress this balance, especially in men, starting with myself.

To support this process, a friend of mine, Marieke de Vrij, helped me to establish a men's group in 2002. I had known Marieke since 1989 and knew her to be a gifted and inspired workshop leader. Funnily enough when I mentioned my idea for the group to her she said that she had been feeling for several months that she wanted to contribute to this idea, too. We started the group with around twenty men, from a variety of different ages and backgrounds.

The group now meets three times a year for a full day. In each session the men share stories and experiences and at the end receive guidance from Marieke. During the time that this group has been active, we have seen some remarkable changes in all of us, as attitudes change and we become more able to open our hearts and express our feelings.

Health Care Experienced Differently

Meanwhile, my gradual healing was reflected in other developments in my life, as I became involved in developing health care further in society at large. Building on my experience with the integrated health care centre, New Stream, and my continuing conversations with Professor van Praag, I was thinking more and more about developing further integrated health care initiatives. I felt strongly that our current orientation for health care, being based on identifying the problem and then fixing it, was inadequate and that we needed to look more at the concept of wholeness in this as in other fields. I wanted to highlight the importance of the whole body and the whole person, instead of just focusing on the diseased part of the body or the illness.

After all, no doctor actually heals a cut in a person's finger—the healing power that comes through our body does it. I felt that health care somehow needed to incorporate the role of our innate wisdom and healing power. I was also stimulated by an encounter with Patch Adams[34], the medical doctor and clown who I had met at the Soviet—American Citizens' Summit in 1988. He had been entertaining delegates in a full clown's costume criss-crossing through the crowd on a giant unicycle! Patch has dedicated his life to bringing the "fun, friendship, joy and service" back into health care, and defines global "peace, justice and care" as his life's mission.

I liked the way Patch interacted with people and appreciated his sense of fun, which has brought healing to people's lives. He has done a lot to revolutionise our

---

34. For more on this, and Patch's work, see: *www.patchadams.org* and also Patch's contribution to this book on page 231.

approach to health. We spoke together at the conference and he gave me his book Gesundheit!: Bringing Good Health to You, the Medical System, and Society through Physician Service, Complementary Therapies, Humour, and Joy (Healing Arts Press 1998). He talked about his Gesundheit! Institute Hospital Project in West Virginia, a proposed forty-bed rural community hospital, with a new model of health care based on compassion and friendship, with free treatment, which was aimed at changing society drastically. I subsequently met him several times in the USA and, impressed by his work and ideals, invited him in 1991 to give some lectures in the Netherlands. This led, some years later, to setting up a conference in The Hague called 'Healthcare Experienced Differently' to explore new ways of approaching health care.

In January 1994, I arranged the conference with the help of some friends. Over two hundred doctors, nurses, caregivers, health charity representatives and political leaders attended. I invited Patch Adams and Freek de Jonge[35] to participate in the conference as well. The idea was for participants to sit together and look at health care afresh.

Increasingly I had become aware of the need to get beyond the 'problem-solution' approach in society at large to a different and more holistic way of seeing ourselves and the world around us. This applies also to health care, where the conventional model is of a patient who has an illness (problem) that needs healing (solution). I make no judgment about this model, but I wanted to explore fresh approaches as well. My idea was based on the fact that a patient, even one who is seriously ill, is alive so they must be at least partly healthy. So we could seek to work to extend that healthy part so that, in the end, the illness vanishes.

One of the outcomes of the conference was the setting up of the foundation, Healthcare Experienced Differently (now called The Healing Company[36]. The original foundation was set up jointly by Lydia Helwig-Nazarowa, Pieter Sluis, Sandra Kloezen and me.

It has now been operating in the Netherlands, in one form or another, for many years, and has involved nearly two hundred volunteers at one time or another. Typically, at a hospital, health care centre, or nursing home, the volunteers go to the wards for one or two days and entertain with music, songs, storytelling, clowns and give aromatherapy and foot massages. Ordinary pillowcases are replaced with coloured ones; all the hospital staff—cleaners, nurses, doctors, administrators—are invited to wear badges with only their first names; everyone is

---

35. Freek is The Netherland's leading cabaret performer and stand-up comic. He is also a novelist, singer and TV presenter. See: *www.freekdejonge.nl*.

36. *www.betergezelschap.nl*

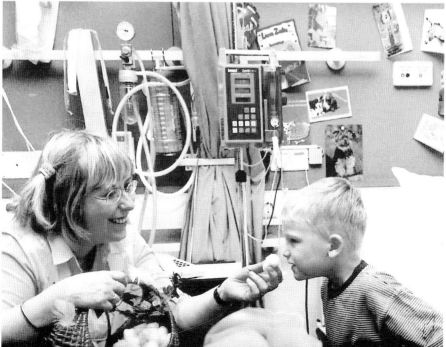

Members of 'Healthcare Experienced Differently' in action

given little gifts, things to taste, listen to, smell and so on. In this way, everyone's senses are stimulated in new ways as part of their healing.

Just these simple little changes can have a profound effect. I remember once taking the lift in a health care centre that was being visited by our group that day and sharing it with a medical professor who was wearing a badge with just his first name in place of his usual formal one with only his surname. A young nurse got on at one of the floors and seeing his label greeted him beamingly with "Hi John!"—something she had never dared to do before. It was interesting to see how this broke down barriers between them.

Another moving example of Healthcare Experienced Differently in action was the experience of my old friend, Dorine Bijl, a singer and therapist, visiting an old people's home one day with the group. She noticed an old man sitting alone in a chair in a corner and wanted to go to him. One of the home's care workers tried to discourage her, saying it would be a waste of time, as the man had not responded to anything for years. Dorine went over anyway, sat next to the man, and started to sing an old song from about the time of his youth. To her surprise she saw tears start to well up in his eyes, which made her realise that he had responded to her song.

This simple action showed the care workers that this man was aware of things and had feelings and, although he did not react much in a normal everyday setting, he was indeed able to respond to certain stimuli. As a result of this experience the man was released from his prison of loneliness for, once the staff realised that he was indeed aware, their attitude and behaviour towards him began to change. This simple story illustrates the importance of changing attitudes for healing to occur.

"I Have AIDS—Please Hug Me"

I experienced something similar in the Attitudinal Healing support groups set up by Jerry Jampolsky and Diane Cirincione at their International Centre for Attitudinal Healing in Sausalito, California. They established Attitudinal Healing groups there for people diagnosed as HIV positive in the early 1980s. People were only just beginning to become aware of this new health challenge and there was a lot of fear, anxiety and ignorance about the disease.

I was privileged to be allowed to sit in on one of these group meetings and was deeply moved by the members' accounts of their experiences. The group, made up of around twenty men, sat in a circle and shared their thoughts and feelings. I particularly remember a man talking about the heart-rend-

I HAVE AIDS
PLease hug me
I can't make you sick

AIDS HOT LINE FOR KIDS
CENTER FOR ATTITUDINAL HEALING
19 MAIN ST, TIBURON, CA 94920, (415) 435-5022

ing loss of his partner, previously a group member, and the realisation that he himself would be dying soon. The loving acceptance of him within the group was very touching. At each meeting the group had to deal with the difficult loss of members who had died from AIDS as well as welcoming new members.

A poster that Jerry and Diane created in 1986 to address psycho-social needs and to educate people about the disease made a particular impression on me at the time. It had a simple drawing of a person and the slogan, "I have AIDS—Please Hug Me. I can't make you sick!" I thought this was very poignant as those suffering from AIDS were as much in need of love, hugs and physical contact as anyone yet they were, in some cases, being shunned like lepers by people who were unnecessarily fearful that they might catch the disease.

The WHO (World Health Organisation) in Geneva reproduced the poster in several languages and distributed it to about 140 countries. In 2008, for the sixtieth Anniversary of WHO, this poster was selected as the best educational tool for taking the message worldwide. It was also chosen to represent all of the AIDS work done by WHO during its year-long anniversary celebration, which began at the United Nations Headquarters in New York City.

My contact with the HIV positive Attitudinal Healing group left a deep impression on me. It seemed to me that this group exemplified Jerry's theme of 'Love is Letting Go of Fear'. Instead of being fearful of the disease, or of those who were HIV positive, loving compassion allowed this irrational fear to dissolve. Studies have shown that fear can lead to physical changes in the body, including depressed immune function, so it would seem that fear can actually play a role in disease and dying. Yet, for me, if one had a hundred more years to live or just one more moment of life, the most important question would be the same: "How can I release my fear and find inner peace?"

Letter in Response to 9/11

At the same time I realised that fear, like love, is contagious, for it is easy to be affected by the fear of others. I have also seen this spread of fear take hold in situations such as the rough plane ride that I had in Colombia, while working with the Red Cross. Each time I have seen how love and trust in God can melt the fear away.

I was also deeply moved how, in the aftermath of the horrendous events of the 9/11 attack on the Twin Towers in New York, so many of the phone messages from people caught in the towers, or on the hijacked planes, were powerful expressions of love. This event inspired me to write a piece that I posted on my website and which I reproduce below. I am reprinting it here because I feel that the principles expressed still apply today.

To ALL women and men of this world.

We all live in this world side by side.
We all experience this world by letting our minds and feelings (through our hearts) be inspired.
I am one of you and I am still perplexed by what occurred on September 11.
Pain and sadness flash through us all. Especially those that were closely involved with the disaster and its victims; they have been hurt deeply.
People are standing up—we call them leaders—who claim they shall retaliate for the injustice that has been committed and the deep pain that has resulted. If we aim for peace and harmony, is that then our direction? Of course we have to find those that are responsible. Of course we have to hold them responsible and bring them to justice.
Yet isn't it just as important to connect from love with one another to emotionally process the pain and find mutual support? Luckily we can do that with our families and our close friends. Could we maybe also extend our horizons and include in our respect people who think and feel differently to us because they are from different cultures or religions? And can we maybe also include them in our love? Do we always have to agree before we can share respect and love? It does not matter if we walk our path as a Muslim, Jew, Christian, Buddhist or Atheist; we all live together on this earth.
In accepting what has happened, we don't have to agree with it. Our differences could rather be an invitation to dialogue, from the mind and through the heart, so we meet with respect for our differences and in the spirit of inclusion—not exclusion. Let us, both men and women, create space so that we can accept the 'female' quality of feeling as well as the 'male' quality of thinking. Maybe we can teach ourselves to connect more with our feelings and then our actions will be different as they will come from the heart. In this way, maybe we can help prevent the products of our think-ing—that is the result of our mental actions without heart—be-coming unguided missiles that fly criss-cross over this world and hit without mercy.
Let us try to look at the things that we have in common rather

than at the things that separate us and the implications of both commonality and separation.

Yes, we are different. Yet the fact that somebody is, or some people are, different does not mean we have to exclude them or change them according to our preferences.

Everybody has their own free will. Accordingly, everybody has his/her own responsibility for her/his choices. Whatever our 'leaders' decide to do, nobody can take over, or take away from us, our responsibility to act, or not to act. I propose that we all consider the option to choose respect for ourselves, others and what inspires us—to remain in our own power, or to come to our own power. Let's anyway choose to remain calm as much as we can and keep our minds and our hearts, and the feelings that follow, clear and open so that inspiration can flow through us.

We can choose mutual support. We can choose to see and process our fears. We can choose to love one another unconditionally and to not let ourselves be excited into emotions of vengeance in order to retaliate.

Our children and our grandchildren observe us. Often they are depending on us. Let us all live from respect for ourselves, for all others and for Existence, of which we all are an inseparable part, so that our children and grandchildren can experience us as an example.

According to my own truth, life is about all that has been given, and not just about the facts of life. Can we be grateful for what has been given? Can we forgive ourselves and others? I am one of us and I wanted to share this with you. I fall flat on my face too—many times a day. Just as many times I get up again, maybe just like you.

Fred Matser

With thanks to all those that have inspired me and all those that are still inspiring me.

22nd September 2001

Reflections

Wholeness and Integration

The Sunday morning walks with my grandfather gave me a sense of the oneness and wholeness that can be experienced in the natural world. I became aware of how nature is both strong and vulnerable and all elements are part of the whole.

Reflecting on this I could see that it is so easy in our daily, urban lives to forget this wholeness or connectedness. Instead, the emphasis on separation leads us to see things in terms of 'them' and 'us' or to see nature as separate.

In relationships too I wondered what triggers us to come together as partners or to separate? Do we select each other on the basis of current attitudes, behaviours or appearance, which are inevitably going to be subject to change? Or, do we base our choice on their essence, the eternal quality, of the person? (I explore this concept of 'essence' later in Part II on pages 164-166). It is interesting to note that the nature of all phenomena is change and yet the dynamic of change can itself create problems in relationships.

Situations of intense personal difficulty can test our belief in the concepts of wholeness and connectedness to the limit. For me, my difficult divorce was an example of this. Terrible world events like 9/11 also challenge us in this way. Yet these experiences may also give us opportunities, challenging us to explore unity in all its aspects.

If we live in a world of separation then we may also miss possibilities for being part of our global family and global home.

This led me to my fifth Key:

KEY 5
We can live in the spirit of unity.

AFFIRMATION
*By learning to integrate different parts of myself
and focusing on our essence and common humanity
we can come together as a whole.*

CHAPTER 6

Spiritual Exploration

As well as the various projects and initiatives that I was involved in, new experiences triggered further personal and spiritual development. These included witnessing crop circles, incidences of synchronicity, healing phenomena and psychic surgery. I will share some of these experiences in this chapter.

Change also came to my personal life when I met a wonderful person, Chris. We first met at the home of our friends, Jerry and Diane Jampolsky and I was immediately struck by her presence. I looked into eyes that were crystal clear and I sensed her deep and gentle soul. I was also touched by her modesty and subtlety as well as her elegance. Chris, who was then living in Hawaii, was to join me on my inner and outer journey, selflessly supporting me in many ways and, sharing her wisdom, humour and abundant love. We shared many interests and were both curious about phenomena that could not easily be explained. One of these was the strange phenomena of 'crop circles'.

Crop Circles

Mysterious formations, which later became known as 'crop circles', started to appear in wheat fields in certain parts of the UK in the early 1980s and attracted large numbers of people and worldwide media interest. Although many dismissed the formations as hoaxes, and certainly hoaxers have been at work in some cases, some serious researchers have also concluded that this phenomenon is authentic and worthy of investigation.

I had seen various photographs of crop circles and both Chris and I were intrigued by their intricate and precise patterns. In 1998 we decided to go to the UK to see the crop circles for ourselves. We were fortunate that Colin Andrews[37], considered one of the foremost research authorities on crop circles, kindly acted as the guide for our group. Colin believes that the circles have been created as signs and symbols to give us information about environmental and other earth changes and about what we are doing to our planet. He told us that most of the circles appear in the UK, although there are a few in the USA and that they are almost always in fields of wheat.

---

37. Colin Andrews, together with colleagues Pat Delgado, Busty Taylor and Dr. Terence Meade, was one of the first people to investigate crop circles. For more information on his work, see: *www. cropcircleinfo.com.*

As part of our trip we took a flight in an ultra light, open-air aircraft and flew over various crop circles near Marlborough in Wiltshire. In this area alone, almost fifty crop circles appeared in 1998. We marvelled at their beauty and structure as we viewed them from above. One example of what we saw was photographed by Lucy Pringle[38] and is reproduced here with her kind permission.

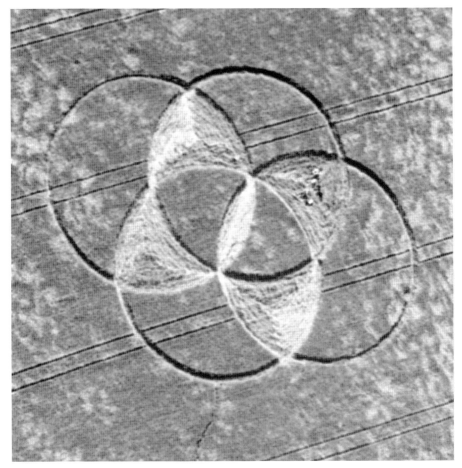

A Crop Circle Photo © Lucy Pringle

In 2004 we returned to the same area and happened to get talking with an elderly man in a shop in the village of Avebury, who also turned out to be quite an expert on crop circles. He very kindly took us in his car to visit one of the newest crop circles that had recently appeared in a nearby field.

---

38. See: *www.lucypringle.co.uk.*

On this occasion, as previously, we were able to walk into the field and enter the crop circle formation itself. Some people have reported different types of sensation when they enter the circles, from feelings of 'energy' and elation to more ominous sensations of discomfort and menace. In my case, I can honestly say that I did not feel anything special or different. However, I did notice that there were hardly any broken wheat stalks where it had been flattened to make the design. This would be almost impossible if a human was deliberately crushing the wheat to create such a pattern. Although I had heard about this phenomenon, it was still very surprising to witness and made me think that there must be something behind the crop circles that we do not yet fully understand.

When you study a lot of the images of these crop circles taken over time, it does seem as if there must be some kind of message, or even a language, that is being conveyed in them, as certain types of formations are repeated again and again. Another possibility is that the crop circles do contain some kind of force that might have a specific purpose, such as healing. We still don't know the real meaning behind these crop circles, but it is certainly a fascinating phenomenon that will no doubt reveal more of itself over time as new crop circles continue to appear.

Synchronicity

Like most people, I have had many experiences of extraordinary synchronicity in my life. One of them occurred around 1997 when I was in Snowmass, a town in the Rocky Mountains, in Denver, Colorado with my partner Chris. It was a weekday morning and we were in the car just driving around and looking for somewhere to stop and go for a walk. Spontaneously I said, "Let's try to the right," and so we took a right turn and found somewhere to park.

We then went for our walk, listening to the sounds of our footsteps crunching in the snow; the place was completely deserted and there was silence all around. After walking for a while we turned and started to go back towards our car. Some way along the path we saw a group of around seven people walking towards us. They were clad in winter garb and woolly hats so their faces could not be made out clearly. However, as they got nearer, to my great surprise I found that I suddenly recognised one of the voices! It seemed to be that of Vincent Harding, a priest friend of the late Martin Luther King whom I had met at a conference[39] with Caroline Myss and Patch Adams back in 1990. I had offered some support for his

---

39. The council Grove Conference—an annual cutting-edge forum on science meets spirituality, founded by Dr. Elmer Green, the biofeedback expert.

organisation, which provides educational opportunities for young black people, but had not had any contact with him since. We soon recognised each other and were amazed that we had bumped into each other in such a remote place, selected purely on the basis of an instinct pulling me up a particular road.

I took this as yet another example of the connectivity of all things. I was also intrigued that I had recognised him purely on the basis of his voice. Considering that I have met many thousands of people over the years, I was amazed that a single voice memory from several years before could be that strong. I wondered if voice memories may be even more distinctive than facial ones.

This incident was one of a number of synchronicities that have occurred in my life. Let me share with you some more of these 'coincidences' that seemed in some way remarkable to me.

One Saturday, around ten years ago, I was sitting working at my kitchen table at home with the doors open to the garden as it was nice weather. Suddenly a racing pigeon flew into the room and perched on the window ledge in front of me. This had never happened before, even though I often had the doors open in the kitchen. I shooed the pigeon outside and went back to sit at the table but the pigeon flew back in and, once again, I had to encourage him to fly back outside.

The pigeon in the kitchen

The next day, a Sunday, it was another beautiful day and I was again sitting at the kitchen table with the doors open, this time reading my paper, when the same pigeon flew in again! On this day it came and perched right on the table in front of me, fixing me with its eyes. I watched it and let it remain there for a while and then again encouraged it to fly outside. Two days later, on the Tuesday, I received a letter announcing that an acquaintance of my father had just died. This man had always been really grateful to my father for saving his company from bankruptcy by giving him some building work when it was most needed. Every since that time he had continued to show his appreciation by sending cards and dinner invitations to my family. I also remembered that his hobby had been pigeon racing.

Now I wondered if the persistent appearance of the racing pigeon in my kitchen could somehow have been a final sign from this man indicating his gratitude once more before he passed on. Of course I will never know and this could have just been a chance occurrence. However it is interesting that once I had made this connection the pigeon did not return and no bird ever entered my house thereafter either.

Birds also featured in my meetings with Professor Van Praag (see page 47). We used to sit talking in a little room at the top of his house, which had a window at one end. One day he said to me, "If you look at the window you will see some pigeons appear." I looked over but couldn't see any birds yet he told me he could feel that they were coming. Sure enough, within minutes, some pigeons appeared and sat right on the window ledge.

This made quite an impression on me because the timing was so amazing—there were no birds in the vicinity and yet they just suddenly appeared, as if out of nowhere, right when he said they would. Again I wondered if this had just happened by chance, or if it was a regular occurrence at a particular time of day that he knew about, or if he actually had some sort of extrasensory perception or psychic ability that I was not aware of. I never found out and he never explained it to me!

Another coincidence, also involving a bird, is one that I always find both touching and amusing. I was at a lunch party sitting next to the father of a friend of mine and somehow the conversation turned to the subject of life after death. He told me that his wife of many years had recently died and said how much he would like to be in touch with her if there was indeed life after death. As we talked I told him some stories I knew of people who feel they have received messages from 'the other side' and which they have taken to be evidence of life after death. This led us to talk about whether or not we believed in God and he told me the following story:

He had been sitting on his terrace at home one day following the death of his wife and wishing that he could believe in God. He decided to issue a challenge to God and formulated the thought in his mind: "If you do exist, then prove it by sending a bird down to sit in front of me within the next three minutes." In less than a minute a small bird flew down and perched right in front of him on the edge of the low terrace wall. I thought that he was going to tell me that this had strengthened his belief in God but, no, he ended the story by saying, "But then I thought to myself—oh it's only a 'musje' (a sparrow, which is the most common garden bird in the Netherlands)." Because the bird was a common one he immediately dismissed the possibility that this could have occurred in response to his challenge to God and instead put it down to an everyday experience. Of course it could indeed have been just that but on the other hand…

I also experienced some extraordinary synchronicity related to the 'female principle' when I attended a conference at the spiritual community at Findhorn[40], in Scotland some years ago. It was the autumn of 1989 and I was invited by Jan Backelin to speak about our integrated health centre (The New Stream). There I had the opportunity to meet Peter and Eileen Caddy, two of the original founders, and I felt particularly connected with Eileen, who was a very warm and friendly person. It was there too that I met Caroline Myss who was also one of the conference speakers.

During the conference I took part in some workshops. One evening I was in a group of twenty-four people and, as part of a group exercise, we were asked to come forward and each take a folded piece of paper out of a box. The papers all had the letter A, B, C or D written on them and the idea was that these papers would randomly assign each of us to one of four groups so that we could take part in some self-development group exercises. To my great surprise, once all the papers had been taken, it turned out that we had three groups with five men and one woman and one group with one man and five women. I was the one man in the mainly female group.

The odds for these configurations within the groups were quite remote and I pondered on the meaning of them. It occurred to me that this was a reflection of my family life where I have been predominantly surrounded by females: my mother, three aunts at that time, two sisters (my father, uncle on my mother's side and two brothers had all died), three daughters, my wife and step-daughter (Chris's son sadly died also).

As I reflected on this alignment, I came to the conclusion that a theme in my life is to contribute to the re-empowerment of the female principle, within my-

---

40. The Findhorn Community was started in 1962 by Peter and Eileen Caddy and Dorothy Maclean. It now operates as the Findhorn Foundation—a spiritual community, eco-village and international centre for holistic education that aims to help unfold a new human consciousness and create a positive and sustainable future. See: *www.findhorn.org* for more information.

self as well as more generally in both men and women. So often I have seen that problems that I have had in my own life, and that we have in society, are related to the devaluing of the female principle. For me, this female principle embodies attributes such as receptivity and openness, which may be present in both women and men. I discuss this further in Part II of the book (see pages 177-179)

Meeting Elisabeth Haich

Experiences of synchronicity sometimes take many years to manifest. An experience long forgotten can suddenly link directly to the present in an interesting way. One example of this for me concerned the authors Elisabeth Haich and Selvarajan Yesudian. Elisabeth was a renowned Hungarian artist, born in Budapest in 1897, who developed a strong interest in esoteric knowledge and yoga and who wrote a best-selling book called *Initiation*. The book tells the story of a twentieth-century European who is initiated into the priesthood in ancient Egypt.

There has been considerable speculation as to how much of the book was autobiographical, fantasy or real memories of past lives, as claimed by the author. I came across the book myself in 1985 while I was living in Switzerland and working for the Red Cross. One evening, when I had almost finished reading it, I attended a dinner and happened to sit next to a lady who worked for the World Council of Churches in Geneva.

During our conversation, I happened to mention that I was reading Elisabeth Haich's book and, to my surprise, my dinner companion not only knew of the book but had also read it herself that same year. As we talked about it, I happened to say how much I would have liked to meet the author as I had assumed that she was no longer living.

To my amazement my companion said, "Oh, she is still alive—she lives in Zurich!" I could hardly believe that the author was alive and even living so nearby, especially since neither of us was native to Switzerland. My amazement was even greater when I learned from this lady that the co-author of several books with Elisabeth, the yoga teacher, Selvarajan Yesudian[41], was living in a village just four kilometres from where my family and I were living at the time. I later discovered that Yesudian was still giving yoga classes in Geneva and I had the good fortune to attend some of them.

When I first spoke to him and our eyes met, something suddenly clicked in my mind. I remembered a yoga book that I had read when I was eighteen years old and practising yoga in the Netherlands.

The book[42] had made a deep impression on me and I still remembered the face of the man on the cover and the intensity of his amazing eyes. I described the book to Yesudian and asked him if he could have been the man on the cover. To my astonishment he confirmed that it was indeed him. It seemed incredible to be meeting the author of a book that had made such an impression on me as a young man so many years later and in a country foreign to us both.

Through Yesudian I was given an opportunity to visit Elisabeth Haich at her home. She was already well into her eighties and yet she proudly demonstrated to me that she could still do yoga poses and even put her leg up behind her neck! However she was not very forthcoming about the book—I got the impression that she had become tired of being asked about it so many times over the years—so I never did find out the truth about the book's source.

Still it was a privilege to meet both her and Yesudian in person and the amazing coincidences that led to these meetings seemed to me an example of the powerful, unseen connections that can exist between people, somehow drawing them together over time and space. Meeting them also reminded me of words written by Yesudian in the introduction to her book, *Initiation*. He relates a conversation he had with Elisabeth, then his spiritual teacher, where she said:

> *"I don't want you to simply follow me on the path I am following to reach the goal," she told me. "Go your own way, on the path you select yourself, corresponding to your innermost inclinations. Don't accept any statement because I made it. Even if it is true a hundred times over, it is still not your truth, it is still not your experience and it will not belong to you. Bring truth into being and then it will belong to you. Regard the lives of those who have achieved truth only as proof that the goal can be reached."*

These words reinforced my own feelings about how to determine truth and the most appropriate spiritual path. I feel grateful that they were a part of my journey which still continues.

When I have reflected on different episodes of synchronicity which I and others have experienced, it seems that they have often revealed a deeper meaning. They may have yielded a spiritual lesson or led to an experience, or meeting, that created

---

41. Yesudian was the son of an Indian physician who went to Hungary in 1936 to study medicine. There he met Elisabeth Haich and they began to teach yoga courses together. They fled Hungary at the end of the Second World War and eventually settled in Switzerland where they established a series of very popular yoga schools. They co-authored some best-selling books on yoga and also wrote books individually. Elisabeth died in 1994 aged 97 and Yesudian followed her in 1998.

42. *Yoga and Health* by Selvarajan Yesudian and Elisabeth Haich (first published 1953).

a shift in my thinking or action. Sometimes they seemed to me to be a wonderful sign of our connection with the Infinite. Often they have focused my attention on phenomena that have no rational explanation and this has encouraged me to question, explore and reawaken my inner senses and reconnect with a deeper knowledge within.

On certain occasions these experiences may even become a type of 'initiation' or 'rite of passage'. In ancient spiritual traditions those seeking spiritual enlightenment were required to go through various initiations to test their level of development and readiness for the next step. Sometimes these initiations, such as those described in Elisabeth Haich's book, involved facing a terrifying ordeal or a great temptation to see if this would deflect them from their chosen path. Only the most dedicated and pure in heart would pass the initiation and therefore be deemed worthy of embarking on the next stage of their spiritual development.

Nowadays some spiritual teachers have suggested that we may go through particular initiatory life experiences in place of some of the more formal initiations of the past. Some may be dramatic events that demand our awareness and appropriate response while others may pass by virtually unnoticed. Yet they are all regarded as significant in their own way and said to exist so that we may learn. It may be something that we need to find out about ourselves—our strengths and weaknesses, our readiness to progress or to surrender—or about life, consciousness or the meaning of truth.

In my own case, one of these pivotal, initiatory experiences was the time when I came unexpectedly close to death.

Experiencing My Own Mortality

The fever that I caught during my Gombe trip with Jane Goodall in September 1997 continued to trouble me after my return to the Netherlands. My condition deteriorated to such an extent that I was admitted to hospital but I was misdiagnosed and sent home. My condition worsened and soon I was so weak that I could not walk or even stand unaided and was confined to a wheelchair. For this reason I was readmitted to hospital. This time I was correctly diagnosed as having a particularly virulent and serious strain of malaria—*malaria tropica*. In the days that followed I was tested to the limit as I came the closest that I had ever been to dying.

On the first day after my second admission I was so ill I felt as if all the life force was leaving my body. I felt like a sack of potatoes and it was hard to take in what was happening around me. I was taken for an x-ray but was so weak I could not even stand up for it and had to be draped over the machine in order for the x-ray to be taken. I felt utterly drained and had no energy to fight for my life and not even any energy to feel afraid of dying. I felt completely helpless yet my consciousness was clear and I remember completely surrendering myself to God and praying, "Father, wherever you want me to be—on this side of life or on the other side—there I will be." At the end of my prayer a feeling of calm came over me and I felt full trust in God.

Gradually the life force started to return to me and I felt deeply grateful to find myself still alive. I continued to be very sick and remained in the hospital for some time. I remember one day lying in my hospital bed and, tired of looking at the ceiling, I turned my head to look out of the window. I was hoping to see a tree or something to remind me of the beauty outside. Instead I noticed a dustbin man lifting up the rubbish bins and emptying them without effort. At the time I would have jumped at the chance to trade places with him. It made me realise how precious life was and I felt I would do anything, and any job, if only I could get my health back.

After some time, I was able to get about in a wheelchair and got to the point where I was due to be discharged to continue my recovery at home. Before leaving I was sent for a final x-ray and, after it had been taken, I noticed that the radiologist was looking at it with a frown. I asked him what was the matter and what the x-ray showed but he wouldn't tell me anything. He just said that he was only newly trained and I should wait to speak with the consultant.

My brain went into overdrive, as this was only a few days since my 'conversation' with God and I became convinced that I must have some serious condition such as cancer. I was then hit by a wave of fear and spent the next twenty minutes, while I was waiting for the consultant, contemplating having cancer and examining how I felt about dying. It was amazing having had no fear when I was on the brink of death to now experience it just when I thought life had been returned to me.

Finally the consultant appeared and announced that my x-ray was clear! I discovered that the earlier radiologist had only been frowning because he was newly qualified and was concentrating really hard as he studied the x-ray! It was a great relief but I also realised that the wait had been a valuable experience too, for it is often only when actually faced with such a crisis that we take time to really consider such issues.

Thankfully, after being correctly diagnosed with malaria I was given the appropriate treatment and eventually recovered fully. Yet this remained an important experience for me. Not only was I, of course, very grateful to have my health back but this experience also made me realise that at any given moment you never know if you are going to live or die—that is truly in God's hands—and you don't know how you will respond until the moment actually comes. I felt grateful to have had this experience, making me more aware of my own mortality and of the preciousness of the life I had been given. This strengthened me in my resolve to put my life to good use.

During my hospital stay another man shared my room for a time and his plight and his conduct really moved me. He was a man in his mid-thirties who had a serious skin condition. Because this condition required daily medical care he had to live in a nursing home for the elderly as this was the only place where such regular care was available. Every two months he had to come to the hospital for more intensive treatment. The nurses would draw the curtain around his bed and I would occasionally hear him sigh with pain during the long periods that they worked on his dressings. When the curtain was opened I could see that his small frame was completely covered in bandages, just like an Egyptian mummy. Every day he would have to endure the whole process again as the bandages were removed and then reapplied.

This man lived with constant pain, discomfort, immobility and suffering yet he never complained and the nurses told me he was always charming and friendly with them. When we talked I was struck by how gently he spoke about his chronic, debilitating skin condition without any trace of anger, pity or bitterness. I wondered how he could be so accepting.

His gracious conduct, gentleness and acceptance of his situation made a deep impression on me and helped me with my own healing. I found him quite inspirational and have never forgotten him.

A Gentle Healing

After recovering from malaria I looked at life differently. Though physically weaker, I began to appreciate things with a greater awareness. I was very happy to be alive and to share life with my partner, Chris. I found her presence, and her loving ways, very comforting. My healing process took a further turn when we decided to move to the country together.

My daughters had by then all graduated from school and I had already decided that I wanted to leave the noise and bustle of the town to experience a more tranquil, slower, rural environment. On one of Chris's visits to the Netherlands we drove to the east of the country and together discovered a beautiful farm for sale in Epse. By this time our relationship was deepening yet the distance between Hawaii and the Netherlands obviously made it a long commute to see one another.

One Sunday morning we were talking about our separate homes and lives with an old friend, Egon, when he paused and said, "But do you have room in

With my wife, Chris

your hearts for each other?" Our friend Jerry Jampolsky had also said something similar. We thought about this and soon decided to let go of our fears and follow our hearts by living together. Chris made the loving decision to make the move to Epse with me in 1997. I thought it was so courageous of her to leave her home in Hawaii, and to come from a bright, sunny, colourful island to the flat and often rainy Netherlands, so that we could share our lives together.

Through Chris I came to know her daughter Mel, who later became my step-daughter. Mel is a beautiful, elegant young lady with a bright mind. Having three daughters of my own it was a new experience to come to know this lovely young woman who already had a whole life behind her. Naturally it took time for us to get to know each other. Over the years we have become accustomed to the different ways that we each look at the world. We have grown closer and now share a great friendship and can also have fun together.

Living on the farm in Epse meant that I had an eighty-five kilometre drive to my office in Hilversum twice a week. On this journey I began to notice how my mind would always start to speed up the closer I got to the city. Yet on my return trip, as I got closer to home, I would relax both mentally and physically. In general, while living a more rural, slower-paced life I felt more detached from my philanthropic and business work and was more able to 'let go' when I got home.

REDISCOVER YOUR HEART | 97

Being in this peaceful part of the country I also felt more connected with nature. My neighbours were mostly farmers and were in tune with the more natural rhythm of the seasons and the land. Chris and I enjoyed the quiet life in Epse and we were lucky enough to have a cheerful man named Ferdi living on the property with us. He would help us tend the cows, vegetable garden and other chores and we couldn't have managed without his help and friendship.

When family or friends came to visit, it was so nice that we had real quality time together as they would tend to come for longer stays, rather than the quick visits that we so often have in towns and cities. This gave us time to really connect with one another.

In 2000 Chris and I got married in the Netherlands. For the wedding we had a house full of family and friends with some coming from as far away as Hawaii. We arranged to have our marriage ceremony and celebration nearby. Everything was planned and organised but on the morning of our wedding we woke up around 5 a.m. and both felt awful. We felt like we were coming down with the flu and wondered how we would get through the day.

Suddenly Chris remembered a CD we had been sent as an early wedding gift. It was a recording of Tibetan singing bowls, created by a friend, and was said to harmonise our energies. We started listening to it and then both fell back to sleep. At exactly 8 a.m., in good time for our wedding, we woke up and found ourselves feeling completely refreshed, calm and ready for our special day.

Tonio—our Dog

As we lived on a farm, people would often ask us what kind of animals we had. Sometimes Chris would reply, "Mice." We got three magnificent Scottish Highland cattle to help us manage the grass in the summer time. As they are hardy animals they could stay outside all year and it was lovely to see them graze in the fields. Yet after getting to know the pug dog belonging to Chris's daughter Mel we began to feel that we would like to have a dog too.

While dining out one evening in a nearby café, Chris spotted a tan and white dog sitting quietly under a table. She thought it was a mongrel but after speaking to the owners we found out that the dog was actually an old Dutch breed called a kooiker. Chris said to me, "Wouldn't it be great to have one of those dogs one day?"

Soon after this we heard of a local breeder who had a litter of seven kooiker puppies. All the puppies had been sold but luckily the first born was available again as the lady who had bought him had changed her mind since she had to move to a flat. We went to have a look at the puppies and we both noticed one particular dog and somehow felt that he was 'our' dog. Later we found out that this dog was in fact the one that was now available.

We brought him home in a box and put him next to our bed that evening on my side of the bed. I woke up several times during the night and each time I put my hand in the box and he licked my fingers. I was surprised to find myself comfortable letting him do this as previously I would have been concerned about the hygiene aspects. Yet he was so affectionate that I couldn't resist!

A few weeks later we received his official pedigree papers and were amazed to discover that he was born on the same day as my birthday. We decided to name him Tonio, after a good friend Ton, who was a very sweet man we knew who had passed away. Tonio is a very sweet dog. He has been with us for many years now and has become an integral part of the family.

With my mother on the farm in Epse

It has been a great experience having Tonio in our lives: he is a real friend and just loves unconditionally. It is fascinating how we have learnt to communicate with each other. Even though he can't talk I know his different moods and he seems to sense when we are unwell and comforts us. When we go into the local village together it is also amazing to see how well he remembers just where he can get little treats such as cookies or a little piece of sausage from the butcher.

After five years of living in Epse, I was finding commuting increasingly draining as I was now having to go to my office three times a week due to increased work demands. As traffic increased the journey was also taking longer and longer. I also felt that I wanted to spend more time with my mother who, for more than sixty years, has lived in our old family home close to my office. She was now living alone for the first time following the sad passing of her partner of more than twenty years. Also, my three daughters now all lived in Amsterdam and the distance from Epse made it more challenging for us to spend a lot of time together.

The reality of living on the farm was that it was time-consuming and Chris too started to yearn for a simpler, easier life. So, for various practical reasons, we made the decision to move closer to Amsterdam. Yet we also made the choice to take the gifts of our peaceful country life with us on to our next home.

Soon after making this decision we fell in love with a charming village on a river between Amsterdam and Utrecht. In 2002 we moved into a historic house there on the riverside. Now it is a short walk over the drawbridge to shops in the village and my office and an easy drive to visit my mother and daughters.

Psychic Surgery

In 2002, my wife and I had dinner with Prince Alfred von Liechtenstein in Amsterdam. During our conversation, he mentioned that he had arranged for a well-respected Filipino healer, Alex Orbito, to come to Vienna and asked if we might like to come and meet him In fact Chris had already met Alex some years ago, while living in Hawaii, when he had treated her teenage son, Zack for a recurrence of his brain tumour. She had been told that there was little left medically that could be done to help him and, although she was sceptical about so-called 'psychic surgery', she decided to give it a try. She had heard from others that Alex was a genuine and gifted healer so she took Zack to see him.

Alex treated Zack four times in two days. Each time Zack felt better after the healing and seemed to be getting stronger. Some weeks later Zack called Alex and said, "I forgot to ask if you removed my cancer?" Alex responded, "When I do my healing work, I am an instrument of God. I can only remove negativity at the time; the rest is between you and God." Chris told me that Alex's words and treatment helped her son a lot during the last year of his life.

Having heard this story I was interested to meet Alex and to learn more about 'psychic surgery'. I had heard that the healer is said to have the ability to enter the body with his or her bare hands and was keen to witness this with my own eyes. Since Alex had been invited to the Academic Hospital in Vienna to give a demonstration to a group of medical professors, this seemed a good opportunity to meet him in a scientific setting.

On arrival at the hospital in Vienna we joined a group of about ten elderly medical professors and physicians who sat together around a large boardroom table. Prince Alfred had arranged the meeting in order to build a bridge between the medical community and spiritual healers. We were all introduced to Alex, who seemed to be a very modest, gentle and soft-spoken man and a kind and warm Dutch woman, Marika Verheijen, who accompanied Alex and helped organise his healing sessions and travels.

Prince Alfred told the group that since first meeting Alex about twenty years ago he had experienced Alex's healing many times. These personal experiences had motivated him to want to make this healing available to others. He also said this day would be a unique chance for the group to witness it for themselves.

We were then shown a short documentary film of Alex doing healing work. The quality of the filming was not very good and it was quite difficult to see what Alex was doing with his hands during the 'surgery'. The film lasted about fifteen minutes and, as I glanced around the room, I noticed that several of the medical doctors were napping. It seemed that they had lost interest.

After the film Prince Alfred asked Alex if he was willing to demonstrate his healing work on a woman who was herself a medical doctor from Vienna. This raised the group's interest once more. This doctor had had a severe skiing accident some years ago and had experienced Alex's healing work previously. Alex was willing to work on her but made it clear that he was not there to do a 'demonstration' but to heal. He said, "My mission is not to convince, but to allow healing."

Alex went into an adjacent room with the doctor to light a candle and pray for five minutes. We were then invited to join them and gathered closely around the treatment table where the woman was lying calmly. She explained that she suffered pain as a result of her accident and indicated where. Alex began by working on her abdomen; his thumb and two forefingers seemed to penetrate her skin, his fingers appeared to move inside her, liquid began to drip down her side and he seemed to extract something from her abdomen.

She appeared to be completely relaxed and free from any discomfort. He wiped her skin off with a tissue and the skin appeared to close up and was just a little pink where he had apparently gone in. It all happened so quickly that it was difficult to absorb what I had just seen. Alex placed his hands on top of the woman's abdomen, bowed his head as if he had just finished saying a prayer, and said, "OK." With that we all went back into the other room, along with the woman who had been lying on the table, to have tea and sandwiches.

Seeing Alex's fingers apparently disappear into the woman's body right in front of my eyes was quite a shock and I felt dizzy. My mind was reeling from seeing what was logically impossible. It was one thing to see such a phenomenon on a video screen and accept it in principle. It was quite another to see it at first hand. After a few minutes I recovered and Marika said that Alex would like to offer others there the chance to experience this for themselves. I was very surprised to see that many of the doctors lined up to take their turn. As I watched each person coming out from having their session with Alex, they seemed to appear younger and more vibrant. It was interesting to note how their seeming indifference had changed.

The following day we went to join Alex for a further healing session and this time one of the first people to be operated on was my wife, Chris. A small tumour had been found on an x–ray of her left breast and Alex now operated to remove it. He put his hand into the side of her breast and as he removed it I actually saw a small, round lump of tissue, the size of a small marble, between his thumb and index finger. After this 'surgery,' Chris was left with a small, pink spot on her breast that disappeared after two days. A week later, back in the Netherlands, she was x–rayed again in the hospital and the tumour was found to have gone.

I had two 'operations' that day as well—one on the right side of my belly and one on my chest near my sternum. It was incredible because I actually heard a pop as Alex's hands seemed to enter my body. It was such a strange sensation to feel his hands apparently moving inside my body but the whole procedure was over so rapidly there was no time to process it fully.

The 'operations' did not hurt at all and I felt that Alex did much more than just operate with his hands. Tremendous love radiated through his eyes and the whole experience gave me a very special feeling that is hard to describe.

That evening, instead of going to a party in Alex's honour to which we had been invited, Chris and I stayed quietly in our hotel room We wanted to allow the feelings and sensations from the healing to work through our bodies. I felt deeply touched and grateful to have had this experience even though I could not fully explain or understand it. That day Alex operated on about eighty to one hundred people and he did the same the next day. Throughout the healing he maintains a prayerful attitude and very quietly moves from one person to the next, speaking only very rarely. He always says his hands are simply guided by God and that he just tunes in and acts accordingly. The outcome of the healing is up to God's will and the individual themselves. He is just an instrument and makes no claims himself about any healing powers.

The next evening Alex was scheduled to go on a chat show on Austrian TV called *Vera*. It was named after the show's host, who also happened to be a medical doctor. Alex was reluctant to appear, as he does not seek to promote himself and usually shuns the limelight, but in this case he agreed to it simply because Prince Alfred had requested it and made all the arrangements.

When he agreed to appear Alex told the Prince that he couldn't promise "any instant operation on demand for TV" since his healing work is very sensitive to surrounding energies. Prince Alfred understood this very well but the TV crew had high expectations for a dramatic 'show'. However, they were also extremely sceptical. When I chatted with the hostess prior to the show and asked if she believed in psychic surgery she replied emphatically that she did not.

There were various items on the programme that day and the audience happened to be full of bartenders as the item preceding Alex was a competition to find the best cocktail mixologist. When it was Alex's turn to appear, Prince Alfred briefly introduced him and his work and then a male volunteer with a certain diagnosis, selected by the programme makers, lay down on the table for healing. Alex placed his hands on the man and tried to concentrate despite all the noise and the distractions from the audience, performers and the bright lights of the studio but nothing happened. We were all sitting in the front row and everyone waited in great anticipation, yet still nothing happened. After a few more minutes Alex simply removed his hands, walked quietly over to the hostess and said that he could not do the healing under such circumstances.

Everyone was shocked and there was a moment of chaos as the hostess did not know how to respond. The show ended soon after and some of the audience started to leave. The producer was quite agitated and said to me that this was going to cause a lot of problems since it had already been announced in the morning papers that Alex's healing would be shown on the programme the next day. (The show was being pre-recorded).

In the midst of all this, Alex caught my eye and I offered myself as a patient if he wanted to have another try in front of the cameras but with less pressure now that most of the audience had left and the atmosphere was quieter. Alex agreed, the cameras were quickly re-installed around us and Alex operated on me. This time, unusually, I found the surgery a bit painful and the post-surgical mark remained for six weeks, whereas in other cases I had found that it was normally only visible for about two days. I believe this may have been because the difficult conditions in the studio made it harder for him to 'tune in' and do his work in the normal way.

Some time later an Austrian medical/pharmaceutical group tried to prosecute Alex for practising medicine without a licence and he has also been similarly persecuted in other countries. Alex is always saddened when this happens but he just quietly continues with what he sees as his mission. It is said that he has now given over a million healings all over the world, and there are countless stories of people who believe that they have been helped or cured by him. These accounts have been written up in several books.[43]

The Visionaries' Circle

Shortly after the terrible events of 9/11 in New York in 2001 Deepak Chopra, the best-selling author, doctor and spiritual teacher, set about creating an Alliance for a New Humanity, which seeks to accelerate a global movement for a better world. It aims to help create global communities for personal and social transformation through connecting, communicating, inspiring and supporting. The Alliance organises various events, and in August 2007 Deepak invited forty people from all over the world, to come together in Taos, New Mexico for a week, to share visions for a new humanity under the theme, 'the Visionaries' Circle'.

I had first met Deepak about ten years ago and then met him again in 2006 when our mutual friend Ray Chambers[44] invited me to join him for an Alliance meeting in Puerto Rico. On this occasion I had the chance to get to know Deepak much better and discovered what a wonderful, loving and spiritual person he is. We made a strong connection with one another and, following on from this, Deepak invited me to join his 'Visionaries' Circle' group.

In Taos we had a week-long programme of talks, meditations and outdoor activities and there was much profound sharing, learning and exchanging of visions. One activity, a ride in a hot-air balloon, had been planned for the middle of the week but was postponed until Saturday morning because of weather conditions. By Saturday some of the group had already left so could not participate. The thirty or so of us who remained got up at 5 a.m., before the sunrise, and went to a place on the plateau above the Rio Grande. There, we had a joint meditation as dawn began to break, just before the start of the balloon ride. As the sun rose, the balloons were prepared for flight, and within about twenty minutes our five balloons took off one by one and then slowly descended into the canyon of the Rio Grande.

---

43. See his website: *www.pyramidofasia.org* for details of these.

44. Ray Chambers is an American philanthropist and the founding chairman of 'Malaria no More' in the USA. In 2008 he was appointed as the first Special Envoy of the UN Secretary General for Malaria.

It was an amazing experience to float down into the canyon, carried by the wind and with just the occasional sound of a hot air blast released into the balloon by the pilot to control our height. Occasionally one of the natural air draughts blew our balloon towards the rock on the sides of the canyon but then we would drift away again. We really enjoyed the truly spectacular views as we followed the path of the river from above.

After about an hour our pilot used the burners to release more hot air into the balloon, making it ascend out of the canyon and allowing it to drift a little toward a suitable landing site. Just as we were about to land we noticed an open ultra-light plane in the distance flying towards us. As it came closer we were able to make out the features of the pilot. He seemed to be really enjoying himself, flying in the early morning on this wonderful bright, nearly windless day. We waved at him and he smiled and waved back as he flew by us. Then we turned our attention to the imminent landing of our balloon. Once on the ground we all helped to deflate the balloon, loaded up our vehicle and set off to meet our companions from the other four balloons for a small breakfast. We then returned to the hotel to continue our meetings together.

The Cycles of Life and Death

We began with some short meditations, with Deepak guiding us through some mantras, and part of that morning's teachings was devoted to the subject of death and dying. I was very struck by how profoundly and beautifully Deepak explained the continuity of consciousness through life and death. I was particularly struck by his explanation of the cycles of life and death in our cells. He pointed out that our bodies are composed of cells that each have a limited life cycle lasting from a few minutes to seven years.

He explained that each cell has a built-in consciousness of its own life cycle, which encompasses the fact that its death contributes to the structure and function of the body as a whole, as old worn-out cells make way for new ones. This reminded me of the concept that we are all symbolically 'cells' in the body of the universe, each one of us making a contribution to the development of the whole. On this planet, when our time comes, we make way for a new generation. What we leave behind—through our relationships or our work, the way we interact with the planet—can benefit, or damage, all humanity and beyond. The parents who take care of their children, the workers who put thought and care into their jobs, the gardeners who tend and nurture their patches of nature—all of these make vital contributions.

We continued to explore these topics as the day progressed and shared a lot of visions for contributing toward a better life for all on this planet. That evening it was arranged that we would have our farewell meal together down in the canyon at the side of the Rio Grande. This meal had been planned for Sunday evening, but was brought forward because some more of the group had to leave early on Sunday.

We were supposed to end our programme at 6 p.m. but collectively decided to continue until 6:20 p.m. so that everyone could have the opportunity to finish sharing their visions. We then took a bus from the hotel that was to drop us at a spot near the edge of the canyon from where we could walk down to our dining site at the riverside in the canyon.

We began our walk across the plateau before descending into the canyon and after a few minutes again heard an ultra-light plane flying towards us. As it came more clearly into view we remarked to each other how it looked like the same plane and the same person that we had seen flying in the morning. A couple of the group members took pictures of the plane, and I again noted the happy face of the pilot who was so obviously enjoying his flight. The plane flew on and, as we began our descent, the attention of the whole group was suddenly, dramatically focused on a rattlesnake that had appeared on the path in front of us. Conversation stopped and we all stood in silence watching it, not wanting to walk around or disturb it. It seemed extraordinary that we had been considering death that afternoon and now here it was, staring us in the face. Luckily the snake then slithered away into the bushes and we were able to continue our descent down the winding path into the gorge.

Less than a minute later, we rounded a bend and I glanced over to the other side of the canyon. Something caught my eye in the rocks and as I looked at it, I realised to my alarm that it was the wings of an ultra-light plane. They were stuck to the rock like the wings of a dead butterfly and it immediately crossed my mind that this must be the plane that we had just seen fly by moments earlier.

I drew the attention of the group to what I could see and some of those in front said that they had heard a bang just before turning the corner. We all began to wonder if this could have been the impact of the ultra-light, smashed against the rock by a sudden air current although there was no wind. We could make out red-and-white markings and the group members who had taken pictures of the plane just moments earlier checked back in their viewfinders and confirmed that these were indeed the colours on the wings of that plane. The realisation that a terrible accident must have taken place dawned on the group. Spontaneously, four of the youngest and most athletic men in our group, Erik-Jan, Patrick, Gabriel and Richard, began to clamber down into the canyon to get across the river and climb up to where the plane was stuck to the rock. Their descent was very precarious as that part of the canyon was very steep and there might also have been other rattle-snakes nearby. Without thoughts for their own safety, these four were determined to reach the pilot to see if they could help.

This descent was beyond most of the group members, including me, so the rest of us watched and waited and held the pilot in our prayers. We also contacted the emergency services. It took the men around forty-five minutes or so to get over to where the pilot had crashed. As the first one got to him, I called across—for the ultra-light was about level with us but around half a kilometre away as the crow flies—"Is he still alive?" One of them, I think Erik-Jan, tried to call back but he was too far away. We then looked through our guide's binoculars and saw him wave his arms and gesture that the pilot was dead. This wasn't a surprise but it was still a terrible shock. Although we didn't know the pilot personally we neverthe-less felt connected with him, having seen him twice.

It was getting dark and, seeing that there was nothing that they could do for the pilot, the four crossed back over the river and began their return journey. Meanwhile the rest of us prayed for the pilot's soul to have a safe journey back to its source, the Infinite. We were all, of course, very saddened by what had hap-pened and also concerned for the pilot's relatives who were yet to learn of his ac-cident. One of our group members was particularly distressed since she had only recently lost her brother in a helicopter accident.

Within the hour the emergency services arrived and the firemen lowered ropes to pull our group members back up the incline as it was so steep. We all walked back to where the bus was waiting for us and, as the dark of night quickly de-scended, the police took witness statements from the men who had gone to the scene of the accident. Once this was over we boarded the bus and went to the bot-tom of the canyon. We were all deeply moved to have been present at this man's passing. We were also amazed at how being confronted by a deadly snake and then being witness to the tragic death of this pilot was linked directly to the topic of death that we had been discussing that very afternoon. The whole evening had been both shocking and profound, and we were all processing the experience in our own way.

Finally arriving at the bottom of the canyon we gathered together at the picnic site. Later that evening Deepak addressed us: "You who are here have all decided to be here and to witness the consequences of this terrible accident. Some of our group decided not to be part of this, since they already left earlier. The events of this whole day are reflections of a higher plan. We would not have been part of this if it had not 'happened' that we changed our plans, brought our farewell meal forward to tonight, and closed our session at the later time of 6:20 p.m. It is clear that today each of us, being here, have had to face death and we all need to experience our own 'deaths' in a way, too. So I invite all of you to go inside and ask yourselves what you need to leave behind here in Taos." He then closed with a prayer for the pilot who had died and ended with the words, "May this man's soul fly into boundless freedom."

At the very moment that he spoke these words and when all our thoughts were focused on the man who had died there was a sudden, surprising rush of wind that seemed to come out of nowhere. This was particularly striking, since the whole evening had been practically wind free. The rush of wind went through our group for around ten seconds and then all was still again. It was a deeply impressive moment, as we had no direct explanation of where the wind had come from and it was as if, by praying for the man, nature was providing the wind for his soul to fly to freedom.

After this, as we all took time to reflect on what we would leave behind in Taos, I realised that I wanted to make the utmost use of my God-given life and to cut out all those activities that do not serve this purpose. We all continued to reflect and share and sometime later we re-boarded our bus and went back to the hotel.

Pete's Gift

The next morning as we prepared to leave I mentioned to our guide, that, if it would be possible to contact the family of the pilot, I should like to pass on how happy this man had been right before his death. Some weeks later, via an email from Carolyn, Deepak's assistant, I received an emailed copy of the service leaflet from the pilot's funeral, which was held on 1 September, and I found out that he was Paul R. 'Pete' Adams, 12 October 1935—25 August 2007. The leaflet also contained a nice photo of his smiling face.

As I read the leaflet, I was touched to learn how much Pete was loved, cherished and admired by his family—his three sons, two daughters-in law, niece, four granddaughters, a sister, brother and sister-in law—and his peers. I also learned that he had graduated from Princeton University in 1957 and that he had had various careers spanning the pharmaceutical industry, restaurant ownership and property development. He was described as an 'unconventional and renaissance man' who was 'creative, intelligent, passionate about life, extraordinary and deeply spiritual'. What was most extraordinary was to read the letter, which he had written a few years earlier, to be read out at his funeral in the event of his death. His son, Mike, whom I later spoke to, most kindly agreed, also on behalf of his other two brothers, that I may reprint it in this book[45]:

Pete's Letter

This service is in my memory but right now I am totally OK—I am in the bosom/arms of God and with all my family, friends and animals. I am totally at peace and far beyond any happiness we have ever known on Earth. I will always be with you when you think of me or need me. Always.

AND mostly this service is for you, the survivors. To grieve, to cry; to be sad and to be happy; to laugh, to love; to open your hearts to one another and reflect on the meaning of your lives. To put aside the differences and see the real beings among you. God is Love.

That true, unfettered, unconditional, non-judgmental love that is beyond all personality and form that we have all experienced at one time or another. If only for a fleeting moment or two. In that moment it doesn't matter if we are male or female, black or white, ugly or pretty, rich or poor, Anglo or Hispanic or Jew, young or old, 'somebody' or 'nobody'.

In that moment we know God.
We are Love.
We are God.

I love you all,
Peter

---

45. I later learned from his son that Pete had written his letter in 2001, the year of the atrocities at the Twin Towers.

I was very moved by his words and struck by how closely the letter expressed, in essence, the themes that we had been discussing during our Visionaries' Circle in Taos, as well as the synchronicity of all the events that had occurred. Everyone who has read this letter since has also been deeply moved by it. It seemed as if this extraordinary and wonderful man had prepared a gift that not only touched his immediate family and friends but which was now 'taking wings' and already touching others around the world. In mid-September I had the chance to speak with Mike, one of Pete's sons, by phone. I felt him to be a very warm, understanding person and we made a good connection. I shared with him how I had seen his father flying in both the morning and the evening on the day of his death and how he had seemed to be so very happy and carefree, taking real pleasure in his flying. Mike in turn told me how much he and his brothers loved their father, how well he got on with his father and how he feels his presence even now, stronger than ever.

A further extraordinary coincidence was discovered by a member of our group, Richard, who was one of those who had gone down to the site of the plane crash. He later spoke with another of Pete's sons, Pete Jnr., and learned that Pete had not only been at Princeton University in the same year as his own father but that they were in the same class and had known each other. Richard had lost his own father seven years earlier so this knowledge and the whole experience affected him deeply. The two men were able to share a lot together about their experiences of loss.

Another strange coincidence was revealed in an email from the group member Erik-Jan, who was also one of the people who had been at the scene of the accident. He had talked at length with another of Pete's sons, Chris, who said he had gone down to the crash site with his brothers a few days after the accident to collect their father's belongings, such as his gloves. On the way down he said that he had suddenly and inexplicably experienced a strong fear of rattlesnakes even though he did not see any during his descent. Of course, he had no knowledge of the rattlesnake that had appeared to us just before his father's death.

The same day that I read this e-mail from Erik-Jan I went for a walk with Chris near our home and I saw, for the first time in the Netherlands, a water snake slithering through the grass into the water. Then the very next day Chris told me that our cleaning lady had found a small garden snake in our kitchen. Again, this had never happened before.

All these sudden sightings of snakes made me think about their symbolism. I discovered that in some indigenous cultures they are regarded as a symbol of wisdom and as guardians between the physical and the spiritual worlds; also that their characteristics are thought to symbolise alertness, vigilance and courage. All of these things seemed to fit so well into the experiences that we had all just shared.

Reflections

The World of Spirit

The experiences described in this chapter have often seemed to defy logical explanation or demonstrate synchronicity. They have challenged me to determine their truth or their possible deeper meaning.

Being presented with phenomena like the crop circles and paranormal healing, I have had to open my mind and consider the evidence. This led to shifts in my perspective as I considered new possibilities.

My close encounter with death through malaria felt like a process of initiation. I was helpless but, drawing on my inner resources and with the support of others, I came through the experience. My trust and faith in God, or the Infinite, were reaffirmed and I saw my life through new eyes.

The experience of being present at the time of Pete Adam's passing seemed an extraordinary incidence of synchronicity that had a greater purpose. Reading his wise words and having contact with his family afterwards were a profound privilege and blessing for all in our group. Perhaps we were all 'meant' to be there at that time in order to learn from his life and words and to help spread them further.

I feel that having an open mind, a pure heart and a willingness to be open to these wonderful mysteries can enable us to explore the truth and meaning behind them.

This led me to my sixth Key:

KEY 6
We can find our own path to Truth.

AFFIRMATION
*May I have the courage to explore the mysteries of life
and seek the truth without judgment.*

CHAPTER 7

Making a Difference?

Today the earth is going through many unique changes and we are faced with huge challenges, both at a global and personal level. Yet I really believe that we can all contribute to building a more caring and sharing society.

To do this I don't think that we need to be powerful, rich or famous; the small changes that we each make in ourselves and in our own lives, as well as contributions that we make to society, can surely make an impact on the world as a whole. We are all one of billions and if each one of us does whatever we can to support positive change then I do believe that our whole planet can move forward and evolve a higher consciousness.

To become involved we need to ask ourselves how can we really make a difference and how can we best 'help' or support one another. In my own life I have become involved many times, both spontaneously and after careful thought, in trying to help others. Reflecting on these experiences I started to see that, even with the best of intentions, the results are not always beneficial. Sometimes the help may be misused and at other times it may even have the opposite effect and hold someone back from taking full responsibility for themselves.

I also saw that there can be problems for aid organisations that aim to help. For example, when I was volunteering with the Red Cross my colleagues and I had a very sincere desire to help others yet I came to realise that we also often exported our own stress and problems. I also observed in various situations that aid organisations may unwittingly impose their own cultural values, or Western models of help, on those they are working with without fully understanding and appreciating local culture and needs. In this context I often feel that we need to learn more from those we were meant to be helping and that we should also learn to help ourselves in order to support those in other cultures and in the 'developing world' most effectively.

As a result of these reflections I started to question what was the best way to help others. I concluded that rather than helping it might be better to think in terms of supporting the person or organisation in their development. I also feel that the support needs to be wanted by the person or institution themselves, rather than imposed on them, and that it should respect local culture, religions, needs and so on. I also learned that sometimes the best way to support is actually to take a step back and let people develop their own capabilities. As is sometimes said, "Help yourself so that we can help you."

In this chapter I would like to share with you five experiences that I have had of helping and supporting others. Some of them occurred quite spontaneously and looking back on them at various stages in my life has helped me formulate my ideas about helping. I hope these accounts may also motivate others to develop further their own thoughts about helping and may even inspire ideas that we can all share to support personal and planetary development.

Sowing the Seeds of Unconditional Love— *The Twinkling Eyes Club (TEC)*

Nowadays we have all sorts of clubs and societies, each catering for different interests or groups. They may be based around a particular sport or hobby or aimed at a certain age group or income bracket. Such clubs and societies can play a valuable role in bringing people, or specialists, together with common interests. But what if we were to expand that principle to what all people have in common—their humanity? We are all already members of the 'club of human beings', sharing all that this planet has to offer us, although we may not be fully aware of this.

One day in 1991 I was in Washington, DC, the capital of the USA, talking with my friend Bill Halamandaris[46] and we happened to be discussing this issue of clubs and organisations. At a certain moment I smiled at something he said, and he observed laughingly, "You've got twinkling eyes!" I replied, "So have you! Maybe we should set up a club for the twinkling eyes people!"[47] We were just joking about it at the time but afterwards I started to think how great it would be to establish a non-exclusive club and aim to make everyone on earth into members[48]. So I decided to create the Twinkling Eyes Club (TEC) and make it open to all members of the human family.

I got the idea of drawing a smiley face on my thumb and then transferring it to other people's thumbs to make them members. I thought that the TEC could

---

46. Together with his brother Hal, Bill Halamandaris is the founder of the Caring Institute in Washington, DC.

47. 'Twinkling Eyes' is a metaphor for our inner smile and need not be taken literally. Thus sight-impaired people are also warmly welcomed within the club's membership.

48. The world population reached 6 billion in 1999 and is projected to grow to 9 billion by 2040. At the time of writing the world population is 6.7 billion, more than double the 3 billion population recorded half a century ago in 1959. Source: The US Census Bureau International Data Base (IDB) World Population Information. See: *http://www.census.gov/ipc/www/idb/worldpopinfo.html.*

aim to spread awareness of the power of a smile, as smiles make life more agreeable, easier and happier for everybody. We all know that an inspiring, authentic smile with twinkling eyes, which comes from the heart, can make us feel good and help us through the day. Smiles can also help deepen friendships and enrich experiences.

Later on I was inspired to create the slogans, 'Miles of Smiles' and 'Sprinkles of Twinkles' and had stickers and T-shirts made with the TEC symbol and these words in order to spread the message about the club. A few years ago my wife Chris also presented me with balloons, pens and travel tags with the TEC symbol and

Jane's 'Miles of Smiles' birthday present

'Miles of Smiles' Detail

slogan. I have now been initiating people into the Twinkling Eyes Club, and giving these items out all over the world, for over fifteen years. I estimate that there are already many thousands of members and the numbers are growing all the time.

Members also appear in the most unlikely places as illustrated by the following story: My step-daughter Mel, who lives in New York, was in Central Park some time ago with a girlfriend, when they decided to stop at one of the small cafés. Most of the tables were taken but they saw a space where a good-looking guy was sitting. Mel asked if they could join him and, as they got talking, found out that he was Dutch. Jokingly she asked him if he was a member of the Twinkling Eyes Club. To her amazement he responded by opening the book he was holding to reveal a Twinkling Eyes Club sticker on the inside!

Another wonderful thing about this club is how the smiles you send out have a way of coming back to you in all sorts of unexpected ways. One birthday my dear friend Jane Goodall came to see me and presented me with a gift: a massive roll of wallpaper. When I unravelled all fifteen metres of it I found she had collected and pasted hundreds of smiling faces on to the paper, making 'miles of smiles' for my birthday! At the very end of the paper she had pasted a tiny mirror that could reflect viewers' own smiles back to themselves. Jane had put so much love and care into her gift that I was really inspired and deeply moved.

How to Join The Twinkling Eyes Club

Wouldn't it be great to have a club that was open to everyone; that is all the nearly seven billion people now in the world? We are all already members of the 'club of human-beings', sharing together all the gifts that this planet has to offer. So why not join the Twinkling Eyes Club, the only non-exclusive club in the world and spread miles of smiles around the globe?

HOW DO I BECOME A MEMBER?

Touch the pad of your thumb to the smiling face symbol on the thumb image on this page. Then draw the smiley face onto your own thumb with a ballpoint pen to confirm your membership. At the same time repeat to yourself, "I am now a member of the Twinkling Eyes Club and I will make other people members too."

You are now a member and can start spreading 'miles of smiles' and 'sprinkles of twinkles' amongst others. Whenever you have the opportunity, redraw the smiley face on your thumb to refresh it.

HOW DO I MAKE OTHERS INTO MEMBERS?

First ask the person if s/he would like to become a member of the Twinkling Eyes Club, explaining that it is for everyone and costs nothing to join and outlining the club's philosophy to share 'miles of smiles' between all the nearly seven billion members of the human family.

Twinkling on the South Pole: Robert Swan (centre) and two others

If the person says "yes" redraw the smiley face on your own thumb with a ballpoint pen, then draw another smiley face on her/his thumb and press your two thumbs together.

As the smiley faces join together tell the person, "You are now a member of the Twinkling Eyes Club!" Ask the person to repeat the phrase, "I am now a member of the Twinkling Eyes Club and I will make other people members too."

Then invite the person to spread 'miles of smiles' and 'sprinkles of twinkles' wherever and whenever possible and to repeat the smiley face procedure often for new members as well as for her/himself.

OPEN TO ALL!

Anyone and everyone can join the Twinkling Eyes Club. It costs nothing and is fun to belong to. To become a member of the Twinkling Eyes Club follow the instructions on the TEC pages printed here or go to my website, *www.fredmatser.com.*

You may also like to think about starting up something yourself that is simple, and costs little or nothing, yet will bring people together. All it takes is a bit of imagination.

Simple Living and Simple Solutions—
Using Alfalfa

The way each one of us lives has an impact on our planet. I believe that we can do a great deal by following the natural rhythm of life and learning to treat nature with both awareness and respect. This involves us both letting go of our excesses and demands on nature and developing ways in which we can nurture the planet's resources. I feel that living simply but well can free us from the endless distractions of consumerism and can increase our focus on what is really important for us and our planet.

One inspiring example of this was told to me by Hamid Hossaini[49] whom I met once through my friend, Jane Goodall. Hamid told me how he grew up in a farming family in rural Iran but managed to secure an educational scholarship. He gained a place at a prestigious university in the USA but instead chose to study in India as he wanted to be in touch with people who lived simply.

There he met a man who became his teacher. Later he found out that this man was one of the very wealthy in India but he never realised this at the time as the man used to walk around in an old coat and give money away. The question his teacher always asked himself was: "Can I do without it?" Yet, his life was one of joy, not deprivation. He had chosen to dedicate himself to a high ideal and had within him an inner richness that was greater than his external wealth.

When I heard this story from Hamid I felt the phrase 'Can I do without it?' was a really useful yardstick to carry throughout life. I started to apply it as much as possible in my own life and this inspired me, amongst other things, to sell the second car that I had at that time (a Mercedes Benz). I realised I could do without it and instead I donated its value to a charity connected to Jane Goodall's environmental work.

I think this yardstick can also be applied in terms of finding ways to preserve our natural resources or of utilising them most effectively. One example of this might be greater use of the humble alfalfa plant to for the undernourished. This idea came to me when I was in Moscow in 1991 visiting several of the hospitals that were recipients of our Foundation's aid. There I saw first hand the problems of inadequate nutrition.

I began to think about how an alfalfa seed programme might help solve this problem. I already knew that it could be grown very easily and had a rich nutrient content. I also knew from my work with the Red Cross on the oral rehydration programme that simple, inexpensive interventions could have profound effects. I felt

49. Hamid Hossaini is an international peace-builder and a special advisor for The Teaching and Learning for Peace Foundation, *www.tlpeace.org.au*

that providing people with alfalfa seeds and simple instructions for growing them at home could make a significant impact on nutritional status for a relatively low cost.

GROWING ALFALFA

Alfalfa is packed with nutrients and a source of high biological value protein, that is it contains all the essential amino acid proteins that the body needs to obtain from food. Alfalfa seeds can easily be grown in glass jars and require only light and water to germinate. They need to be rinsed daily and left to drain. Within four to six days they sprout into nutrient-rich and chlorophyll-rich shoots. These simply need to be rinsed of loose seeds and can then be added to salads or sandwiches or simply eaten as a snack.

The seeds can be stored for many months or even years and can be used to provide a good source of nutrition all year round—even in sparse winter months.

Nutritionists working with alfalfa in India have found that just the simple dietary change of consuming a handful of alfalfa daily can significantly contribute to decreased infant mortality, improved maternal health and better child growth and development.

Therefore, this simple, low-cost seed has very high potential. It can give health and can empower all, including the poor and underprivileged, with a cheap and easy, self-sufficient source of good nutrition.

The same year a Dutch national newspaper, the NRC-*Handelsblad*, published an article describing this idea but so far it has not been taken up. It is interesting to note that sometimes there can be a lack of interest in simple solutions such as these because there is little profit to be made or because more 'high-tech' solutions are preferred. Yet I remain convinced that simple solutions can sometimes be highly beneficial as well as economical.

Essentially I believe that there are many different ways that we can choose to live our lives more simply and in harmony with nature and that some simple solutions from nature may be highly beneficial and cost-effective. If we can learn to take less and grow more, freeing ourselves from the consumerist mind set, we may create new paths for living sustainably and well on this planet.

Spreading Peace and Caring and Sharing—
Taking the Peace Flame to Sarajevo

In the early 1990s, as Yugoslavia was breaking up, wars broke out in its various states. In Bosnia, Serbs, Croats and Muslims were engaged in a bloody civil war. Sarajevo, its capital city, was under siege for almost four years[50] during which time electricity and water were cut off and food and medical supplies dwindled. The city was reduced to rubble and people struggled to survive. In fact, so many died that a football field was converted into a cemetery to accommodate the dead.

Day after day pictures of the devastation and suffering appeared in the TV news. On one programme I saw this football field cemetery and behind it I caught a glimpse of the stadium where Sarajevo had hosted the Olympics in 1984. This was followed by another news item featuring the Winter Olympics in Lillehammer, in Norway. It was 18 February, 1994 and as I watched the juxtaposition of these two news items I suddenly had an idea.

Here's what I later wrote about what happened:

I am at home.
8 o'clock news.
Again images of the war in Bosnia.
A few minutes later an item celebrating the Olympics
in Lillehammer (Norway).
A flashback: ten years ago to the Olympic games in Sarajevo.
Lillehammer now. Sarajevo now.
Sarajevo then.   Sarajevo now.
  Two comparisons.
  Two, or rather, three realities.
How in the world is it possible that these co-exist?
The violence of war and the joy of sport?
What does the Olympian in Lillehammer feel right now?
Does he think of his own performance?
Or does he think of the people in Sarajevo?
    of their pain?
    of their deep suffering?
Maybe he has all these thoughts?
Maybe he feels confused. Like me.
Then a plan came to me:

We'll go to Sarajevo with ten gold medallists from
Lillehammer and ten from the Sarajevo Olympics of 1984.
We'll light the Peace Flame as a sign of our empathy, as a remembrance
of the eternal flame that burns in all our hearts.
Peace Flame '94 was born.

I watched the images on the news of the winning athletes proudly receiving their Olympic medals in Lillehammer. I recalled the images of Sarajevo (1994) that had just been shown; ravaged by war and with people suffering and living in fear. I thought back to the Sarajevo Winter Olympics in 1984, with the city and its inhabitants standing proud and celebrating. These thoughts and images triggered my idea to take the Olympic Flame and Olympic athletes back to Sarajevo so that we could stand in solidarity with the suffering people there and remind them that we had not forgotten them. Rationally this was a seemingly impossible task since Sarajevo was still a war zone and the logistics for making such a plan happen were mind-boggling. Yet I felt sure it could succeed.

I called a Norwegian friend, Katarina Thome, who put me in touch with the Olympic committee in Lillehammer and promised to help in any way she could. Within two weeks I found myself outlining my plan to Gerhard Heiberg, the Head of the organising committee for the Lillehammer Winter games. He liked the idea and gave the OK for the flame to be taken. Even though we hadn't yet got permission to fly into the war zone, he asked me to announce the plan at the Closing Ceremony for the Olympic and Paralympic games the next day. It was quite an experience to deliver a speech about this plan in front of the ten-thousand-strong crowd that included the King and Queen of Norway and the President of the International Olympic Committee, Juan António Samaranch. Then, just before the Lillehammer Olympic flame was extinguished at the end of the games a flame was taken from it for us to take to Sarajevo. We were not allowed to refer to it as the Olympic Flame so we renamed it the 'Peace Flame'.

All the details had to be finalised very quickly. Katarina continued to work on the project and, with her wonderful help, athletes were contacted and we started to negotiate a plane and flight crew and tried to obtain a permit from the UN to land in the war zone. We needed the co-operation of the UN forces in Sarajevo, had to find musicians and organise the ceremony and had to contact local people in Sarajevo who could publicise and participate in the event. These arrangements

---

50. The Siege of Sarajevo lasted from April 5th 1992 to February 29th 1996 and was the longest siege in modern history. It has been estimated that 12,000 people were killed and 50,000 wounded during the siege—85% of them civilians—and that the post-war population decrease was 64%.

all took place in the days before mobile phones or emails were in common usage, so communications were not easy and it was all very time-consuming.

The arrangements were also fraught with difficulties. At first we were told that only planes with anti-missile detection systems were allowed to land in Sarajevo, yet we were unable to gain access to one. However we discovered that the UN official who had told us of this requirement had been permitted to land in a plane without such a system. When we presented him with this information he agreed that the requirement could be waived for us as well.

In the end the Dutch government agreed to provide us with a military plane and crew, although officially the mission would not be done in their name. It was agreed that we could take off and land from Belgrade airport and arrangements were made for the athletes and musicians who had agreed to participate, and the Olympic flame, to be flown there from countries all over the world. However, just one day before our departure, this permission was withdrawn. We then had only twenty-four hours to find a new airport, make new travel arrangements, find new accommodation for all the participants coming from many different countries and reschedule the arrival of the Peace Flame from Norway. Many obstacles like these—too many to mention here—presented themselves but a way was found through them all.

Finally, on 29 March, just thirty-nine days after I had first had the idea, thirteen Olympic and Para-Olympic gold medallists, three musicians, and various other supporters took off from Ascona airport in Italy en route to Sarajevo[51]. As we came in to land in Sarajevo airport, which was being held open by peace-keeping forces, I remember the plane weaving down and swinging from side to side as it descended. We were not sure if this was to avoid making the plane a target for missiles or if it was because the pilots were hung over—we had, to our great shock, found them drunk in the hotel the night before take-off. I had needed to go to the plane ahead of our group in the early hours of the next morning to check that they were ready and fit to fly. Their behaviour had nearly jeopardised the entire project and was yet another obstacle that had to be overcome.

On agreeing to participate in this mission each person had been required to sign a declaration confirming that they understood their safety could not be guaranteed. So we descended into Sarajevo knowing that our landing was potentially dangerous. Once on the ground, we were moved rapidly across the tarmac to behind a wall of sandbags and then immediately placed into armoured vehicles. We were then driven in convoy straight to the city square where our event was to be held. As we peered out of the windows we saw destroyed buildings and rubble in every direction. It was deeply shocking to see the extent of devastation that the brave people of Sarajevo were being forced to endure[52].

29 March 1994

39 days and 390 near dead-ends later we were standing there.
In the middle of Sarajevo. In the midst of around 2,000 people;
the women, men and children of Sarajevo.
The sun shone.
There also stood thirteen Olympic and Para-Olympic medallists
and three musicians.
Sixteen wonderful people.

Our message:

> *We want you to know that we have not forgotten you.*
> *We know that you are in great pain,*
> *although right now things are a bit calmer.*
> *We cannot really experience your pain,*
> *Yet we want to give you sparks of light and hope.*

While we were surrounded by many UN soldiers,
We have also seen trees and bushes starting to bloom.
Signs of new life.
Through every barrier, be it earth, asphalt, rock, hate,
jealousy or anger, the life force still asserts itself.

It is this inspiring force,
which is beyond growth, flowering and decay,
that I wanted to remind the people of.
New connections are made.
New friendships sealed [53].

At the square, all had been prepared for us. As well as the 2,000 or so local people there was a ring of 400 UN soldiers for security. We went straight onto the stage

---

51. The medallists and musicians who participated are listed in Appendix B on page 154.

52. Reports have stated that shell fire in Sarajevo was so heavy—with an average of 329 shell impacts per day over the four years and 3,777 impacts in one single day on July 22nd 1993) —that virtually all buildings in Sarajevo had suffered at least some damage and an estimated 35,000 buildings were completely destroyed.

53. Diary entry written at the time.

and told the crowd that we wanted to let them know they were not forgotten. We wanted to support them at this difficult time. Each Olympian spoke briefly, saying why they had been inspired to come. The musicians played and sang, local children staged a dance display and various local people spoke. Then the Peace Flame was lit from the flame that had travelled by plane all the way from the Olympics in Lillehammer. It was then placed in a special fixture on a nearby bridge, its light a symbol of our united hearts and minds.

During the event it was heart-warming to see the joy in the faces of everyone present, especially at such a time of suffering and struggle. At the end I promised the people that we would come back and help them restore peace and harmony. I kept this promise but, at the time, I did not realise how many years it would take to bring my promise to fruition.

As soon as the ceremony was over we were whisked away in the armoured vehicles once again and were shown some other parts of Sarajevo en route back to the airport. We saw the market that had been hit by shelling and where more than eighty people had been tragically killed in one missile blast the month before. We also visited the Olympic stadium from the Games ten years before, including the indoor ice skating rink. This had been partially demolished in the fighting, a point that particularly struck the two skaters in our team who had won medals on that very rink. Then we arrived back at the airport and were immediately flown out.

Driving in an armed vehicle through Sarajevo, 1994

Addressing the crowd in Sarajevo, 1994

The day was so full it passed very quickly. On the return flight we quietly absorbed all the emotions we had experienced as well as our feelings of hope for the future.

The Peace Flame House in Tuzla

Our visit had occurred during a lull in the fighting, but the Siege of Sarajevo continued for another two years. I had made a promise to the people that I would not forget them and soon after I had the idea of establishing a centre where their pain could be acknowledged, accepted and released. I thought that this could be helpful to the survivors in Sarajevo who remained deeply traumatised and emotionally scarred by their experiences of war. With this is mind, our Peace Flame Foundation was established in 1994 with the aim of contributing to sustainable peace in areas of conflict.

Later on we began negotiations with the authorities in Sarajevo to build such a centre. However, after almost eight years of negotiations, we had still not been granted permission due to all kinds of red tape and some corruption as well. As

The Peace Flame House in Winter

an alternative, Maurits van Heek, a co-worker with considerable experience of the Balkans, suggested building the centre in nearby Tuzla instead. This town had a history of inter-racial harmony and a mayor who was well-regarded for his reconciliation work, so it seemed a good choice.

In due course we received permission to build in Tuzla and over the next eighteen months the project was realised. My friend, the Dutch architect Ton Alberts[54], known for his beautiful organic designs which mirror natural forms, very kindly agreed to design the building as a gift. Ton very sadly passed away on 19 August 1999, just after completing his sketches for the Peace Flame House. However, his colleague, the architect Marius Ballieux from Alberts & Van Huut Amsterdam, and the Bosnian architect Kenan Haracic, did a great job in bring-

---

54. The innovative and beautiful organic architecture of the late Ton Alberts is well regarded in the Netherlands and abroad. He and his colleagues, Max van Huut and Marius Ballieux and their team (*www.albertsenvanhuut.nl*) have created many renowned buildings including the ING Bank Head Office in Amsterdam and the Gasunie Head offices in Groningen, northern Netherlands. Ton's approach was based on the principle of 'healing through form' and he once said, "A building only starts to live when all the materials together in harmony mean more than each of the materials separately."

Official Opening of the Peace Flame House, 2003

ing Ton's designs into form. Lani van Petten, Ton's widow, painted the interior in natural colours in her unique style and Isabel and Frans Smeets helped 200 children in Tuzla to design and construct a playful and colourful floor mosaic.

The Peace Flame House[55] was officially opened in October 2003, consisting of a ninety-seat theatre, three therapy rooms, a studio for all kinds of creative activities, a multi-purpose room, and a kitchen. It was a great day, with people from different ethnic groups who had been set against each other during the war all enjoying music, laughter, performances and refreshments together.

I initiated many new members into the Twinkling Eyes Club (see page 115) that day, too, and 'miles of smiles' were spread everywhere.

Since its opening the Peace Flame House has hosted many arts, drama and dance programmes and other courses as well as therapy sessions. A documentary on sports activities for those with disabilities has also been made there and shown on Bosnian TV. All these have been great achievements. However, the centre is not without its problems. I have observed that in countries that have been used to a Communist regime, where everything has been 'taken care of' by the State, it can be quite hard for people to feel empowered and really take the initiative.

---

55. *www.peaceflame.nl*

This has been reflected in the fact that it has been quite hard for the Peace Flame House to become self-sustaining.

The centre itself was a gift funded by our Foundation but the idea was always that it should slowly become independent and self-financing with regards to maintenance and running costs. However it took a long time to become so and our Foundation continued to provide funding and guidance until March 2008. Since then the centre has been self-sufficient but it seems to be a continuing struggle to keep things going. I still hope that this independence can be further developed in the future and that more trauma-resolution work can also take place there.

Sarajevo Now

Although the Peace Flame House was finally built in Tuzla rather than Sarajevo, I wanted to keep my promise of aid to the people in Sarajevo as well. Therefore the Peace Flame Foundation committed funds equal to the initial cost of the Peace Flame House for supporting various other projects and initiatives in Sarajevo itself. These have included setting up a halfway house for children leaving orphanages at eighteen, which helps to prepare them for independent life in the outside world, and co-financing the Vladimir Nazor Centre[56] for the education and rehabilitation of severely handicapped children. At the Centre, the children are treated with love and respect and encouraged to develop new learning skills, while their parents are given some much-needed respite. Today Sarajevo has been substantially rebuilt and the Peace Flame Foundation remains committed to playing a small part in aiding its recovery.

Working With Mind and Heart

My decision to respond to the plight of the people of Sarajevo came from the heart. At the same time, I knew that I would have to be intensely practical from the outset for anything worthwhile to be achieved. Thanks to the team of people involved we were literally and metaphorically able to get the project off the ground. The innumerable obstacles we faced required everyone in the team to stay very focused on our goal. Thankfully, we got through it all and were able to hold the Peace Flame ceremony in war-torn Sarajevo as planned. Our mission

---

56. Named after the Yugoslav poet and novelist, Vladimir Nazor (1876-1949) who was born in Croatia.

represented one small triumph of the human spirit against despair and isolation.

But our task did not end there. To make our contribution solid and long-lasting, we had to negotiate the difficult process of setting up the centre in Tuzla and supporting projects in Sarajevo. Hopefully these have contributed to improving life for those who have survived the years of bitter civil war in Bosnia. Yet, this experience also taught me that, however much I might wish to see people empowered to shape their own destiny, I had to accept that the process can take time.

I realised that, in supporting others, I need to be aware of my own expectations and not fall into a very common trap of attachment to the result. I can take responsibility for my own actions but not for how others respond or make use of the opportunities given to them. If people are empowered to make choices, I must accept that I may not necessarily be in full agreement with the choices made. I also realised once more that local people always hold the key to success in any initiative.

Personal Development—
My Journey to Peru

In 2005 I had my 60th birthday and to celebrate it my wife and daughters and I went together to spend time working on a rural social project. On my actual birthday we sat outside at a simple wooden table enjoying a farmer's meal when my daughters surprised me with a wonderful medley of songs they had put together as a story of my life. I was so touched by their singing and by all the love that I felt from them that I was moved to tears. It was the most wonderful gift and I appreciated it more than I can say. I also loved receiving my step-daughter Mel's subsequent gift; a wonderful photo album with photos of the event. It was a true work of art and I was deeply touched by that, too

Turning sixty helped me to reflect on my life—not only on what I had accomplished so far but also on what I still had to do. As a young man I had seen many friends set off on foreign adventures before finding their life's purpose. I had never really taken the time off to venture away from my responsibilities, family and full agenda. As much as I appreciated my full life, I yearned to know what it would be like not being 'my mother's son', 'my wife's husband', 'my children's father', or 'my employees' boss'. Being interested in spiritual development, I felt that I wanted to discover my inner self further. So my sixtieth birthday was a good reality check for me; I was healthy, curious and realised that I still wanted to explore my dreams of travelling to an unknown territory and tasting freedom.

I wondered where I should go on this personal quest and, for some reason Peru kept surfacing. I did not know much about its history and indigenous culture, nor do I speak Spanish, but still I felt strongly drawn to going there. I contacted a Peruvian friend who lives in Spain for advice on making such a journey and she suggested that I should meet Victor Estrada. She told me that he is a shaman (medicine man) from Cusco, a large city 3,000 metres above sea level. I still had not decided on my plans when Victor's name came up again via another friend. It struck me that this was perhaps more than just a coincidence. Of all the many spiritual teachers in Peru, what were the chances of the same person's name coming up twice? I took this as a sign that I was to meet him and began to plan my trip to Peru.

Through a series of further synchronicities occurring a week prior to my departure, I began to trust this intuition even more. I happened to be in touch with a Belgian woman who was an experienced guide for remote areas of Peru and who gave me further suggestions about places I should visit. I was also able to speak with Victor on the phone and arrange to stay with him. He also suggested an interpreter who could travel with me.

Everything seemed to be falling in to place without much effort. I had experienced this sort of thing before in my life, and it felt right to go with the flow and allow my journey to unfold. However, when I first set out to meet Victor in Peru, I encountered a number of obstacles.

Encountering Obstacles

Just before my departure from the Netherlands, I suddenly experienced intense abdominal pain. It came right out of the blue and was so severe that I could hardly walk and couldn't even put my socks on. Eventually the problem was diagnosed as a damaged muscle in my abdomen and with a mixture of orthodox and alternative healing, I became fit enough to travel, albeit in some discomfort. I don't know if this was meant to be an inner test of my resolve, or pure chance, but it was the first of a number of strange experiences that occurred.

When I reached Lima, the Peruvian capital, I went to the home of two artist friends who had kindly agreed to have me to stay for a few days. We would meet once a day for lunch and the rest of the time I stayed mainly in my room, meditating and writing while they were out at work. Nearly all houses in this part of Lima are fenced in and have guards and I felt this created quite an oppressive atmosphere. However I would forget about this by immersing myself in reading and, during my stay, I was particularly inspired by reading a book describing one man's experiences with his Indian guru, Yogananda.

One day I decided to go for a short walk and tried to open the door to get out but it wouldn't open. I tried it again and then realised that I was locked in the house compound. I couldn't get out or make any contact with the outside world, since every room was sealed with separate locks. My hosts were not due back until the evening and there were no people nearby to call out to—and in any case I don't speak Spanish—so I was imprisoned there.

This felt strange but, as I tried to make sense of it, I realised that both my abdominal pain and now my 'imprisonment' could just be interpreted as obstacles or 'tests' on my way to greater things on my journey. So I decided to just accept my confinement and settled down to a day of more reading and quiet contemplation until my hosts returned home that evening. When they did, they were shocked to discover that their housekeeper, unaware that I was inside, had locked me in.

Meeting Victor

After four days of resting and acclimatising in Lima I flew to Cusco, with Mary-Ann—the translator, and healer, who had kindly agreed to accompany me—to meet Victor Estrada. Victor was waiting to greet us at the airport. He looked like a friendly man and had short, dark, curly hair and clear, dark eyes. As we drove through town I began to feel the effects of the high altitude and heat. Cusco moved at a much slower pace than Lima and seemed to be filled with tourists.

We parked on the unmade road next to Victor's large house. He opened the big, solid doors and I found myself in a dark hall from where they also sold hand-made jewellery. After putting my things in an upstairs bedroom, we went to the kitchen where Victor's wife, who was busy cooking, greeted us. We sat together around the table and drank the coca tea[57], which many people drink in Peru as it is thought to ease altitude sickness and other ailments.

Victor invited me to come up to the top floor of his house, where he has a room for teaching and holding ceremonies. We sat down and talked, via the interpreter, so that we could get to know one another a little better. He said that he had to get a sense of me in order to determine which sites to take me to and what experiences I could benefit from.

Afterwards he stood up, selected some feathers, stones and beads and chanted some words in his language. He performed a short ritual to prepare the path for me and then we sat in silence and meditated together.

---

57. Coca tea, also called Yerba maté, is a herbal tea made from the leaves of the coca plant.

Touching the Volcano

Victor took me on a trip to experience some of the ancient sacred sites in his area. The morning we left I was woken at 5 a.m. We ate a hearty breakfast, as we would travel far that day. Victor's son-in-law drove us and Mary-Ann joined us as translator for the journey. We drove through the lively and chaotic city to an ancient sacred site higher up in the Andes that was once the centre of Inca rituals but was now in ruins. Victor asked me to enter a circular area, marked by standing stones, and to stand in the centre. He told me to raise my arms horizontally and to spin to the right while holding my breath. When I had done this he asked me to do it again and he continued to do this several times. At first it was hard to do this without feeling unsteady. I was also aware of the thinness of the air as we were around three thousand metres above sea level. Yet after a while I found myself spinning effortlessly. It seemed that I was 'being spun', faster and faster. My awareness started to shift and I felt free from limitations. It was as if the spinning somehow accelerated everything within me and at one point I felt in union with the earth, the sky and everything beyond. Eventually the spinning slowed and I fell to the ground. Yet the dramatic sense of connection that I had experienced stayed with me.

A few days later we went on a long journey and it was pitch dark by the time we stopped the car at a high point in the mountains. Victor said we were at the spot where the three mountain ridges of South America joined together. We got out of the car while our driver remained inside waiting for us. We were surrounded by ground fog and, standing there for a few minutes, we felt the silence and solitude of the place. We walked through the darkness and came to a fence and then, walking along it, arrived at a gate. Victor shouted a name and, after hearing some noise in the background, we saw an old woman emerge from a hut carrying a torch with a weak light. I was rather surprised to find such an aged woman living alone in this remote place without any electricity or amenities. Yet she and Victor greeted each other like old friends and then she unlocked the gate for us so that we could enter.

In the darkened fog we made our way across some uneven ground and ascended a hillock about six metres high. Mary-Ann waited at base while Victor and I clambered up to the top which revealed itself as a four-metre wide crater. As we lay on our bellies peering over the rim I could hear some gurgling sounds down below and realised we were at the summit of a dormant volcano. Victor looked at me and said something reverently in Spanish which Mary-Ann translated from below as "This is the womb of the earth".

As we lay there the mist cleared and revealed a sky with the most dazzling array of twinkling stars that I had ever seen. I was in awe of the beauty and solitude of the place. Then Victor spoke again saying that, if I was lucky, the dormant volcano would 'speak' to me. This sounded a bit odd but after my earlier experience of the spinning I was prepared to be open to all experiences and see what happened.

We focussed our full attention on listening to the sounds of the bubbling inside the crater. Suddenly Victor said, "Fred, did you hear it? It is saying your ancient name. Listen well . . . it is meant for you."

I could not make out any specific name but Victor repeated the sounds that he had heard and told me what he understood to be the name and its meaning. Again he spoke reverently for he held this place to be very sacred and regarded the name as a gift from mother earth herself. He explained that the vibration of the sounds from within the crater could be translated into words from ancient Inca language. He also said that the name was something to hold dear and private and that its purpose was to help me reclaim inner power and strength. Then he motioned me to put my hands inside the 'womb', the crater. As I let my hands fall down over the edge I realised it was full of liquid that felt warm and soft.

After a while Victor indicated that it was time to leave the crater. Our walk back down was easier as the mist had cleared. The old woman was waiting for us by the gate and once again she opened it for us to pass through. She then locked it and went back to her hut. Again I wondered how she could exist in such a place but she seemed quite content as the keeper of this sacred place.

As we walked back to the car we suddenly noticed a brilliant light shining in the sky. Its brightness was highlighted dramatically against the dark mountains yet its form was hard to distinguish. On noticing the light Victor knelt on the ground saying, "There they are!". He started to offer coca leaves towards the light and passed some of the leaves to Mary-Ann and me so that we could do the same. Then he stretched his arms out, with palms up, and said, "We are open for contact".

I was not sure what to make of this but waited quietly in anticipation. I recalled the book by Shirely MacLaine, *Out on a Limb*, where she claimed to have encountered extra-terrestrial beings and wondered if this was something similar. I didn't feel afraid—just intrigued. I was curious but calm.

As we watched the light it seemed to hover in one place but then it suddenly gathered speed, darted across the sky and disappeared. Its movement was extraordinary and quite unlike the steady lights of a flying plane that you would expect to see in the sky. I was unable to explain what I had seen but Victor was in no doubt that we had had extra-terrestrial contact. He said that 'they' had been aware of our presence and that such sightings often occurred in this area.

In wonderment, but not knowing quite what to make of it all, I got back into the car and we began to drive away. There were no other cars on the road and as we drove down through the darkness the moon started to appear over a mountain ridge on our left side. We were looking at it when, a few moments later, Mary-Ann exclaimed, "Look on the right. There's the light again. It's following us!" A light had appeared again about a mile away from our vehicle and for a short time it seemed to follow us. Then, just as suddenly as it had reappeared, it again vanished. I have never been sure of the explanation for what we had seen but there was certainly a remarkable quality to the light and the way in which it moved. It was completely unlike the movement of any type of aircraft or star, so could it have been a UFO flown by extra-terrestrials? I have no way of knowing.

On one of our last days we drove out to the site of an old, ruined temple. While walking among the remains of this sacred site old memories kept coming back to me. Having been with Victor for some time I was becoming accustomed to the fact that some places we visited seemed to have a special energy that somehow activated inner experiences. I therefore trusted this process and just let the feelings emerge. It was a very peaceful place with no distractions so it was easy to focus within.

As I approached the edge of the site, near some trees, I noticed a large standing stone and felt particularly felt drawn to it. It was almost as if it was silently calling to me. I went over to it and sat down on the ground with my back against it. It felt very natural and safe and I felt as if I was in the warm embrace of the stone. I allowed myself to sink into the stone, relaxing and letting go and as I did this the feelings that had been stirring inside me began to come to the surface. Tears began to flow as colourful images from different parts of my past played before me in my mind's eye.

At a certain point an image of my former wife, Ineke, appeared and all the pain and sorrow of our difficult divorce welled up inside me. Along with these painful memories came more tears. Yet, after a time, I found my attachment to some of the unresolved issues of the divorce beginning to dissolve along with my tears. I was able, once again, to feel her original sparkle and the honesty and trust that we had shared in the early stages of our marriage. I was able to forgive and started to release the pain that I felt over not having been able to reconcile our differences. As this process developed I began to feel freer. I do not know how long I sat against the stone but I was aware that somehow a profound healing had taken place inside me.

After some time I rejoined Victor and shared my experience with him. He told me that I had been sitting on a very special spot and that the stone I had been leaning against is known as 'Killa Rumi'. Killa is the Quechua word for 'moon' and 'Killa Rumi' is translated as the 'mother' stone. He suggested that the special properties of this stone had played a part in my experience.

On our way back into town I continued to cry and felt that these tears were the continued release of my old pain. Mary-Ann and Victor's son-in-law seemed to understand the process I was going through. When we got back to our hotel they came to my room and gave me some laying-on of hands healing, which I found comforting and helpful.

Machu Picchu

For many who visit Peru, the 'Lost City of the Incas', Machu Picchu is a must-see—and that included me. With my backpack on, I boarded a train full of fellow tourists from around the world and headed up towards its location high in the Andes Mountains. After our arrival at the nearest railway station, we found ourselves in a bustling village with a colourful market packed with all kinds of tourist souvenirs. I headed straight for the bus that was going up to Machu Picchu itself. The bus was very crowded and had seen better days but it managed, slowly, to chug up the narrow unmade road. After our arrival we disembarked like a herd of sheep on to the sacred grounds of one of the world's most breathtaking sites. I stood in the midday sun trying to take in the panorama of peaks of the Andes that provide the stunning backdrop to this ancient site.

I had been advised to book a place in the only hotel at this altitude far in advance. Checking in, I saw it had a large dining area that was packed with people enjoying the incredible views. The hotel had a library of Western videos and that night I watched the classic film *Gandhi* which I had not seen before. I was moved by the simple, peaceful and effective methods that Gandhi used and how he did not allow obstacles to block what he believed was right. I went to sleep full of these impressions of his life and work, and have found that these still resonate with me today.

I woke early and walked out into the ruins of Machu Picchu. The sun had just risen and the majestic Andes seemed to be reaching for the sky. This sight, and just being in this unique place, took my breath away. It also felt such a gift to be there in the stillness of the morning without others around. I climbed on to the different terraced levels and looked at the remains of some of the grey stone houses and temples. The buildings no longer had roofs and were open to the elements. I wandered along the maze of small paths amongst the ruins and found a place to sit on the dry, clay ground. Leaning back onto a small rock wall I closed my eyes and felt the sun's heat getting stronger.

As I sat there quietly I imagined the many challenges the Incas must have endured to build this city. It occurred to me that perhaps they wanted to live on these precariously high terraces, where the edges fell away to sheer drops, as a sign of their devotion. I felt so grateful for the opportunity to visit this place and to be in the ruins quietly and alone. Then the sound of distant voices started to come closer and I realised the first buses had arrived depositing their full loads of visitors. It was time for me to leave.

After my time in Machu Picchu, I stayed on in Cusco for another week. I wanted to have some quiet time to absorb my recent experiences and to have the opportunity to write and read. While there I learned how the Incas had been overcome by the Spanish Conquistadors who destroyed their temples and built Catholic churches on their foundations. I thought how very intimidating this must have been for the indigenous people; these churches still stand to this day.

While I was in Cusco, there were two days on which there were military parades and, at the end of each, I was surprised to see Catholic processions of nuns, priests, voluntary groups, and so on, carrying banners. This strong Catholic presence made me realise how powerful the indoctrination must have been. The local, indigenous, Quechua-speaking people have become second-class citizens to the urban Spanish dwellers and their native religion is no longer given any prominence.

This reminded me of the patterns of hierarchy and control that you see in so many parts of the world; indigenous people are often excluded from the local power structure even though they carry many generations of wisdom in their culture. Yet this situation may also be changing—for example, the dramatic election of an indigenous coca farmer, Evo Morales, as President of Bolivia in December 2005.

I went on some leisurely strolls through the city's colourful markets. My trip was all about living differently to my usual active lifestyle so it was nice to wander around slowly just taking in the sights and sounds. Walking through the centre of Cusco, I noticed that many people seemed to be leisurely chatting in cafés or sitting on park benches. They didn't appear to be caught up in the rat race as many of us are in the West.

On one of the busy city squares I noticed an ATM cash machine at the entrance of a shop. As there were not many of these around, I decided to get some money out. I had been warned about pick-pocketing so I scanned the area to see if anyone was lurking who might want to take advantage of a tourist with cash. I noticed a thin, dark fellow leaning against the wall opposite. He didn't look that tidy, nor did he seem to be doing anything in particular, which made me wonder about him. However I ignored this feeling, opened my wallet and inserted my card into the machine.

Then the thought surfaced—what if this man tried to take my wallet? I quickly punched in my pin number, took the cash and walked away. After putting the money deep in my pocket I heard a voice behind me calling out "Señor, señor!" I turned to see the same man and jumped to the conclusion that he must have seen me taking the cash and was now following me. So I kept on walking but so did he. When I eventually stopped he came up to me and to my utter surprise handed over my credit card. I had forgotten to take it out of the cash machine and he had followed me to return it. I was so thrown off guard that I forgot to thank him before he walked away. As soon as I realised what had happened I began to hunt for him in the crowd. I was so happy when I managed to find him and could give him my heartfelt thanks.

Meeting the Shipibo

I next travelled to the jungle town of Pucallpa, a two-hour flight north from Lima, together with a translator, Mia. There we were met by our new host, Mateo. He first took us through the busy town, packed with noisy scooters, and we then got into a car with five others and had a six-kilometre bumpy ride to his home village of San Francisco. This area is populated by Shipibo Indians—a very modest and delightful people with their own language, colourful clothing and rich culture.

Mateo's home is just a one-roomed hut with a thatched roof. Up to eight members of three generations of his family live there and they spend much of their time sitting together out on the front porch. The family were all very warm and hospitable and I was given an adjacent hut in which to sleep on the floor. Meals were taken on an outside table at the side of the hut. The dogs and chickens roamed freely around us and birds often alighted to share our meals. I was given the one chair to sit on but had to balance quite precariously, as much of the seat was missing. The others sat on a bench. One of Mateo's daughters did the cooking while the other had the job of washing both dishes and clothes.

Hardly anybody in the village has electricity and after sunset it soon becomes pitch black everywhere, so we took our evening meals by candlelight. There was no running water in the village. Water was drawn from the pump in the centre of the village several times a day, brought to the hut and often used more than once. To my relief, the drinking water was brought in huge, sealed plastic containers collected once a week by Mateo from Pucallpa.

Most days local women and children would come to the hut and urge me to buy their colourful bead necklaces—I ended up with quite a collection! I also walked around the village every day and would be accompanied everywhere by a flock of pre-school, bare-footed and smiling children. It was great fun to be with all these cheerful little children. They were very curious about my hair, the beard

I had grown and the hair on my arms, as they are a smooth-skinned people. They constantly wanted to touch my hair and it must have seemed as if I came from another planet.

I learned a lot from being with the Shipibo people. I was particularly struck by how they never said anything bad about each other and how they rarely complained. For example in the village, which had around 2,000 inhabitants, there were blaring loudspeaker announcements that could be heard all day long throughout the village. The first announcements started at 6 a.m. and were about getting to school. Then at weekends an Evangelical group used another loud-speaker to preach to the village. They held their services in a huge shed but normally only a handful of people turned up.

I found these constant noisy announcements very intrusive and they disturbed me quite a lot, but the Shipibo never seemed bothered by them at all. I was also impressed by their patience, modesty and simplicity. I found them to be wise and loving people.

During the three weeks I spent with the Shipibo I was grateful for the real sense of freedom that I experienced and the opportunity to get more in touch with my own thoughts and feelings. Even after I returned home and resumed my daily life I found that the memory of this period and this sense of freedom would often sustain me.

Preparing for my Return

I loved the Andes but was not very comfortable in the jungle area where Mateo lived, as I found it so hot, humid and mosquito-ridden. While I was there, I began to long for the ocean, for fresh air and a sense of space, so I decided to leave a little early. I travelled back through Pucallpa and Lima and on to the Caribbean island of Bonaire, which I had first visited in the 1960s with my parents.

It was wonderful there to walk along the water's edge and feel the ocean breeze on my face. While walking I also really enjoyed listening to a selection of music compiled for me on an iPod given to me by my children before I left. The selection was wide ranging—from Billy Joel to Mozart. I've always been aware that music can have a very uplifting effect on me, even transporting me to different states of consciousness. In this context, it really revived my spirit.

While in Bonaire my longing to see my wife, Chris, became stronger. She was on retreat in a place a few hours' drive north of Atlanta, Georgia and my daughter, Lyke, also happened to be working in Atlanta at that time. So I decided to fly to Atlanta where it was great to first meet up with Lyke and I then went on to where my wife was staying. In the week before her retreat ended, I thoroughly enjoyed several long walks, taking in the seasonal autumn leaves. It was marvellous to be immersed in nature and to experience all the leaves' glorious colours. At the end of the week Chris and I had a heartfelt reunion and spent a few beautiful days together. We travelled back to the Netherlands at the end of November.

I was very much looking forward to seeing my other loved ones again but was also apprehensive about going back to the old routines of my Dutch life, as I had so much enjoyed my freedom. The challenge was going to be how to maintain this sense of freedom within a Dutch context. Before starting back at work at the beginning of December 2005 and tackling the pile of work that had accumulated in my absence I had a few quiet days of adjustment.

Recharging Batteries

In 2006 I went back to work on existing projects but continued to reflect on my time away. I realised how low in energy I had been before my trip and how valuable it had been to have had the opportunity to recharge my batteries and to reconnect with my inner self. I could see more clearly how important it is to have a balance between giving and receiving, activity and stillness and how in this stillness the Divine, or the Infinite, can be more readily experienced. I also continued to re-evaluate my life and took time to consider what should be my next step.

My trip increased my awareness of the need to utilise both inner and outer resources and to maintain some balance in my life. On the one hand I wanted to be less 'busy' while on the other I still wanted to support and co-operate in different ways and contribute to society. I also wanted to be open to what the Infinite might send my way—to act according to whatever my true 'soul' purpose might be.

Two things then became the main focus. The first was the writing of this book. I had been making notes on my philosophy and experiences for some time and the work of turning them into a book was already underway before my trip. Now the challenge of completing this task became more prominent. Synchronicity played a part and the right helpers and encouragement came my way to support me in this process and to convince me that the book would serve a purpose in inspiring others.

My motive was to share experiences that I have had in order to inspire others to rediscover all our hearts so that we can co-operate to bring about change in the world. I did not feel that I held all the answers and have been aware throughout the process of writing this book of how much I still have to learn. I make mistakes and learn new things every day. I also believe that learning and caring and sharing together can help us make great strides forward. I hoped that my book might play a small part in this. The second focus that emerged unexpectedly occurred as a result of a phone call from my friend Ray Chambers[58] in late October 2006.

New Initiatives for Old Problems—
Malaria No More!

Ray invited me to develop a Dutch initiative as part of a wider campaign started in the USA to prevent and treat malaria[59]. He told me that 350 to 500 million cases of malaria occur annually and that at least a million people die from malaria worldwide each year, most of them children under five years of age in sub-Saharan Africa. Yet, he said, malaria is both treatable and preventable by means of effective interventions currently available.

These include long-lasting, impregnated, anti-malarial bed nets and anti-malarial drugs such as Artemisinin-based combination therapies (ACTs)—that is, drugs based on an extract from the Chinese herb, *Artemesia annua* (sweet wormwood). On the advice of the World Health Organisation (WHO) moderate spraying of DDT is also part of the policy.

A big campaign, under the banner 'Malaria No More!', was being set up in the USA and network partners were being sought in other countries to join the initiative. Would I like to be involved? I took some time to think it over. I felt a strong affinity with the campaign, since I had miraculously survived a severe bout of malaria—malaria tropica—ten years previously (see page 93). I was also motivated by my experiences with the Red Cross nearly twenty-five years ago, where I had seen at first hand how our campaign to promote oral re-hydration therapy salts had significantly reduced child mortality due to dehydration from diarrhoea. I felt it would be marvellous if the incidence of malaria could also be reduced by means of simple interventions. On the other hand, having just entered my sixties, I also felt a strong desire to take more of a back seat and to simply focus on my existing Foundations and their charitable activities.

---

58. See footnote 43 on page 103.

59. The United Nations Millennium Declaration in September 2000 set out eight development goals to be reached by developed and developing countries by 2015. The goals include targets for reducing hunger, improving education, resolving environmental problems and so on, with the overarching goal being the halving of poverty by the year 2015. Millennium Development Goal No.6 is aimed at health issues and, in particular, seeks to halt and begin to reverse the spread of HIV/AIDS, malaria and other major infectious diseases. This goal prompted a global campaign to control malaria.

However I felt that since I had been given a second chance after recovering from malaria, I was now being given the opportunity to prevent others from suffering and dying from this disease. So I researched the topic a bit further and explored the possibility of mobilising a team that would be committed and capable of establishing the campaign in the Netherlands. After careful consideration, I decided to say "yes" to my American friend and set about establishing the Dutch foundation, 'Malaria No More!'

The American campaign had decided to focus on the provision of bed nets, as well as education, monitoring, and treatment. They aimed to ask for $10 donations per bed net emphasising that each gift of a bed net could save a life. For the Dutch campaign I wanted to have a slightly different focus working closely with existing Dutch organisations that were already involved in implementing health initiatives at a grassroots level in Africa, such as the Netherlands Red Cross. A key characteristic of our approach was to build bridges of trust through an attitude of true respect and patience. We aimed to co-create sustainable and effective methods for dealing with malaria, in the context of primary health care, in the most affected African countries.

As part of my commitment to the campaign, I attended the White House Summit on Malaria in Washington, in mid-December 2006. Ray had mobilised support for this initiative from influential circles. This initiative was launched by President George W. Bush and the First Lady, Laura Bush, and it brought together 250 political and charity leaders, medical scientists and supporters from around the world to discuss new opportunities for combating malaria and to kick-start the combined public-private initiatives supporting the campaign.

Those present included: the then Secretary of State, Condoleezza Rice; many African representatives, such as Nigerian Minister of Health, Dr Eyitayo Lambo and the Principal Secretary, Ministry of Health and Social Welfare in Zanzibar, Dr Mohamed Saleh Jiddawi and many others[60]. This event helped to raise the profile of malaria on the global agenda and, since then, more funding has become available and many more people have been mobilised to support the anti-malaria projects.

Dancing to the Music

As part of the Summit, we were entertained by some really good African musicians and singers, including Yvonne Chaka Chaka. While she was singing, an elderly lady, seated next to me, stood up and started dancing in the aisle. I thought this was a wonderful response to the African music, so I got up and joined her but was surprised when no-one else followed suit. We danced to the end of the song and then sat down. Immediately after the song ended President George W. Bush walked on stage and addressed the audience. Later someone came up to me and said, "That took some guts to dance in front of all those people and keep the President waiting!" I had no idea that was what we had done!

Starting the Dutch Campaign

In April 2007, on World Malaria Day, we officially launched the Dutch foundation, Malaria No More! (Netherlands)[61] in The Hague in alliance with the following Dutch organisations: the Netherlands Red Cross (NRK)[62], UNICEF (Netherlands), Médécins Sans Frontières (Netherlands) (AzG)[63], AMREF Flying Doctors (Netherlands)[64], the Royal Tropical Institute (KIT)[65], CORDAID Memisa[66], and 'Drive Against Malaria'[67]. I feel privileged to be involved in this campaign and am delighted to work with a really committed Dutch team and a wonderful group of people on the Advisory Board, including Ruud Lubbers (Prime Minister of The Netherlands, 1982–94), Jane Goodall, and the 1992 Nobel Peace Laureate, Rigoberta Menchú Tum.

Since then our team and supporters have worked really hard to try and increase awareness of this issue and to raise grass roots support for this initiative. It has been encouraging to make some progress and to develop good links with our dedicated partner organisations in Africa.

On an international level things are also gathering pace. In September 2008 the first World Malaria Summit was held at the United Nations and I was privileged to participate. This meeting was again attended by many influential people including several African Heads of State, the UN Secretary-General, Ban Ki-moon, the British Prime Minister, Gordon Brown and Microsoft founder and philanthropist, Bill Gates. At the meeting it was announced that the stunning amount of US$3 billion was being made available for the fight against malaria.

---

60. Melina Gates, co-chair of the Bill and Melinda Gates Foundation has committed $83.5 million in grants to fight malaria. Ann Margaret Veneman, the Executive Director of UNICEF, is helping spearhead the campaign. Paul Wolfowitz, the then President of the World Bank, and Dr. Richard Feachem, the then executive Director of the Global Fund to fight HIV/AIDS, Tuberculosis and Malaria, both headed organisations that are assisting with funding. There were also representatives of the American Red Cross, Millennium Promise, United Nations Foundation, the Global Business Coalition, United Way of America and others.

61. *www.malarianomore.nl*.

62. NRK is the abbreviation for Het Nederlandse Rode Kruis, the Dutch name of the organisation. For more see: *www.rodekruis.nl*.

With the leadership of Ray Chambers, malaria has really gained a prominent place on the world health agenda.

However so much more support from individuals, groups and corporate organisations is still needed. It is my sincere hope that many more will be inspired to become involved to help stop the spread of malaria and to prevent suffering and death due to this disease. Perhaps, as a result of reading this book, you may decide to become involved in this worldwide campaign. Why not find out more at *www.malarianomore.org* or on our Dutch website, *www.malarianomore.nl*.

63. AzG is the abbreviation for Artsen Zonder Grenzen, the Dutch translation of 'Doctors without Borders'. For more see: *www.artsenzondergrenzen.nl*

64. AMREF is the abbreviation for the African Medical and Research Foundation. For more see: *www.amref.nl*

65. KIT is the abbreviation for Koninklijk Instituut voor de Tropen. For more see: *www.kit.nl*

66. CORDAID Memisa is the abbreviation for the Catholic Organisation for Relief and Development AID and Memisa stands for 'Medical missionary action'. For more see: *www.cordaidmemisa.nl*

67. "Drive Against Malaria" was started by David Robertson in 1998. He drives the length and breadth of Africa informing and educating about malaria and distributing bed nets. He is accompanied by Julia Samuel who records and produces documentaries abut the journey to raise awareness about malaria. For more see: *www.driveagainstmalaria.org*

Reflections

Making a Difference

In this chapter I have shared some of my experiences of ways in which we can support one another. I have learnt that sometimes the simplest ideas and solutions can have far-reaching and beneficial effects. For example alfalfa is readily available, cheap and easy to grow yet it provides a highly nutritious food that can have a profound impact on health. We can also support each other with encouragement, a hug or a smile. The Twinkling Eyes Club requires only the willingness of two people to share and a pen. Yet it provides a light and humorous way of reminding us that we're all part of one human family and one planet. It's a way of remembering the inner smile; the soulful spark that lies inside and which connects us all.

I have also learnt that supporting one another is not necessarily easy. The many obstacles that we encountered in Sarajevo and Tuzla for example were challenging and it can be hard for projects to become self-sustaining. Yet I have also seen what tremendous achievements are possible when we work together and share with one another.

I have also realised that self-awareness and self-development are important aspects of helping others too. If we are willing to explore our own thoughts, emotions and feelings, to forgive and release old pain then I believe we become more compassionate and able to support others in the same process. Sometimes we may need to go beyond our existing belief systems. I can see that my journeys and experiences in Peru were a way of going beyond my daily patterns and normal comfort zone. This, and the contact I had with wonderful people closely connected with nature and the Divine, helped me to see the world in new ways.

The experiences that I've had in supporting others through the work of our Foundations have often come from seeing potentials and possibilities and then allowing myself to be inspired. When this inspiration fills my heart it seems to give me a type of courage that doesn't entertain doubts. I can then enjoy being part of this creative process.

I am not saying that all my inspirations and ideas have always worked out because they haven't. Much of what I have been able to accomplish has been through co-operation with other inspiring and dedicated people. Global challenges like fighting malaria take co-operation between many people and organisations on different levels in many countries and progress may be made with tiny steps. Yet, if there is a willingness to change and make a difference then I truly believe that transformations are within our reach.

KEY 7
We can make a difference.

AFFIRMATION
My personal development is linked to global transformation;
each one of us counts and can make a difference.
I cherish and support the global family of which I am part
and the home planet that we all share.

CHAPTER 8

Looking to the Future

I was delighted when one of my daughters was happily married in 2007 and when she and her husband had their first child, a wonderful little boy in 2008. I can hardly express how thrilled I am to be a grandfather for the first time and the great joy that this baby gives us all. I am once again awed by the power of creation and the commencement of this new life. His birth has also made me so aware of how my generation is now preparing to step back, my daughters' is coming up and my grandchild's peeks around the corner. This is an exciting process!

Another important landmark for me has been the fact that, also in 2008, I reached the same age as my father when he died. Realising this has enhanced my sense of gratitude for the gift of life. I feel so fortunate to be in relatively good health and able to do so many things that my father could not on his latter years due to his serious illness.

I also feel fortunate that I do not have any particular problems with ageing at this time. I notice that I have a bit less energy so I now value my twenty-minute 'power naps' in the afternoon as I find they give me increased vitality. I also feel the importance of exercising, if possible on a daily basis, in order to keep my body flexible. When I see sports people in the peak of fitness I sometimes miss having the athletic ability that I had in my younger days but, in general, my philosophy is to catch any negative thoughts about ageing, or anything else for that matter, and to replace them with positive ones. Consequently, I have no fear of getting older. I see it as all part of the evolutionary cycle through which we pass in our journey back to the Infinite.

I am so grateful as well that the members of my extended family are all in reasonable health and good spirits and doing well too. We have so much to be thankful for, not least the opportunities we all have to support each other as well as other people who may have greater needs than our own.

Rediscover Your Heart Launch and Awards

In July 2008 the American first edition of this book was launched, along with the first Rediscover Your Heart Awards, in New York. The Awards were offered by The Fred Foundation in collaboration with Global Youth Action Network (GYAN)[68] and Chat the Planet[69]. The aim was to empower young people in carrying out projects that mirrored the principles outlined in this book.

Twelve inspiring winners each received $2,500 to carry out their chosen project for contributing towards a more functional and peaceful society. The projects ranged from educational and garden projects to empowering those with disabilities and encouraging dialogue through music and drama[70].

I was honoured to have the event co-hosted by the New York Society for Ethical Culture (NYSEC)[71] and held in the beautiful theatre of their landmark building on Central Park West. We had a wonderful evening that included speeches, music, presentations and sharing. Dr. Phyllis Harrison-Ross, President of the Social Service Board for NYSEC, renowned author and speaker, Dr. Deepak Chopra and Jonathan Granoff, President of the Global Security Institute, all gave addresses. Jonathan also read a letter from the Nobel Peace Prize winner and former Soviet President, Mikhail Gorbachev, encouraging and honouring the awardees.

I was touched by the great music from celebrated musician, composer and Oscar nominee, Charles Mack who performed a 'Rediscover Your Heart' song that he had specially composed for the evening and from awardees, the Mahina Movement. My friend, Donna D'Cruz, founder of Rasa Living, also chaired an on-stage question and answer session where I was joined by book contributors Dr. Jerry Jampolsky, Carolyn Myss and Deepak Chopra[72]. It was a unique experience to be gathered together on stage exploring spiritual questions together.

At one point Jerry spontaneously invited me to stand on the edge of the stage and to make eye contact with each person in the theatre. It took quite a few minutes to do this with each the 200-plus people who were present. It was a remarkable and moving experience to stand in the silence and make this connection with each and every person present.

It was also great to hear all the awardees briefly describe their projects and to chat with them and their families at the reception afterwards. I was also grateful to all the wonderful volunteers and NYSEC staff who helped make the event possible

---

68. Full details of these inspiring and award-winning projects can be found on *www.rediscoveryourheart.org*.

69. GYAN, founded by Benjamin Quinto, is a youth-led organization that unites the efforts of young people working to improve our world. For more see: *www.youthlink.org*.

70. Chat the Planet is a global dialogue company founded by Laurie Meadoff and Kate Hillis in 2001. It connects young people from around the world to talk about everything from politics, prejudices and war to sex, music and life in general. For more see: *www.chattheplanet.com*

71. *www.nysec.org*

72. For more on each of these please see their contributions in Part III.

and to The Works who provided organic, vegetarian food and drinks and donated their profits towards care for homeless New Yorkers living with HIV/AIDS.

Now we are in the process of planning a similar launch and award event in London, UK to coincide with the publication of this new, English edition of the book. This time it is hoped to 'grow' the Rediscover Your Heart awards by inviting other corporate sponsors and individuals to also fund them. Over time we hope to launch more Rediscover Your Heart awards in other countries too.

I hope that in this way many people can co-operate in inspiring and supporting young people with their ideas for change. I feel this is especially needed in the challenging times that we are currently facing.

The Economic Crisis

Even when life throws up really challenging experiences, I believe there is always the opportunity for learning and development. An example of this for me is the economic crisis that first gripped the world in early autumn 2008, shortly after this book was first published. To many this situation is a disaster of great magnitude and certainly its effects cannot be underestimated. I too have suffered personal financial losses as a result of the crisis and the financial status of my charitable foundations has also been affected.

However I do also feel that many good things can also come out of these challenging times. On a corporate, governmental and global level the greed, irresponsibility and mismanagement that contributed to the international credit and banking crisis may be curtailed, the whole process of providing and managing mortgages is being re-evaluated and more responsibility and accountability may come in. On a more personal level a curbing of excesses and wastefulness and a return to greater economic watchfulness and frugality is also not necessarily a bad thing.

This is not to deny that some people have experienced, and are experiencing real suffering and hardship as a result of the crisis. Yet this too brings opportunities for caring and sharing and for supporting each other in a productive and loving way. Already there are many examples of individuals, groups and communities coming together to help each other through these difficult times. Governmental and other leaders are also exploring and creating initiatives to protect some of the populations most affected.

In fact you could say that situations like these are a real opportunity for the philosophy and keys outlined in this book to be put into action. For example letting go of the fears associated with this crisis can enable us to rediscover our hearts and find new ways of working together for the benefit of all. I have a deep trust that all will be well in the end.

It could also be said that we are living in exciting times of transition. Who could have imagined just a short time ago that Barack Obama would go from being a relative unknown to be elected President of the United States of America? His calm demeanour and principled stance have inspired millions and he carries the hopes of a whole new generation of Americans, as well as those abroad, who look to him to change the role and actions of the USA on the international stage as well as at home.

And Finally…

In my own life I am still trying to find a balance between maintaining my inner peace yet also dealing with my responsibilities and requests to be involved in new initiatives. I am still often very busy but am learning not to over-stretch myself. I am mainly occupied with my philanthropic activities but also continue part-time involvement with my business interests. I am entering a more reflective period where I prefer to carry out supportive, advisory roles rather than more active ones.

I continue to try and integrate my heart and mind and to grow spiritually. With my trust in the Divine, I continue on my journey as a student of life…

In the next part of the book I share some guiding principles that I feel could transform the way that we live on this planet and which could enable us all to 'be the change'.

PART I - Appendices

PART I - APPENDICES

1. Thinking 'Outside the Box'—
the Shopping Centre 'Hilvertshof'

In the early 1950s, my father had been thinking about creating a new project to rejuvenate the centre of our hometown of Hilversum. He started acquiring land for this from the early 1960s onward. The challenge was to create a business environment that would serve the needs of the people of Hilversum and the surrounding area and which would be economically viable. Given the high cost of land in the town centre this was no easy task.

Shopping Centre the 'Hilvertshof' Hilversum, (opened in Spring 1973)

We had been thinking about this project for some time but had been unable to come up with a successful formula for realising it when I suddenly had a flash of inspiration. At the time, I was twenty-three years old and happened to be in Glasgow on a trip to Scotland with some colleagues on a shopping centre study trip. I was just mulling over the challenges of the Hilversum project in my mind when I suddenly 'saw' that we could solve the problem by creating a multi-layered building. In my mind's eye it had different activities going on at different levels, including shopping, thus making best use of the available space. It was also carefully integrated with existing buildings around it and offered parking on the roof!

At this time, Hilversum had a population of 90,000 and a catchment area of 300,000 consumers. My idea was that consumers could start their shopping trip in the very centre of Hilversum by parking on the top floors of this new building. They could then walk down through the shopping floors below and also visit shops in the surrounding old parts of the town via linking pedestrian alleyways. The centre would also contained a large fitness club to help meet the health needs of the local population—at that time also a new concept in the Netherlands.

To realise this project we needed to get agreement from the public authorities as well as cooperation from existing stores and other businesses. Some saw the opportunities it would provide straight away while others were more cautious.

With my father at the Opening Ceremony for the 'Hilvertshof'

In the end we secured the necessary consents both at local and national level and got planning permission for building the new shopping centre to be called, "Hilvertshof". It was a very risky project, as we had to start the building work before having the leasing and finance in place. Otherwise we would not have been able to complete it within the planning permission and government subsidy deadlines. Its construction lasted from 1971–2 and it was opened in the spring of 1973. Nearly forty years later, it is still a very successful shopping centre.

Today, these kinds of inner-city projects are common. However in the 1970's this was a very innovative approach and enclosed malls did not really exist in the Netherlands. In fact our Hilvertshof project was, to my knowledge, the first Dutch multilevel, major, inner city, enclosed shopping centre that was not attached to a main railway station.

Our company was responsible for developing many shopping centres (twenty during my time with the company). We also built several thousand homes, recreational parks, many office buildings and even a football stadium designed with integrated office space. Our achievements were possible through the cooperation of many dedicated people within the company and other contibutors.

2. An Innovative Football Stadium —
'Galgenwaard'

In 1981 our company got the opportunity to develop a new football stadium in the Dutch town of Utrecht. Once again we wanted to explore how to make the best use of space for the occupants and how to make the building multi-functional.

We decided to develop the area under the stands into office space and also built four office buildings into each of the corners of the stadium. These different functions for the building complex meant the parking facilities could also be used optimally. On Sundays and in the evenings, when there were soccer matches, the parking facilities could be used by supporters and players while, during office hours, the parking was available for office workers.

This use of the space under the stands and timesharing of the parking space are commonplace nowadays but, at that time, this was unique in the Netherlands and, to my knowledge, in other countries as well. Once again, many capable people in our company co-operated together to realise this project.

The 'Galgenwaard' Stadium, Utrecht, in 1980

3. Taking the Peace Flame to Sarajevo —
The Olympic Medallists and Other Participants

The Olympic Medallists:

Gaetan Boucher—Canada
Marjorie van de Bunt—Netherlands
Yvonne van Gennip—Netherlands
Stine Lise Hattestad—Norway
Paul Hildgartner—Italy
Bill Johnson—United States
Eirik Kvalfoss—Norway
Kristin Otto—Germany
Adrienne Rivera—United States
Alexander Spitz—Germany
Vegard Ulvang—Norway
Bart Veldkamp—Netherlands
Cato Zahl Pedersen—Norway

Others

Lenny Kuhr—Netherlands (Singer)
Noreen O'Ryan—Eire (Singer/Musician)
Markus Stockhausen—Germany (Musician)
Kai Tidemann—Norway (Paralympic Committee)
Fred Matser—The Netherlands (Initiator)

The Seven Keys for Personal and Planetary Transformation

*During the writing of Part I of this book
I was inspired to formulate Seven Keys
for Personal and Planetary Transformation.*

*On the next page they are presented altogether
with their corresponding affirmations.*

The Seven Keys for Personal and Planetary Transformation

KEY 1 - **We can trust in the guiding hand of the Divine.**

AFFIRMATION - *I trust that everything has a divine purpose from which it is possible to learn and grow.*

KEY 2 - **We can free our minds to explore new horizons.**

AFFIRMATION - *I can go beyond my conventional belief systems and open up to infinite possibilities.*

KEY 3 - **We can rediscover our hearts and serve humanity.**

AFFIRMATION - *By expanding my consciousness I can integrate my mind and heart and serve humanity compassionately.*

KEY 4 - **We can empower ourselves.**

AFFIRMATION - *I choose to free myself from fear to allow changes within and without. In supporting myself and others in this process, we can together develop a caring and sharing society.*

KEY 5 - **We can live in the spirit of unity.**

AFFIRMATION - *By learning to integrate different parts of my being and focusing on our common humanity, I can work for the interests of all.*

KEY 6 - **We can find our own path to truth.**

AFFIRMATION - *May I have the courage to explore the mysteries of life and seek the truth without judgment.*

KEY 7 - **We can make a difference.**

AFFIRMATION - *My personal development is linked to global transformation and I am aware that each one of us counts. I honour the global family of which I am part and cherish the home planet that we all share.*

PART II

Philosophy—'Being the Change'

PART II

1. Introduction

On the basis of my life experiences, some of which I have described in Part I, my own personal philosophy started to take shape. I began to think about how our human systems, based on having, on power and control and on separation and exclusion, are not working for us. I started to explore how we might create new systems based on empowerment and what I call 'self-response-Ability' (that is, experiencing fully in the present, and having the Ability and willingness to interact with the world around us while being aware that we are all part of the Infinite and accountable for our actions). Also how we might work together for change, developing a more functional society here on earth.

In this part of the book I will explore the ideas and concepts that have evolved which give meaning and understanding to my life and which I hope may also be of use and inspiration to others. I will share ideas on (amongst other topics):

- going beyond our belief systems
- accessing new types of experiences and information
- the role of fears, and judgements
- the differences between thoughts and emotions or feelings
- ways of expanding the mind
- the nature of truth
- the use of free will and authentic power
- ways of caring, sharing and connecting
- the experience of unconditional love.

I have thought long and hard about these topics and have also learned to view them in different ways through the transcendental experiences that I have had. In other words I have approached them with both the intellect and the heart and I am still learning about them every day. Mahatma Gandhi said "You must be the change you want to see in the world". I believe the topics explored in this part of the book contain the potential for transforming our lives and our society. I hope you will enjoy exploring them with me.

I also love to play with words, explore their meaning and create new ways of using them. I have used a few words in different ways in this section so I have also included a glossary of them at the end of Part II that you can use for easy reference.

Being the Change

So how did my philosophy develop? Some of it came about through reflection on past events and on lessons that I learned in my private life, business dealings, and philanthropic endeavours. Other perspectives were stimulated through discussions with, and learning from, inspiring teachers, some of whom I mention in this book. Other sources were the moments of revelation that I experienced when everything became clear and all the pieces of the jigsaw fitted into place. These included the life-changing moments that I described in Part I when I experienced what I have called 'the Infinite'. I have used this term as, from my perspective, these experiences transcended any form of dogmas, such as religious ones.

In these moments of experiencing the Infinite I was given a glimpse of the wholeness and the workings of our universe. I have already described my experience during a healing session when I suddenly found myself opened up to dimensions beyond normal day-to-day life. Also the moment when I sat in the concert hall and suddenly became one with the music and entered an altered state of consciousness. There have also been other experiences such as one sunny morning when I was just driving to work in my car and stopped at a traffic light. I was looking out of the window appreciating the beauty of nature and the dancing sunlight when, all of a sudden, I again had this overwhelming experience of oneness. I lost my immediate physical presence and instead my consciousness was one with the universe and beyond. The experience only lasted a few seconds in this finite universe yet I entered a timeless state of bliss.

These experiences led me to think a lot about how our finite universe and the Infinite interact, how we relate to them and how this could be incorporated into my philosophy. Finding the words to describe my experiences of the Infinite is a challenge in itself. Logically, we can accept that the Infinite can encompass the finite but it is not easy to describe a larger concept in terms of a smaller one. I have therefore tried to explain the Infinite with regard to my own experiences and then tried to relate how the insights that I received, when in these states of bliss, have inspired my life philosophy.

I do believe that access to the Infinite is open to all and that every experience of it is unique to each person and may lead them to different conclusions. What I offer in this part of the book are the fruits of my own journey. I am merely a student of life and I have done my best here to write down and explain quite a complex subject as I understand it. My philosophy is a work in progress and I don't claim to have all the answers; I am simply sharing the way that I look at the universe and beyond and exploring ways that we can all 'be the change'.

I have also found it fascinating to read the inspiring philosophies of others and to find many elements in common with my own. In the same way I hope that reading this part of the book will support and encourage you, dear reader, to reflect on your own experiences and ideas of life and the Infinite.

You may choose to read this part of the book in its entirety or simply select sections to which you feel most drawn. I hope you will enjoy the journey…

2. Exploring the Infinite

Many of us like living safely within our familiar comfort zones, treading the same paths, doing the same jobs, following the same routines day after day and holding onto the same beliefs and patterns of behaviour. There is nothing wrong with following these routines, as they can give us security, and comfort. Yet I think it is also important to be open to change and willing to explore what is outside our normal experience of life and not be scared of it. Although life is all about change and openness to the new, we often try to resist it. However new experiences give us a chance to evolve in consciousness.

For me a belief system is a limiting thought which often prevents us from expanding our minds and hearts towards new horizons where new information and knowledge can be found. We often handicap ourselves by apparently only being willing to accept information that we can explain in so-called 'scientific' or 'rational' terms. This means that we tend to exclude the inexplicable, even though such phenomena occur in our daily lives.

However, by having the courage to be open-minded and to go beyond our conventional belief systems into the unknown I believe that we may access valuable new information and knowledge. Indeed, we may even have a personal experience beyond the known. This might feel uncomfortable at first but, on the other hand, it may lead us to new levels of understanding that we never even imagined.

Perhaps we have limited ourselves by trying to explain everything in finite terms rather than encompassing infinite possibilities. By this exclusion we may be ruling out wider concepts of reality. This is like those who were convinced that the world was flat and who initially greeted the idea that it was round with disbelief and ridicule. This disbelief occurred only a few hundred years ago and our thinking and understanding has since expanded rapidly to encompass ideas that could not even have been dreamed of in the not -too-distant past.

Many of us have had experiences that have caused us to re-evaluate completely the way we think about life. It could have been a serious illness, the loss of a loved one, a huge win on the lottery, a major sporting success, or another type of challenge. Or we may have been fortunate enough to encounter teachers who led us to new ways of understanding, beyond the everyday world of our five senses. Life-changing experiences like these can enable us to go beyond the fear of the unknown, to change our attitudes and to live our lives differently.

In my case it was a single life-changing transcendental experience that was the trigger for resetting my existing belief systems. This spontaneous experience, which occurred during a healing session, took me completely outside of my day-to-day beliefs, and I could not rationally explain what had happened. This experience was so simple and fleeting and yet so magnificent, that I could not forget it. I started to look at life quite differently.

Going Beyond the Finite Universe

We are all familiar with the finite universe that surrounds us. It's the one we experience every day as we go about our life, work and social interactions. It is the day-to-day events and phenomena to which we are accustomed and which we experience through our senses. It includes everything that physically exists, all forms of matter, energy and momentum, all that is time and space, even air.

However, my experiences, as described in Part I, showed me that encompassing this finite universe, is something limitless and all-encompassing which I have termed, 'the Infinite'. As mentioned earlier I use this term here instead of 'God' because, what I experienced did not have reference to any existing religion, culture or other finite form. My experiences were moments of illumination, when I sensed that everything is connected and everything is alive; above all, these were experiences of what I call, 'unconditional love'.

This abstract term is often used but rarely defined and very hard to put into words. I had no clue to what it really was until the experiences I had during my healing session in Switzerland and in other experiences since. The best way I can find to describe it is an all-encompassing, wonderful sense of being loved in every aspect of my being without any conditions or limits. To me this unconditional love is the very essence of the Infinite and it is the power of this love which can enable us to go beyond our fear and grow spiritually. I will refer to this love at various points throughout Part II.

I feel that as we go about our daily lives in the finite we are often unaware of the unconditional love that surrounds us or any of the other marvellous wonders of the Infinite. We have become so used to living in the finite by exclusion of the Infinite that this blinkers our consciousness. My own experiences of this love from the Infinite made me feel as if we are living in a huge box of which the walls, floor and ceiling are formed by our conventional thinking. Yet I don't believe that these confines are actually solid. Rather I see them as 'curtains' that we may draw aside at any time to experience the Infinite that is beyond.

Of course this would also require letting go of the illusion of certainty that the box provides. It might mean letting go of rigid forms of thinking, or limiting self-belief and welcoming uncertainty. Above all, it would mean letting go of the fear that underlies such thoughts and emotions. As a consequence, we might have to let go of some of our finite attitudes and behaviours such as:

- Fear of death
- Being in a hurry
- Having no time for one another or oneself
- Values being expressed in terms of money rather than in love and care.

This might involve some sacrifices for we may be attached to our existing ways, even though they often leave us dissatisfied or miserable. Yet, in my view, we do have a choice; even though we may not fully understand the Infinite we can still entertain it as a possibility and be open to experiencing it.

Another key aspect is forgiveness. I see forgiveness as a part of unconditional love and a part of letting go of fears and judgements. If we harbour resentment, ill will and negative feelings about others then I believe this can also block us from experiencing the Infinite and unconditional love. Learning to forgive both ourselves and others is therefore, from my perspective, an essential part of our journey of rediscovering our hearts.

To make my ideas about the Infinite easier to understand I have tried to illustrate them in Figure 1. I will now talk about some of the elements shown in this figure in some more detail.

Being a 'Human Being'

One way we can try to understand the correlation between the finite and the Infinite is to look at our nature as human beings. When we were born on this planet I would say that we came from the Infinite into the finite. This means that within each of us is the essence of the Infinite—unconditional love—a sense of connection with the Divine, a feeling of oneness, even though we may be unaware of this.

As human beings you could say that our 'beingness' (or 'infiniteness') is expressed through our 'human-ness' (or 'finiteness'). However many of us seem

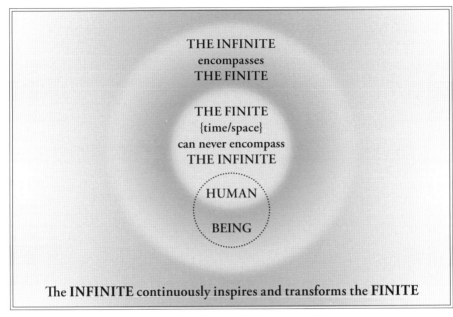

Figure 1. The Infinite in Relation to the Finite

to be unaware of, or have forgotten about, our 'beingness'. As a result everything becomes reduced to 'human-ness' and the Infinite is excluded. We may not even be aware that the whole finite universe, with all its galaxies including

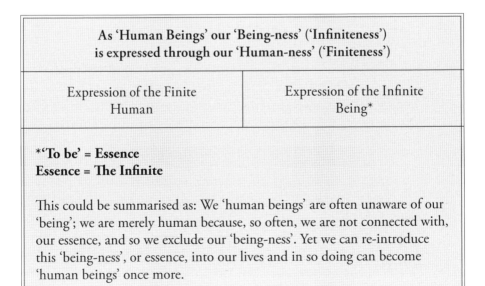

Figure 2. The Meaning of the Human 'Being'

our own planet, is an expression of what I call Infinite creation. (See Figure 2).

In this respect it is interesting to note that the roots of the verb 'to be' encompass those of 'to exist', 'to come into being' and link to the Sanskrit words, 'bahavat' ('becoming') and 'bhumi' ('into the world'). Yet we have almost forgotten about our Infinite existence and have tended to reduce our world to finite, limited experiences. However, based on my own experiences, I believe that if only we can expand our belief systems from the finite to the Infinite, then our whole perspective on life and death will change dramatically.

Synthesis

Most people, including me, at one time or another ask themselves: "Why are we here?" It's one of the great mysteries of life, and it may be that we can never understand fully the answer whilst we are limited by our human consciousness. One way of approaching this question might be to see it in terms of our journey from the Infinite to the finite.

In my view, we can only truly experience our sense of connection with the Infinite when we become aware of the feeling of being separated from it; some describe this as a sense of separation from God. Just as I have argued that we come to learn about love through letting go of fear so too I believe that by becoming aware of separateness we can gradually come to realise that we are a part of the whole of Creation and our connection with our Creator is never lost.

You could say that we learn through a kind of cosmic theatre; one in which we are both the actors and the audience. Like all good theatre, this cosmic drama has both meaning and purpose. We may experience all kinds of reactions as we watch and participate in the play. It may provoke many thoughts or provide any number of insights. Or we may stubbornly refuse to learn anything, sitting there with our minds firmly closed. Or perhaps we may even try to sleep through the whole performance.

It is the process of going, with trust, through resistance or fear to discover— I think of this word as dis-'cover' where 'covering' is a characteristic of the finite universe that we go beyond—and experience unconditional love. Thus we can go beyond seeing love and fear as opposites to embrace the whole, which has no opposites—only the oneness of unconditional love. You could say that the finite, of which we are all part, conceals the Infinite and so it is up to each of us go within our 'inner light' to discover the treasure of the Infinite for ourselves.

3. Rediscovering the Heart

Much of the love that we give and receive in the finite is conditional. Yet, as I have said, I believe that unconditional love is also there to be experienced by all. For this to be possible I do believe that we need to open our hearts completely to the Infinite. We then have the opportunity as human beings to channel and express that unconditional love in our finite universe.

'Rediscovering the heart' for me also involves letting go of our judgements and replacing these with discernment, wisdom, and compassion. It also means evolving through our emotions and allowing our feelings to shine through. In this section I would like to share how I feel this can be achieved.

I believe that we can integrate our hearts and our minds so that they can work together harmoniously. In a wider sense you could say that we can then bring together the 'male' and 'female' sides of our being—which I discuss later in Part II. Isn't this a journey of rediscovering our hearts?

Letting Go of Judgements

Letting go of judgements does not mean that we would stop seeing ourselves and others as we are, with all our qualities and challenges. Instead I would suggest that we may be able to see ourselves even more clearly as this 'letting go' means that we are no longer drawn into personal drama.

For example we may see people who bully and cheat their way through life. We may see the fear that tells them that they must always put down others first, lest they be put down themselves. We see them believing that they must win at all costs, no matter how, so that they can stay on top, terrified of the humiliation of being ranked below. We see how this behaviour can be fed by their sense of worthlessness.

At the same time we may see deep inside them small, frightened children who feel—or have been made to feel—that they are not good enough as they are. In truth, I do believe that we are all fully loved by our Creator, yet many times we cannot, or simply will not, allow this realisation.

Seeing all this play out it is possible to let go of our anger or sense of judgement and to simply feel compassion instead. This does not mean that we think bullying or cheating is defensible or that the bullies' internal pain justifies what they do. However, we can also gain another perspective by seeing the bully as just another struggling soul, one very like so many others on this planet. With this perspective we may then be able to support them wisely, lovingly prayerfully and with detachment. Instead of judging them we can use discernment to create opportunities for them, while also letting go of any attachment to the result of our efforts. We can allow them to take responsibility for their own life without trying to fix their life or feeling the need to do so. Isn't this unconditional love expressed in the form of loving detachment?

Freeing Ourselves from Fear or Attachment

So how can we reach this point of loving detachment? I believe the first step is to let go of our own fears. It is important to realise how much fear can permeate our lives without us being aware of it. For example it can affect our behaviour and actions, can interfere with out relationships or can block our creativity. I have listed some other expressions of fear in Figure 3. Sometimes fear can serve a useful function, such as keeping us out of danger. However, in many cases it works against us.

Examples of Manifestations of Fear	
Arrogance	Jealousy
Greed	Addiction
Anger and aggression	Deception
Laziness and procrastination	Doubt
Stress	Lack of confidence
Impatience	Guilt
	Being in love

Figure 3. Examples of Manifestations of Fear

For many of the words in Figure 3 the connection to fear is obvious. We have already seen how fear can lead to deception and aggressive behaviour. Laziness and procrastination can also mask the fear that we will not succeed at our enterprise. Yet what about the example of 'being in love'? At first glance, this seems to make no sense. Surely, love is the reverse of fear? We all know that being in love is the most wonderful feeling and a marvellous gift. However, if we look deeper we can also see that it may cloud our clarity of mind and give us tunnel vision. We may see only what we want to see about the other person, situation or relationship and be afraid to consider anything outside of this view.

Being 'in love', as opposed to loving someone, brings us into the world of attachment. When we are attached, much is seen in terms of possession: "You are my partner/wife/husband/etc". So often we do not love unconditionally but rather we experience a love that is actually based on fear; the fear of losing the loved person. As the Polish writer and poet, Kazimierz Wierzyński, once wrote: "Love is a constant terror of loss."[1]

We become attached because our belief systems are exclusively anchored in the finite. However, in my own experience of the Infinite, I found there is no fear—only unconditional love. So by accessing Infinite (unconditional) love, it may become possible to go through fear, let go of it, and reach a state beyond it. Yet I wonder how many of us have achieved this type of love without fear in real life? If we can consciously choose to let go of our attachment, and of the fear which underlies it, maybe we can then learn to love more freely.

An example might be a situation where a man is jealous of his wife, fearing her unfaithfulness and the possibility of losing her. If he can focus his attention lovingly on the jealousy and explore it, he might discover that it springs from a fear of loss that he developed after being rejected, for example, by a former girlfriend or a parent. At that time if his sense of self-worth was defined by such relationships, then being rejected would lead to a sense of worthlessness and emotional pain. By becoming aware of and understanding this process, he may become able to dissolve the emotional block caused by the jealousy, move on and re-anchor his sense of self-worth in himself. In this way, the emotion has enabled the man to learn about a blockage that he needed to work on and to evolve through the experience.

Freeing ourselves from attachment has wider implications for us in our daily lives. This principle of attachment—that is, having fears, judgements, and opinions expressed through emotions—is used by industry on a massive scale. Through the manipulation of emotions, desires, and wants, people can be triggered to purchase goods and services that they may not need—a kind of emotional blackmail if you like. This effort to manipulate and bind people diminishes their autonomy; it clouds their consciousness and takes away clarity of thought. On the other hand, if we can reconnect with our pure feelings and have a clear mind, we can enter a state of real being-ness. When I sat in the concert hall in Amsterdam and had the experience of merging with the music as I listened to it, I felt a wonderful sense of detachment, not devoid of feeling but rather experiencing pure feeling without the clouding influence of emotions.

---

1. Kazimierz Wierzyński's, (1894-1969) *'A Word to Orphists'* in Czeslaw Milosz (Editor) (1983) *Postwar Polish Poetry,* University of California Press.

If we could become better at, and find new ways for, integrating our thoughts with our feelings, thus free from attachments, then maybe feelings could once again become valued as subtle information carriers that can guide and inspire us. This peeling away of attachments may well be a life-long process. I have encountered a good example of just such detachment when the renowned Indian yogi, the Maharishi Mahesh Yogi[2] was asked in an interview how he felt about the death of somebody he was close to. The interviewer asked the Maharishi, "Did you cry?" The Maharishi answered, "No", and when asked, "Why not?" he said, "The sun goes down at night and the next morning it rises."

This answer seems to me to convey a transcendental view of life and death, namely that the individual is seen as a drop of water returning to the ocean, or source. Since the yogi experiences himself as, at least part of the time, in the Infinite, he feels no need to have emotion, fear, or any form of attachment to humans. He knows that the connection with the Infinite is there before life, through life, and after life.

The Difference between Feelings and Emotions

As I have used the words 'feelings' and 'emotions' several times I thought it would be useful to discuss these further.

If we listen to music, smell a rose, or feel the coolness of a gust of wind then the resonance of the musical notes, the scent of the flower, or the movement of the wind, in its purest sense, are devoid of opinion or emotional content. You could say we are simply allowing ourselves to 'be felt'. In a way, our body is used as an instrument. This is what I regard as pure feeling; it involves no judgement or opinion.

On the other hand emotions involve judgements and fears and all these are forms of attachment. They add a layer to the feeling and cloud our clarity. The emotion blocks our perception and limits our understanding so that we are no longer aware of the whole picture.

Emotions are linked directly to past events or future expectations whereas feelings are a resonation of the present moment. However, from another perspective, I believe that emotions can also serve a useful function, as they can help us understand what the blocks to our real feelings are.

I have found that an analogy of a cello and some chewing gum can help explain these concepts (see Figure 4). If some chewing gum (representing fear or emotions)

2. He passed away in February 2008.

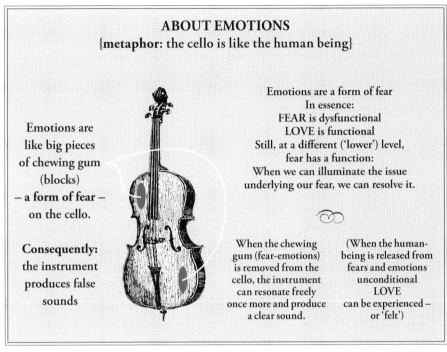

ABOUT EMOTIONS
{**metaphor:** the cello is like the human being}

Emotions are
like big pieces
of chewing gum
(blocks)
– **a form of fear** –
on the cello.

Emotions are a form of fear
In essence:
FEAR is dysfunctional
LOVE is functional
Still, at a different ('lower') level,
fear has a function:
When we can illuminate the issue
underlying our fear, we can resolve it.

Consequently:
the instrument
produces false
sounds

When the chewing
gum (fear-emotions)
is removed from the
cello, the instrument
can resonate freely
once more and produce
a clear sound.

(When the human-
being is released from
fears and emotions
unconditional
LOVE
can be experienced –
or 'felt')

Figure 4. The Metaphor of the Cello

is placed in the cello, it can no longer resonate clearly, but when the gum (the emotional blocks) is removed, the sound produced is clear once more. So too, as our emotional blocks are removed, we can allow in feeling and full consciousness.

Working with our Emotions or Fears

If we can understand the issues that lie behind our emotions then we can start to dissolve the blocks that they create for us. First we need to become more aware and accepting of the emotions themselves. Instead of suppressing or denying them, in the words of Deepak Chopra, "we need to become friends with our shadows". Then by exploring the fears underlying them, we can, in the light of greater consciousness, express gratitude for how they have served us thus far. We can then let them go, as they are not needed any more, and can replace them with thoughts or behaviours that come from this new level of consciousness.

To sum up these steps for working with our emotions or fears which I have found helpful:

1. We first recognise and acknowledge our emotion/fear and bring it into our full awareness rather than denying it.
2. Next we try to unravel the kind of emotion/fear since it often hides its true nature. Rather like unwrapping a present, we can strip it down and shed light on the main issue(s) underlying it.
3. By shining a light—paying attention—to reveal the real underlying issue(s) behind the emotion/fear, it already begins to lose its potency and dissolve.
4. After some time (it may be almost instantly or it may be a while later), the emotion/fear dissolves completely. Then we can express gratitude for the learning from it, say goodbye to it and at last be free from it.
5. If wished we can then use an affirmation to take the place of the emotion/fear.

For example, if we let go of, anger or jealousy about something/someone, we might say "Now that my anger/jealousy has been dissolved, I allow myself to radiate peace, calm and love". Or, if we have let go of the fear of having to speak in public, we might say, "Now that my fear of public speaking has been dissolved, I fill myself up with the joy of sharing information with others."

Releasing ourselves from the attachment of fears or emotions can, in my view, create greater clarity in our thinking and feeling. This can then pave the way for bringing heart and mind together as we learn to value both. To examine this possibility further we need to look at how differently we value thoughts, and the intellect, and our feelings.

Overvaluing Thoughts and Undervaluing Feelings

An important milestone occurred for me one ordinary workday in the latter part of the 1980s. I was just sitting at my desk in the office, about to dictate a letter to my secretary when, out of the blue, the following expression popped into my head: "The chaos in the world ('en-vironment') is a reflection of the disorder in our minds and hearts ('in-vironment')."

I was a bit surprised by this phrase at first but, after a moment I could see its meaning. I looked out of my office window and saw stressed car drivers scurrying about in traffic, fighting for space or trying to speed ahead of other cars. I noticed how much time was being spent chaotically 'doing' and so little in simply 'being'.

As I thought more deeply about the words of this phrase, I started to think about how much our modern world is dominated by the intellect, and what comes from it, rather than by feelings. "Yet we also all have feelings" I thought to myself, "and feelings are sensors too. Don't they also give us important information? Why do we take our intellect so seriously and yet not our feelings? Aren't they equal but different?" Then I thought, "Why have we put the intellect on a pedestal and regard it so highly, while feelings are so undervalued?"

I wondered if this might be because thoughts can be externalised and so the products of our thinking can easily be ordered, compared and therefore communicated. On the other hand feelings are just as real but we cannot measure them easily or compare them externally; they are experienced in the moment and so cannot be communicated satisfactorily to others. This often means we do not know how to handle or express them.

We have no real point of reference for feelings outside of ourselves but we can compare them internally with other feelings we have had; for example, we might determine that "I feel better today than I felt yesterday." Even so it is hard to equate one feeling with another. People often say to each another, "I know how you feel." Yet can this really be true? While we may relate to a person's experience and what this triggers in our own feelings and emotions about similar experiences, can we ever feel exactly the same as another person?

Feelings can also serve a vital function, namely as subtle information carriers, transmitting and receiving messages to the body. For example they may be feeding back to us that we are in harmony or out of balance. Or, they could be giving us information about our surroundings as we enter a room with people or letting us know how we respond to a person as we make eye contact and, maybe unconsciously, also communicating something back to them.

In my view feelings encompass not only the normal senses but also the more subtle ones, such as intuition, and even the so-called 'paranormal senses', that is, information perceived by means other than our five senses. An example of this would be extrasensory perception (ESP) whereby someone might 'see' a person arriving in the mind's eye before they actually see them with their eyes and actual visual sense. I also believe feelings can serve us by connecting us with the silence that lies within and that they may have a role in connecting us with higher dimensions. Figure 5 summarises some of these ideas on thoughts and feelings.

Learning to Value Feelings

As it became clear to me how important the dynamic balance between thoughts and feelings must be for our well-being, I wondered if there could be a way in which our feelings could become as valued and well-regarded as our intellect.

Thinking Faculty	Feeling Faculty
Thinking is real	Feeling is real
The products of thinking can be expressed in comparisons and/or equations	The products of feeling cannot be expressed in comparisons and/or equations
Because of this we can communicate our thoughts	Because of this we cannot deal with feelings as we do with the products of our thinking
We can compare our thoughts with those of others and with previous thoughts	We cannot compare our feelings with those of others; we can only compare with our own experiences/feelings in the past
We can examine and agree or disagree with our thoughts	We cannot agree or disagree with our feelings

Thinking ◄——————— of equal value ———————► Feeling
External ◄——————— measurement instrument ———————► Internal
OVERvalued ◄——————— belief system ———————► UNDERvalued

Figure 5. Thinking and Feeling Faculties

This is something that could be addressed from our earliest years. We come into this world as newborns with our senses and faculties open, and this continues during our time as infants. However, in the West, from the age of four or five, we enter the formal education system, where the mind and the intellect are more highly trained and valued while feelings and emotions tend to be neglected and undervalued.

We are taught to evaluate, analyse, and criticise but are not educated in how to feel and trust our feelings, how to work with our emotions or how to be compassionate and kind human beings. Nor are we encouraged, or sometimes even allowed to explore a sense of openness to the possibility of other dimensions; an openness which seems to be quite natural in children who have not yet been what I call, 'en-veloped', that is wrapped in the confines of limited belief systems rather than encouraged to develop fully.

So, in the process of growing up and becoming educated, it could be said that we human beings lose our 'being' and may start to develop into human-'havings' instead. As such we are taught to be more concerned with materialistic outcomes than interested in personal and spiritual development. This can also limit our openness to the concepts of different dimensions of reality and levels of consciousness.

Because of all this we may also lose confidence in our ability to connect with and express our feelings. This is illustrated in my version of a story about Mary, which I once heard on a tape by Barry Neil Kaufman, the co-founder of the Option Institute in the USA.[3]

Mary was a toddler aged about three years old. She woke up early one sunny morning and, seeing a box of crayons on the floor, started spontaneously to express her feelings of happiness and joy by drawing lots of colourful squiggles all over the wall in her bedroom. In a way, she was one with her creation and was so totally absorbed in what she was doing, that she did not hear her mother get up and come to her room.

When her mother opened the door, Mary turned to her with a beaming smile, ready to show off her creation. However, her expression of joy froze when she saw the angry look on her mother's face as she towered over her. "Mary, what on earth do you think you're doing, you naughty girl!" cried her mother as she grabbed the crayons from Mary's hand and told her severely, "Get back into bed! We have only just decorated your room and now you have ruined it!"

From this experience, Mary learned that expressing her feelings was bad, so she shut off her heart and suppressed her feelings and emotions and instead focused on her intellect, which was praised by her parents. She got top marks in all her studies and achieved great academic success. Yet, in doing so, she became cut off from the creative power that underlies her feelings and heart while focussing only on her mental activities.

How different her life might have turned out if her mother had opened the door, sat on the floor at her daughter's level and said something like, "What a great picture! Next time it would be better to do your drawings on paper. We can go and buy you a sketchbook, as that is a good place to put your drawings in the future."

In contrast to Mary's story, I remember Jane Goodall telling me how her mother supported her adventures. As a young child Jane was curious about where chicken eggs came from. So she got up very early one morning and went inside the family's hen house to sit and wait and to watch for the eggs to appear. Meanwhile, her mother woke up and found her daughter missing and looked everywhere for her.

On finally finding her, instead of being angry or fearful, she listened enthusiastically to Jane's story about her discovery of where the eggs came from. Jane told me how much this experience, and her mother's encouragement on many other occasions, stimulated her to explore and ultimately led her to travel to the forests

3. *www.option.org*

of Africa and study chimpanzee behaviour. It is so important to nurture and encourage children to express their emotions and feelings, rather than to deny them and to provide a safe haven for doing this. This enables them to explore and be creative and stay in touch with their inner nature, and true selves. If this doesn't happen in childhood such denial of our emotions and feelings can be carried into adulthood with profound consequences.

Expressing Feelings and Emotions

These stories resonated deeply with me as I thought about my own childhood. My parents did their very best to bring up their children but they found it difficult to express their emotions and feelings and this had an effect on all of us. In my own case it has meant that I have also found it hard to connect with, and express, my own emotions and feelings. It has only been much later in life that I learned to reconnect with and become more able to express and share them. This is something that I continue to work on.

This point was illustrated to me in a powerful learning experience that I had over ten years ago when I took part in a workshop on living and dying. During the workshop we were given an exercise in which we were asked to lie down and imagine that we were going to die in twenty minutes. One workshop participant was asked to 'sit by our bedside' to hear our 'last words', while another was to sit on the other side simply as a silent witness. When it was my turn to lie down, I had no difficulty imagining this scenario; and almost immediately I had the overwhelming realisation that there were so many things that I had not yet shared with my three daughters.

I felt that I had not told them enough how deeply I love them and I was aware of how I had allowed barriers to remain between us. I felt deep sadness and my crying was so intense that I could not speak. As the waves of emotion eased, I was able to communicate with the workshop participant joining me in the exercise; I spoke as if to each of my children and expressed my deep feelings of love to them.

I also thought of my partner, Chris, felt the profound love connecting us and had a wondrous sense that there was an easy flow of this love, with few blockages between us. My mother, who is still alive, also came to mind and I felt our long-established love for each other, which has had full expression. My father, who had passed away, was part of the process as well and I saw his smile.

Expressing myself in this way was a profound and moving experience for me. I realised I had been able to express these feelings and emotions fully because of being in a 'safe' environment where I could allow myself to be vulnerable. This experience, amongst others, taught me how important it is not to miss opportunities to express love fully toward loved ones and not to procrastinate or hide the feelings and emotions. As a result I now have greater awareness and make the most of such opportunities to express my love and/or appreciation, in many different ways.

Integrating 'Male' and 'Female' Principles

Bringing together the heart and mind, and integrating thoughts and feelings, is, from my perspective, part of a wider process of integrating the 'male' and 'female' sides of our being. From my perspective the concept of the 'male' and 'female' principles goes well beyond the idea of gender. Rather they are different qualities or aspects of consciousness that exist in both men and women, to a greater or lesser extent, and they are interconnected and in constant dynamic interplay with one another. I summarise how I see this in Figure 6.

Human Consciousness Human Consciousness is defined as awareness of one's own existence, sensations, feelings, thoughts and surroundings	
(+) positive, 'male'* principle dense energy mental/mind giving	(-) negative, 'female'* principle subtle, fine energy feeling/heart receiving
* These expressions imply no judgement about 'male' or 'female, plus (+) or minus (-), 'positive' or 'negative'. They are just a description of qualities and phenomena as in, for example, the positive and negative charges in electrical circuits or the poles of magnets. 'Positive' and 'negative' thereby do not have any association here with 'good' or 'bad' but are rather of equal value, in this case as building blocks of our very existence. The 'male' and 'female' principles here refer to different qualities that are present in both men and women to varying degrees, rather than to differences between the sexes.In my view, these qualities are all manifestations of consciousness.	

Figure 6. Defining Human Consciousness and Integrating 'Male' and 'Female'

These qualities are also described in ancient Chinese philosophy as '*yin*', associated with 'female' qualities of softness, darkness, stillness, and receptivity; and '*yang*', traditionally linked to 'male' qualities such as hardness, lightness, movement, and action. This is often represented in the well-known Tai Ji symbol shown in Figure 7.

Figure 7. The Tai Ji (Yin/Yang) Symbol

I also associate the 'male' principle with the (over-valued) mind and intellect and the 'female' principle with (under-valued) feelings, intuition and the heart. Examples of words that can represent 'male' and 'female' qualities are given in Figure 8.

'Male' Qualities	'Female' Qualities
Mind	Heart
Intellect	Feeling
Analytical ability	Intuition
Giving	Receiving
Active	Receptive
Having an 'overview'	Attention to detail
Focused	Multi-tasking
Comparing	Sharing and caring

Figure 8. Examples of Words Representing
'Male' and 'Female' Qualities

In my view we have an imbalance between the 'male' and 'female' principles in our society as a whole and this affects the way in which we live our lives. Dysfunctional 'male' qualities, such as competitiveness or dominance, appear to be more valued and rewarded amongst both men and women. Thus we are encouraged to compete with each other on an individual, group, national and global level. This also affects how we as businesses and nations exploit the natural world; we are focused on selfish needs, scarcity and on 'taking' from nature. For example we exploit all the oil reserves that we can, profit from water resources and carve up the rainforests.

Yet I do believe that we can rebalance ourselves both as individuals and as a species by developing the 'female' side of our natures more, such as our sharing and caring sides. For example we could ensure that we replenish whatever we take away from nature. In our personal lives too we could create greater harmony by making a balance between these contrasting principles, for example between giving and receiving.

Giving and Receiving

It is said that 'in giving we receive' and vice versa. Therefore we do need to both give and receive in order for there to be a dynamic balance with an exchange of loving energy back and forth. A person who just takes all the time could be regarded as selfish and self-centred but equally someone who always gives is denying others the pleasure of giving too and could also eventually become resentful and burnt out.

Expectations and values are also important in this dynamic. People may give because they expect something in return, but this is not the same as unconditional giving, with no expectation of any reward or return. Being able both to give and receive unconditionally without any expectation could be seen as an example of living with the values of the Infinite in a finite universe. These same principles are at work between the finite and the Infinite in every area of life.

For example, I see this in the concept of life itself. For many scientists life is perceived as a given, a natural fact of biology. Yet for me, and many others, life can be perceived not only as a given but also as a gift. Isn't this a completely different realisation and what might be the implications of this awareness?

In my personal prayers I acknowledge and thank God, the Creator, for giving me this gift of life. In my view I received life, born from the Infinite in the ultimate sense, and in return I give thanks from my finite universe back to the Infinite, from whence my life came. This is therefore an example of both giving and receiving. It also reflects the dynamic connection between me, the human (finite) and my being (merged with the Infinite) in the cycle of life.

I also see the dynamic balance between giving and receiving as playing an essential role in our relationship with the Divine. For example we may receive inspiration and ideas from the Infinite and these can stimulate our creativity here on earth. In return we may express our thanks to the Divine and the cycle continues as we receive further and again express our gratitude.

Synthesis

To sum up, I believe that we can rediscover our hearts by learning to connect with, and express, our emotions and learning to value both our feelings and our intellect. Letting go of judgements and freeing ourselves from fear or attachments can also give us clarity and enable us to be open to the experience of unconditional love. We can then become channels for this love in the finite. The apparent polarity between heart and mind, or 'female' and 'male' principles, are manifestations of our finite universe. Yet in reality, everything is connected and I see everything as part of the oneness of the Infinite.

My own experiences have taught me that:

- Releasing ourselves from judgement, fear or attachment, frees us to love unconditionally.
- Integrating thinking and feeling enriches our lives.
- Balancing 'male' and 'female' principles in both men and women can create greater harmony both in ourselves and in society.
- Learning to express our emotions and feelings in safe environments can enable us to make the most of opportunities for expressing our love and appreciation
- We need to both give and receive.

4. Expanding the Mind

In my experience, once we open the door to the endless possibilities of the Infinite here in the finite we can start to explore unknown territory beyond our five senses. To embark on this I believe that we not only need to rediscover and open our hearts—we need to open and free our minds as well. By releasing ourselves from judgement, fear or attachment we can also bring clarity and loving detachment to our minds.

In my opinion this principle holds true for all seekers of truth, whether in the fields of science, religion or other academic endeavour. Everyone is subject to the same human tendencies that can cloud perceptions of reality. Yet by opening up to the Infinite in the way I have suggested I believe that everyone has the potential to expand their consciousness and the ability to access ideas and information from higher dimensions. Let us now consider how this might be possible by looking at how we access information and our perceptions of truth and reality.

Altered States of Consciousness

In the finite we are surrounded by external information sources such as the internet, radio, TV, newspapers, books and conversations with others. We take this information in via our five 'normal' senses, sight, hearing, smell, taste and touch, and process the information internally. We believe that these external sources represent all the information available. We become so attached to our 'normal' every day ways of accessing information that it hardly crosses our mind that there could be other transcendental sources that we might access using 'extraordinary' senses. Might we, for example, also be able to access information via dream and meditative states, altered states of consciousness or so-called 'paranormal' abilities such as telepathy and precognition? What type of information might this represent and where might it be coming from? Let's explore some of these.

An example of someone who was able to access information outside of normal day-to-day consciousness was Galileo. This renowned Italian physicist, astronomer, and philosopher lived in the seventeenth century. I have read that when he was searching for the solution to a scientific, astronomical, or philosophical problem, he would sit in a rocking chair holding a ball balanced between his fingertips. He would then rock to and fro, to the point where he became very relaxed and was almost falling asleep. In this relaxed state he would often get great inspirations and solutions to problems but he needed to stay awake in order to recall them fully. By holding the ball, just as he was on the point of falling asleep and forgetting the ideas, the ball would fall from his hands and this activity would bring him back into a waking state. He could then recall the ideas and think them over. In this way you could say that he was able to access information from beyond the 'here and now' of his conscious mind (the finite). Was he somehow accessing the Infinite via his subconscious or 'supra-conscious' mind?[4]

Brain research has long shown that different patterns of electrical activity predominate in our brains when we are engaged in different types of activities. Four main types of what are popularly known as 'brainwaves' have been identified[5]. The *beta* brainwave predominates when we are in an active mode and focusing our minds on a task such as speaking, concentrating, thinking or worrying about something. Slower *alpha* waves occur when we have completed a task and are resting, relaxing, or walking in nature. As we get drowsy and start to daydream or go on to automatic pilot, such as when jogging or while soaking in a bath, *theta* waves start to predominate—at this time we often get our best ideas and feel positive. This state also occurs when we first wake up but are not yet fully awake.

So it seems likely that by relaxing and rocking in his chair, Galileo was shifting his brain from a conscious, *beta* brainwave state to a slower, predominantly *theta* one, where he could go beyond thinking and allow himself to 'be thought', thereby accessing new ideas. As the ball dropped the *alpha* and then *beta* brain wave activity would have been reactivated, enabling him to concentrate his conscious mind on the new ideas.

The fourth type of brainwaves, *delta* waves, occur when we are asleep, with the faster waves being associated with dreaming and rapid eye movements (REM) and the slowest of all with deep, dreamless sleep. These different brainwaves occur in all human beings, regardless of race or culture, and although a given brain wave may predominate at a particular time, components of all the brainwaves are always present in different areas of the brain.

Dreams that occur during the *delta* REM periods may also be valid sources of information, and we have the choice whether to pay attention to them or not. Yet you never see dream information as part of formal education in the West. Some information that arises in dream states may simply be manifestations of old mem-

---

4. Supra-conscious mind is for me higher consciousness and is linked to the Infinite.

5. *Beta* brainwaves are fast, with a frequency usually above 12Hz (12 cycles per second) and low in amplitude. *Alpha* waves are slower (usually 8-12Hz) with a higher amplitude. Theta waves are slower still (4-8Hz) with a greater amplitude while *delta* waves are the slowest of all (up to 4 Hz) and have the greatest amplitude. In very deep sleep states, delta frequencies may drop as low as 2-3Hz but they never reach zero as this indicates brain death.

ories or buried thoughts. However other information in dreams cannot be so obviously or easily explained. Certain dreams appear to have an element of premonition or pre-cognition for there are various accounts of dream events later occurring in real life. No one knows exactly where such information may come from but I wonder if, in the dreamlike state, we are able to extend our consciousness beyond the limitations of our normal range of thoughts and emotions and somehow tap into what I have called the Infinite, the ultimate source of all information?[6]

No one really knows exactly how information is accessed in these different brainwave or consciousness states or from where it originates. Interesting work on brainwaves, which are imaged electronically on a screen (neurofeedback), suggests that it may be possible to retrain the transition from one wave pattern to another, for example enabling a shift from alpha to *beta* brainwaves. At the Neurofeedback Centre[7], which was established in Hilversum as an offshoot of one of our foundations, we have seen dramatic, therapeutic results using this technique, especially with children suffering from Attention deficit hyperactivity disorder (ADHD).

Since all brainwave frequencies operate at all times, perhaps we can train ourselves to switch from one predominant frequency to another at will. We might then use our thinking capacity, regulated by *beta* frequencies, as well as our feeling capacity, to express thoughts and feelings about information received and to determine appropriate actions.

Sources of Information

Might it be that by opening our hearts and minds and connecting with the Infinite we can open up to a whole new range of experiences? I wonder if we can make a bridge between the finite and the Infinite by allowing ourselves to 'be thought' and 'be felt' in order to receive information. I have represented this idea in Figure 9 and also explain it further on page 185. In this way we could perhaps choose to allow ourselves to be informed transcendentally from the Infinite. Thus the Infinite could be recognised, and used, as a source of vital information.

Examples of individuals who have been considered geniuses or prodigies can further illuminate this idea. Mozart for example is probably regarded by most

---

6. This may have links with what psychologist C.J.Jung called the 'Collective Unconscious', or what the Cambridge scientist, Dr Rupert Sheldrake has termed 'Morphic resonance'—that is collective wisdom and learning into which we may all tap. It may perhaps go even further on many levels to a Divine power at the source of Creation itself.

7. The Neurofeedback Centre continues today as a privately run clinic under the guidance of Guusje Roozemond who was, for many years, a highly valued co-worker within the Fred Foundation.

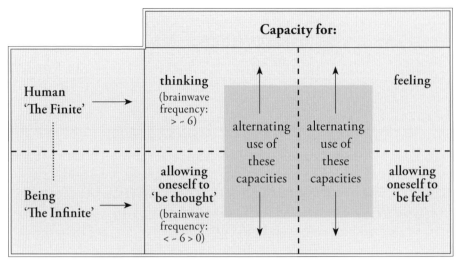

Figure 9. Sources of Information

people as a gifted prodigy who just happened to be able to write wonderful music from a young age. However, perhaps there is more to it than that. Maybe he was able to somehow easily enter a *theta* brainwave state and thereby have ready access to potentially wider fields of information. Perhaps this access enabled him to compose extraordinarily beautiful music far beyond the normal abilities of someone of his age. Similarly Einstein and Michelangelo are people who seem to have somehow been able to access fields of information beyond their normal mental processes in order to inform and inspire their great works. A further example is the scientist Nicola Tesla who—in the earlier part of the twentieth century—is said to have received some visions of different types of devices. It is said that it was only after he actually constructed these devices, on the basis of what he had 'seen', that he was able to explore and fully understand their use.

Accessing the Infinite

I have experienced glimpses of these transcendental fields of information myself and believe that they are potentially open to all. I have found that sometimes I am able to empty my mind and then receive information and guidance from a source of greater knowledge than myself. In that moment I am not thinking of the past, nor having any expectation for the future, but am simply being fully in the present, free of fear and emotional attachments. As the mind empties I have found it is possible to enter a state of quietness. It is such a simple process and yet it is not always easy to do.

Brainwave analysis has shown that in this state, brainwave frequencies slow down and the *theta* range predominates. When I open myself up in this way it feels as if I am directing my human 'antenna' towards the Infinite or, for me, God. In this state, and also sometimes in dreams or meditation, I feel that I receive help and inspiration which, once received, can then be brought into the world of the finite and used creatively.

As I have said, I believe this process is open to anyone. Yet I also feel that, to receive information in this way, we have to be willing to open our minds and take the risk of going beyond our normal belief systems to enter the unknown. If we are not willing to open our minds in this way then I think it would be rather like God calling us up on the phone but constantly hearing the beep-beep-beep of the engaged tone; we are so busy thinking our own thoughts that it is just impossible to get through. To make a connection the phone line has to be accessible and this means our minds and hearts have to be open if we want to be able to access these transcendental fields of information. From the examples quoted above it seems that this connection occurs most often when we are in a relaxed state with low levels of brain activity.

The process of allowing ourselves to be informed and inspired by the Infinite is like being satellite dishes. We can direct our satellite dish horizontally to detect and gain information from anything or any living being around us in the finite universe. We can also direct it upwards (or transcendentally) to create a connection and access the Infinite source of information. In my view we each have the power to direct our own antenna and so can allow ourselves to be informed directly from the Infinite rather than just from the finite. These two ways of accessing information can be symbolised in the form of a cross, whereby 'horizontal', or lateral, thinking, accessed from the finite, can be successfully integrated and alternated with 'vertical' or 'transcendental thinking' (or 'being thought') accessed from the Infinite—as represented in Figure 9 on page 184) accessed from the Infinite. Our connection can enable us to 'go with the flow' of the Infinite.

I believe that many of us have actually had experiences of accessing information from beyond the usual five senses although we may not have been fully aware of it. For example, we may 'sense' a person and then uncannily receive a phone call, letter, or e-mail from them almost immediately afterwards. Or two people may suddenly, simultaneously get the same inspiration or idea not knowing from where it came. Or an intuition or feeling may suddenly prompt us to do, or say, something without really knowing why and it is only later that a definite meaning or purpose is revealed. These things seem to occur quite frequently yet no-one can really explain them. Can they really all just be 'chance' occurrences as some suggest or could they be examples of accessing information transcendentally? It is strange that we take for granted the operation of phones, televisions, satellites and other technological wonders and yet we barely explore the power of our own minds and consciousness in sending and receiving 'signals'.

Perhaps the ability to access information transcendentally is something that can be learned and developed. Just as we can develop the ability to listen to music while performing a task, maybe we can learn to 'tune in' and alternate between receiving information from both the finite and the Infinite. As a result our level of awareness might change and we might also be able to increase what I call our 'response-Ability' (I like to emphasise our ability to respond by using a capital letter) in relation to each other and to God.

Even when using the finite senses there have been some extraordinary examples of people who have developed them beyond what we conventionally imagine is possible. One such case is the blind Belgian detective Sacha van Loo. His sense of hearing is so acute that he can apparently use it to gain vital information from wire-tapped terrorist phone calls. For example, it is said that van Loo can listen to the tones being dialled and can then identify the actual number. Also, by listening to the echoes of the voice, he can apparently deduce whether a suspect is speaking from an airport lounge, a crowded restaurant or other venue. If the suspect is calling from a car, he can apparently determine its make from the sound of the engine in the background. He can also identify people's native tongue even when they are speaking in a foreign language.

This shows us that even our 'normal' senses have great potential for development and refinement, so might we not also consider what could be the potential of our so-called 'para-normal' senses? If we were able to do this what information might we receive about the true nature and meaning of life? It is an intriguing question.

Religion and Science

Traditionally, when we seek answers to the deeper questions in life we turn to science and/or religion. I believe that both serve us in many different ways, helping us to make sense of our existence and perhaps giving meaning to our lives. Yet, for me, neither have all the answers and each has its limitations.

In seeking truth, their approaches seem at first very different. Religion relies primarily on what is termed, 'Divine revelation', with varying amounts of room for interpretation according to the particular school of thought. It also relies on tradition, built up over the centuries through religious scholarship. Religions generally claim to have found 'absolute truth' and thereby the human quest is about working out that truth within our individual lives.

Science, on the other hand, seems quite different in its methods. Truth is found via a process of rational thought and experimentation. A theory is put forward and put to the test under controlled conditions. Proof is determined when a set of circumstances can be repeated under specific test conditions. Theories are revised in the light of new evidence. Truth is thus constantly evolving. Consequently many people revere science as the absolute truth.

However, the conditions and the parameters of scientific experiments are created within certain agreed standards advocated by the scientific community at any given time or place. This can mean that there is a tendency for scientists to find results that fit into the predetermined limited worldview of conventional science. When Columbus set sail across the Atlantic to find the westward route to India, he decided that the islands that he came across in the Caribbean must be part of India, because that's what he expected to find. In the same way, scientists may tend to find the kind of things they are looking for.

Scientists can also become quite attached to their own theories and may see alternative ideas as a personal or professional threat. Disputes between scientists from rival institutions can become ill-tempered, and may block illumination of the truth. Theories can develop into scientific orthodoxy while new ideas are seen as heresy. Original thinkers have sometimes paid a heavy personal and professional price for sticking their necks out against the prevailing winds of opinion, such as Galileo in asserting his new discoveries about the earth's orbit round the sun. Furthermore, some of the great breakthroughs in science have actually come about by intuition or accident rather than through standard scientific methods. Therefore even what scientists regard as 'truth' is still relative.

For its part, religion does not necessarily have the rigid 'once-and-for-all' revelation of the truth that is sometimes portrayed. Religious doctrines evolve over time and new consensuses amongst scholars emerge. Individuals may also seek to find their own way to God, whatever the prevailing dogma. Just as with scientists who question orthodox opinions, religious seekers may also come into conflict with the established authorities.

For example, St Francis of Assisi, one of the greatest Christian saints, hovered on the borderline between orthodoxy and heresy. He came into considerable conflict with the Church yet he made a significant impact in his own time which endures even today. On the scientific front a recent example is the work and claims of the scientist, Dr. Rupert Sheldrake[8]. His theories on morphogenetic and morphic fields, and what he terms 'morphic resonance', have been frowned on by many in the scientific establishment as 'unscientific' as they go beyond the boundary of their orthodox beliefs. Yet many others believe his work is groundbreaking.

This should not surprise us as fear of change and the need to control are part of a finite mentality that excludes the Infinite. A free-thinking scientist willing to go beyond the accepted conventions, or the mystic whose spirituality leads them beyond the confines of dogma, are, in my view, both on a journey to experience the Infinite—albeit in different ways. As they do this their thoughts, ideas and experiences may even start to converge. Religious commentators have long observed how mystics of different faiths seem to experience their spirituality in similar ways and some of the latest scientific findings seem to touch on the mystical.

An example of religious convergence can be seen in these two extracts written about the experience of union with the Creator:

> "This highest stage of union is an indescribable experience,
> in which all idea of images and forms and differences has vanished.
> All consciousness of self and of all things has gone,
> and the soul is plunged into the abyss of the Godhead
> and the spirit has become one with God."

> "I have ceased to exist and have passed out of self.
> I am become one with Him and am altogether His."

The first quote is from a fourteenth-century Christian mystic, Suso[9], from his *Book of Truth*' The second is from a poem by Rabi'a al-'Adawiyya, an eighth-century Sufi and Islamic mystic from Iraq. Yet despite coming from different times and backgrounds the essence of their experiences appears similar. Meanwhile an example of the convergence between religion and some areas of science can be seen in Fritjof Capra's book, *The Tao of Physics* (published 1975), which highlights parallels between quantum physics and eastern mysticism. Though controversial, this book has inspired many.

This idea has been taken further by Dr. Hiroshi Motoyama, the scientist, mystic and Shinto priest whom I met and hosted in Europe in the 1980s. He has developed what he calls 'subjective-objective science', that is science that goes beyond its normal conventional outlook to incorporate understandings of reality gained from direct spiritual, paranormal, and also psychic experience. He be-

---

8. Rupert Sheldrake originally worked in developmental biology at Cambridge University and is best known for his theory of morphic fields and morphic resonance. These suggest that the universe has its own inherent memory and is both living and developing. He is currently Director of the Perrott-Warrick project.

9. Henry Suso 1295–1366, also named Heinrich Seuse, was a German mystic and Dominican friar.

lieves that we need to work towards integrating science and religion, or rather spirituality that goes beyond the confines of religious dogma. In my own opinion this might be achieved if both science and religion could integrate their 'male' and 'female' aspects, combining heart, feelings and intuition with intellect and inner experience with external observation.

The Search for Universal Truth

There are scientists who hope to formulate a 'Theory of Everything' (TOE) to explain all the workings of the known universe and beyond, and also some religious leaders who claim to have found the answer to everything through Divine revelation. Yet can either approach really lead to absolute truth?

As I have already suggested, I believe that, scientific 'truth' only represents a partial view of the whole; it can be a wonderful tool which helps us explore and explain the finite, physical universe and gives us new and different perspectives. However it also limits our belief systems to the finite universe.

Similarly, religious or spiritual beliefs can inform and inspire but may again limit our perceptions and worldviews and our understanding of truth. If religion is experienced only through the intellect as a doctrine, and/or purely emotionally, then there is no real inner experience; this can limit understanding and may lead to a competitive approach between the followers of different religions.

When religious experience is limited by fear and attachment to the finite, this inevitably leads to rivalry and the need to control. As a result, people may debate the superiority of different religions and even fight wars over them. One of my friends and former teachers, Peter Goldman, once told me, "If religion is experienced, it can never be the subject of fighting or discussion; when religion is subject to discussion you can fight about it and it is not experienced."

However, if religion is fully understood and experienced beyond the finite, then the 'being' of the human can be revealed to each of us individually and no thought of competition, or the superiority of one religion over another, remains. It wouldn't make sense for everyone who was unwell to receive exactly the same medicine regardless of their condition. Similarly it doesn't make sense to insist on the same spiritual medicine for everyone. What works for one person may not work for another.

In the same spirit, perhaps the scientific world can go beyond a finite view of reality whereby Western science is seen as having all the answers and as being automatically superior to say indigenous beliefs. In the so-called civilised world where we have a strong belief in science we sometimes forget that it may be based on concepts that are specific to our own culture. We may also focus on finer and finer details and lose sight of the whole. An example might be scientific research into a particular drug and its action at a cellular level. We think that we understand the workings of the drug and yet, when it is tried on a whole person rather than cells in a Petri dish, it can have unpredictable results.

In traditional cultures the emphasis seems to be more on the whole person and there often seems to be a deep understanding of the way the universe works.

This may include not only an understanding of the present, cultural environment in which people live but also awareness of a connection to the deceased and of universes beyond the finite.

To me, scientific ideas represent particular viewpoints held at certain points in time within the finite, and shared with others within a certain scientific community according to mutually agreed rules and terms of understanding. Yet throughout the history of science we can see that it evolves. That is to say, as scientists deepen their understanding of the finite universe, what was perceived to be true a thousand, a hundred or even ten years ago, is not necessarily perceived to be true today. Similarly, what is believed to be true now may be disproved in ten, a hundred or a thousand years from now. So we might ask ourselves, what really represents truth in the finite universe?

Instead of trying to find absolute answers about our existence through conventional science or religious doctrine, we could seek answers from other levels, such as in the Infinite. For what we perceive as truth on earth is merely an expression and a part of a greater creative blueprint from an unseen universe that lies beyond the limited dimensions of the finite.

This blueprint is for all the forms of creation in our finite universe and explains how they interact. If we choose to open ourselves to the Infinite, then a totally different awareness can be experienced. As our perceptions change, our 'under-standing' (to me this literally means 'standing-under-God'—that is, having a greater realisation and awareness of the true nature of reality and of Divine Will) and inner experience of creation or reality also change. In this way, we may be able to go beyond the finite to embrace unity rather than always focusing on the things that divide us. I believe ultimately that truth is only fully accessible in the Infinite.

Experiencing Time and Space Differently

Contemplating the Infinite opens up another key area of our perception of reality—time and space. One of the apparent certainties of the finite is that it is determined by time and space. We look at our watches and see the minutes and hours tick by. We rest secure in the belief that everything happens in a time sequence, one moment after the other. Our perception of space also gives us a sense of order. We can measure distances, know where things are, and learn how they constantly move and change. Thus we see time and space as fixed phenomena that we can rely on and arrange our lives by. However, this is only part of the story because time and space are, in fact, relative.

What do I mean by this? I am not a physicist but I have found that Albert Einstein's Theory of Relativity can help us to understand time and space differently. As I understand it, if we relate his ideas to the finite universe then it can be seen that every star, planet, person, animal, plant, mineral, element, atom, molecule and so on, occupies its own space and has its own time; it cannot occupy the space and time of any other expression of creation.

The concept of everything having its own 'space' can, I think, be easily understood; we can readily accept that in the universe every expression of matter, from subtle to dense, occupies a different physical position in regard to any other. However, understanding the concept that everything has its own 'time' is, I think, more difficult for many people, including me.

Again, I have found that Einstein's theories are helpful here. He suggested that time can be determined in terms of the speed of light and the reference point of the observer. So, for example, if someone is standing in front of me, say a metre away, and a light particle is emitted from the sun, millions of kilometres behind that person's back, it will travel towards us and will reach the person in front of me before it reaches me. Since light travels in a straight line at the speed of 300,000 km/sec, the time difference is infinitesimal, as we are only a metre apart. However the fact that there is a difference is crucial to our understanding of time.

Accordingly, there is also a time difference between any two points on my skin, or between my two nostrils, or between whatever elements we define in time and space. We too easily take the objects around us for granted. We also tend to forget that everything in time and space is subject to change and therefore embodies continuous movement. I discuss this further in the next section.

This understanding of time and space has had dramatic consequences for me. When I really understood this I came to realise how each one of us, indeed each particle in the universe, co-exist with our own unique place in the matrix of time and space. Also, as each point in space-time is different from any other I realised that, of course, we cannot compete for it; a person can never sit on exactly the same spot on a bench at exactly the same time as someone else—and there is no need to compete, as an abundance of points exist in space-time. This fascinating conclusion also made me think deeply about the wider concepts of competition and scarcity and to question their reality. I re-evaluate them on pages 210-214.

I also concluded that as we learn to experience time and space more profoundly we learn to expand our consciousness and, in my view, grow towards a greater understanding of the Infinite.

Synthesis

Through our minds we shape our perception of the world we live in. For the mind does more than simply record internal and external events; it interprets all the information it receives through the senses and orders it. This includes not only deciding what kinds of phenomena are being experienced, such as sorting things into animal, vegetable, or mineral categories but also determining values, such as good or bad, pleasant or unpleasant. It will also place events in sequence and understand them in terms of cause and effect.

From this we can see that the way the mind experiences our inner and outer environment—our consciousness—is key to our personal development. Experiencing time and space differently and re-evaluating the 'truth' of science and religion can shift our perceptions and mental processes. Furthermore, if we can open our minds to accessing information from dream, meditative and transcendental sources we may expand our consciousness and develop a greater connection with the Infinite. This is the invitation that lies before us.

So my key ideas about expanding the mind are:

- Information and ideas from the Infinite can be accessed transcendentally.
- When science and religion can be integrated then our consciousness will expand and true wisdom can emerge
- Every element and every person co-exists in space-time with every other element and person, so in essence there is no competition or scarcity.

5. Utilising Free Will and Authentic Power

As I continued to think about the Infinite as the essential source of all information I also began to think more about free will and power. I see the Infinite as the source of all-encompassing, creative power that governs all of creation and life on earth. From my perspective this great, creative power is embodied in what I have termed the Natural Law of Cyclical, Evolutionary Creation. As human beings we are part of natural creation and thus subject to this Law and, in fact, an expression of it in time and space.

In my view this Law can help us to determine our deepest reason for being here in the finite universe for it represents what I will call 'Divine Will' or 'God's Will' . I began to understand that our purpose is, with our own free will, to follow Divine Will or, in the Christian concept, to allow that 'Thy will be done'. For me this means attempting to be a hollow reed for God's love or, in other words, allowing Divine Will to be expressed through us.

To achieve this I believe we have to find ways of putting aside our blocks of fears, emotions and judgements and allowing our thoughts and actions to be informed and guided transcendentally. In other words maybe we need to find ways of aligning our personal will with Divine Will and of utilising our free will with greater consciousness. This could allow us to reclaim the authentic, personal power which I believe resides in each of us.

I have had glimpses of how this might work through spiritual experiences that I have had and from learning and reading about the experiences of others. In this section I will explore these ideas in more detail. Let's start by considering in a bit more depth the Natural Law of Cyclical, Evolutionary Creation.

The Natural Law of Cyclical, Evolutionary Creation

As I have said I see this Law as the one that guides all of natural creation and life on earth and I see us human beings as an expression of the Law in time and space. I see the Natural Law of Cyclical, Evolutionary Creation as different to man-made laws in several ways. For me, man-made laws:

- are more narrow and rigid
- relate specifically to a given culture, population or area
- incorporate the concepts of obedience, consequences and punishment if not followed

- are based on an anthropocentric view.

In contrast I see the Natural Law of Cyclical Evolutionary Creation as:

- broader
- universal in application
- more related to 'cause' and 'effect', self-development and self-responsibility.

The concept of 'cause' and 'effect' has been described in Indian philosophy as the 'Law of Karma', that is, any action will also create a response at some point in time. Therefore, I see embodied in the Law the concept that—according to our level of development—we need to take responsibility for our thoughts and actions and the effects that they will produce.

I also see the Law expressed in patterns that are natural, cyclical and evolutionary. The fundamental principle is that all life forms evolve naturally through a series of cycles of conception, birth, growth, flourishing, decay, death, new conception, birth and so on.

The evolutionary and cyclical aspects of the Law can be seen in, for example, the life cycle of a deciduous tree. The tree grows from a seed into a sapling and then eventually becomes a fully developed tree. Each spring buds appear on its branches and from these new leaves grow which are then shed in autumn to decay and die along with seeds that generate new saplings. Thus, the seasons themselves represent a cycle of birth and death in the life of a tree. Yet the tree's growth and development during these cycles is also affected by seasonal elements such as temperature, wind and rain. Thus the evolution of the tree—its life and death—form part of a wider cycle of evolution in nature as a whole.

Another example of this, on a larger scale, is how the continents on which we live are constantly evolving and changing. Long ago they were united in a single supercontinent, known as Pangaea, but they drifted apart over hundreds of millions of years to form our present landmasses. Now they are apparently slowly moving together again and geologists estimate that in around 250 million years a new supercontinent may develop. The process of continents breaking up and coming together again in new forms—natural, cyclical evolution—has happened many times before and may happen again.

The evolutionary and cyclical aspects of the Law can also be seen in examples such as the development from an egg into a caterpillar, into a chrysalis, into a fully-fledged butterfly or the transition from a human egg into a foetus, a baby, and then from childhood into adulthood. In both cases, at maturity, the natural life cycle can begin again as new life develops from new eggs. Cycles of low and high tides, heart beats, the orbits and life cycles of planets and so on are also natural expressions of Creation.

On another level I also see the evolutionary aspects of the Natural Law of Cyclical, Evolutionary Creation reflected in the evolution of consciousness. In humans I see this as the development of our consciousness from a limited, finite perspective through to a wider perspective that includes greater awareness and understanding of the Infinite. To me this evolution of consciousness is key to our understanding of the natural Law.

I believe the Natural Law of Cyclical, Evolutionary Creation is reflected in even the smallest elements in the universe. At the most fundamental level, there is a constant exchange of particles going from one place to another. Even in space, a particle of matter and another of anti-matter (its mirror opposite) will appear, as if from nowhere, will exist momentarily and will then come together to annihilate each other.

Furthermore, I see the Law reflected in the dynamic polarity between the 'male' and 'female' principles discussed earlier (page 177) and illustrated in Figure 10. All matter is in motion, irrespective of whether it is subtle or dense, and this motion exists in the cyclical movement from 'plus (+)'— known as the positive, 'male' principle —to 'minus (–)'—the negative, or 'female', principle. The Tai Ji symbol mentioned earlier (page 178) also illustrates these principles.

In addition I see the cyclical and evolutionary principles of the Law operating in a transcendental way. For example, in Figure 10 (page 196) the vertical, open oval in the middle of the diagram demonstrates a transcendental cycle of giving and receiving: from the human perspective you could say that we have received life and we can give our gratitude in return while from the Divine perspective life has been given and gratitude is received in return. The evolutionary principle here, for me, is that the more aware we become of this transcendental cycle and the greater insight that we get into the functioning of the Law of Creation, the more we may develop our own consciousness. With this increased consciousness, we can realise that, while being human, we still contain an essence of the Infinite within the finite.

So there are, if you like, two cycles that human beings participate in: one, in the finite universe, through nature, along with all the other elements in the universe. Then there is another, going from the Infinite to the finite, giving and receiving at the deepest level through transcendental exchanges.

Both of these 'horizontal' and 'vertical' cycles of information exchange and evolution are depicted in Figure 10. In fact this figure summarises many of the principles that underlie my philosophy and illustrates what is, in my view, the most significant understanding of the Natural Law of Cyclical, Evolutionary

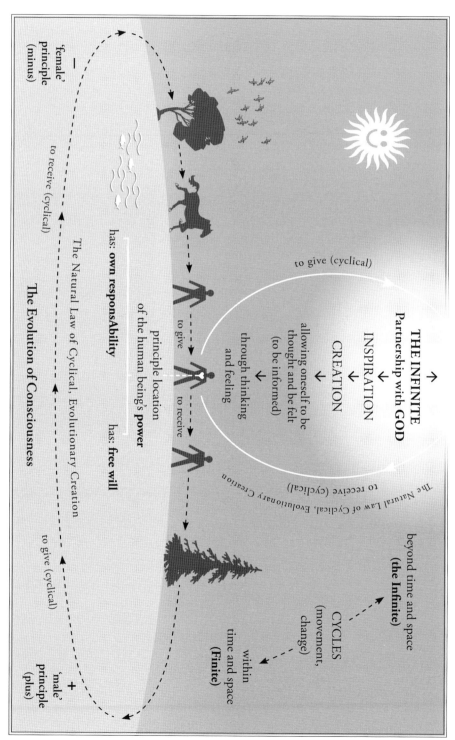

Figure 10. The Natural Law of Cyclical, Evolutionary Creation (simplified representation)

Creation: the connection between ourselves and our Creator, or between the finite and Infinite. As shown in the diagram and mentioned earlier I see us as coming from the Infinite (as 'beings') into the finite (as 'humans') and then evolving in the finite into 'human beings', only to ultimately return to the Infinite (as 'beings') from whence we came. I believe that in this way, during our given lifespan, we are offered the opportunity to develop our consciousness, through our thoughts, feelings, actions and experiences, in order to ultimately gain a deeper understanding of, and participation in, unconditional love.

Learning through Resistance

In my opinion the Natural Law of Cyclical, Evolutionary Creation exists by the grace of the phenomena of resistance. Let me explain what this is and what it means to me.

Resistance can be defined as the push and pull between two forces, attraction and repulsion. A simple example of this principle is weightlifting in a gym. As a person lifts an iron bar they push against the weight of the bar with their body and encounter resistance. Through this repeated resistance the exercised muscles develop and grow. In the same way we encounter 'resistance' in the finite universe, for example in the form of emotional blocks and lessons, and it could be said that this allows our 'spiritual muscles' to grow towards higher consciousness.

We can also relate this concept more abstractly to the example I gave earlier of the dynamic polarity between positive (plus (+)) and negative (minus (-)) forces and of the 'male' and 'female' principles that are implicit in all matter in the universe. These too can only operate by the grace of resistance.

I see resistance as equal to matter because the two are inseparable and so, for me, the existence of the entire finite universe is based of this principle. At the deepest level the finite exists in contra-distinction to the Infinite and is also a part of it. We could say that the finite represents resistance to the oneness of Creation and is expressed in a universe of duality or opposites.

Put another way, I see the principle of resistance which precipitates our separation from the Creator into distinct forms such as our universe and all it contains, as the underlying cyclical principle of life and death. We can also see this at work at a cellular level, where the cell wall separates it from the surrounding environment (or other cells) so that it can function properly. Without the cell wall, all the necessary chemical reactions could not occur. Life began on this planet with single-celled organisms so from the simplest of these to the most complex cellular structures of the human brain, the phenomenon of resistance is at work.

Resistance is, in my opinion also vital for the development of human consciousness. I see us as learning through the contrasts afforded by the principle of resistance. For me one of the most powerful examples of this is the learning that we gain from the contrasting experiences of unconditional love and fear. I feel that resistance is the very essence of fear.

Reflecting on Jerry Jampolsky's book, *Love is Letting Go of Fear*, I saw how we are repelled by our fears and anxieties but also attracted to them. We allow them to determine certain aspects of our lives and find it hard to let go of them. If we can look at the phenomenon of fear with detachment, we can see that it is just a form of resistance and can deal with it by letting go. By learning to do this we become open to experience unconditional love. In a way, we need the contrast that this resistance gives us in order to be aware of the difference.

I began to wonder if fear—resistance—might be seen as a gift from God to humanity to enable us to learn and develop. Might it be that we choose to be born into the limitations of the finite in order to learn about unconditional love? The paradox is that unconditional love from the Infinite can only be recognised when brought into contrast for us by resistance. Though we are bound to the earth by the physical forces of gravity, attraction and repulsion, I feel we are tied in this way so that we may learn about transcendence as well. That is, by working through our fears and emotional attachments, we may transcend them and experience the unconditional love of the Infinite.

We could say that as human beings we are operating at two levels. The first is learning through resistance; experiencing polarities of the finite universe and spiralling through cycles of evolution. On another level, there is no polarity, no opposites, and no resistance—just the oneness of unconditional love that is the Infinite consciousness. This concept is summed up beautifully in the introduction to the renowned text, *A Course in Miracles*,[10] where it is stated, "The opposite of love is fear but what is all-encompassing can have no opposite."

Learning about Unconditional Love

The process of learning about love generally seems to go slowly, one experience building on another as we progress through our life experiences. This sequential learning process is, in my opinion, a gentle gift from God; I feel that if we learnt to access unconditional love too fast we might not be able to handle it. We might

---

10. A self-study spiritual workbook that teaches that the way to love and inner peace is through forgiveness. For more see *www.acim.org*.

literally 'burn-up' in the process. Maybe we are on this planet, in human form in time and space, to learn and grow at our own pace. Through moments of reflection we can assess how we feel internally and this gives us the opportunity to grow in consciousness. As mentioned earlier we also learn and grow through accessing transcendental information.

I believe that in coming to this planet and taking human form, we have chosen to lose our conscious connection with the Infinite and to exist in the finite, with all its limitations, so that we can learn about, and experience, unconditional love.

In my view the lesson is to learn to live here, in the constant flow of all that we have been given, without being attached to any part of it. If we are able to be in this flow then we may detach lovingly from our past, no longer bound to memories nor carrying guilt, and become able to use our free will in a functional way. I will go into this concept of functionality in more depth in the next two sections.

Free Will, Discernment and Functional Choice

As human beings, we have the gift of free will, and we use it to make our daily choices and decisions. Yet how do we exercise this free will and what is the nature of our choices? I suggest that we can make functional or dysfunctional choices depending on our ability for discernment and our level of awareness of the working of the Natural Law of Cyclical, Evolutionary Creation.

I would define a functional choice as one that is in harmony with The Law of Creation, while a dysfunctional one is not. The choices depend on our level of consciousness. Put another way, we can use our free will functionally when we align it with the will of our Creator.

I see discernment as being free from judgement or emotional attachment and it allows us to develop an open mind and heart to decide upon the appropriate course of action. As our power of discernment and level of consciousness increases, we become more aware and more able to make decisions and choices that are functional in nature. When we no longer have self-interest, then our interests will merge with the whole.

Developing a Functional Culture

I define 'culture' as all that humans take from nature to make into new combinations and creations. I am aware there are many other definitions of culture but I am using it here to refer to all elements that are taken in their natural form and then used differently according to a man-made process. Examples of this culture might be cars, chairs, buildings, clothes, computers, food combinations and so on. All involve humans taking elements from nature and then processing them into new forms.

Nature existed on this planet, as an expression of Divine Will if you like, long before humankind appeared. When humanity came into creation we were given, and then developed, the ability to make use of natural elements. I sometimes think of these as elements that God gave us to play with, using our free will creatively to take them out of their natural context and make new combinations and forms. Our interventions can create forms and combinations that nature herself cannot.

Essentially this means that we have the choice of whether to use our free will to take and use these natural elements in *functional* ways—in harmony with the Natural Law of Cyclical, Evolutionary Creation—or in *dysfunctional* ways which go against this natural Law.

An example of functional culture might be deciding to grow some alfalfa seeds. By exposing the seeds to light, air and warmth, and giving them water, it is possible to create a very nutritious food in less than two weeks. This is a highly functional use of natural elements since a tiny seed with a huge potential—it is cheap, readily available and easy to grow— can be used to provide the body with valuable nutrition within a short space of time, using minimal natural resources and creating no damage or toxic side effects. Furthermore, the ingested alfalfa, ultimately results in human faeces which are then recycled back into nature. In this way the natural, creative cycle is brought full circle without any wastage and can be repeated over and over again.

Certain technological developments could also be regarded as 'functional culture' if they operate within these principles such as a processing plant that recycles processed materials and brings them harmlessly back into nature and natural cycles. The plant itself, and its components, should also be considered for re-use at the end of their lifecycle.

There are also corporate examples of this functionality such as the Body Shop, created by the pioneering Anita Roddick, who sadly died in 2007. The Body Shop tries to use ingredients from sustainable sources and offers refills for many of their toiletries and cosmetic products. Many companies also use biodegradable materials in their products nowadays.

In contrast, an example of 'dysfunctional culture' is the creation and use of the atom bomb. We have no way of bringing the elements used for the bomb back into their natural cycles—we cannot heal the damage caused by the radiation fallout from the bomb and just have to wait for it to gradually dissipate over time. Other examples of 'dysfunctional culture' include some modern industries that take little responsibility for the damaging, environmental consequences of their businesses. This has included mobile phone and computer companies that have taken little or no responsibility for the recycling of old models, although thankfully this is now changing in many cases.

'Dysfunctional culture' is widespread. In fact, if we think of our planet as a business, The World plc, we could see that our company is in bad shape since we have depleted our natural resources, threatening the future sustainability of the company. You could say that our emphasis on this type of culture has been due to our egoism and anthropocentrism. What do I mean by this?

I understand egoism as an attitude that focuses on the end result for the individual and which excludes consideration of the effects on the whole. Anthropocentrism on the other hand is the egoism of the species rather than the individual. It means viewing humanity (just one of the millions of expressions of life) as the centre of the universe and focussing on our own interests to the exclusion of those of other species or other manifestations of nature.

As a result of egoism and anthropocentrism, we tend to view other species and natural elements, such as the oxygen that enables us to breathe, or the force of gravity that enables us to stand upright and walk, as a given instead of also appreciating them as a gift. We therefore take things for granted and do not think twice about dominating other species, even to the point of their extinction, or using natural elements for our own ends at the expense of nature generally.

Yet this is, in my view, just another result of the over-valuation of our intellect and the technology to which it gives birth. In reality surely we are stewards of nature and it is our task to take care of her with respect and understanding. As we are not educated to value our feelings and our sense of connection with nature, I feel that we grow up increasingly disconnected from nature and any sense of the Infinite. In the process, as I have said earlier, I think we lose our 'being-ness' and risk becoming 'human-havings', rather than human beings.

As a result, it appears that the majority of decisions that affect our planet are ones based on 'taking' and 'having'. These lead to the destruction of nature, depletion of our natural resources and serious environmental imbalances such as the problems of global warming and the unusual flooding, drought and soil erosion that are now being experienced in many parts of the world. You could say these natural disturbances are nature mirroring our dysfunctional culture back to us. Our collective actions could even lead to the extinction of our own human species.

Most of these dysfunctional decisions are made by working adults, such as politicians and businesspeople. Few are made by children, young people or elders yet I believe that these groups should be included in decision-making processes.

In my view children and young people are more likely to still be in a state of 'being-ness', while elders may have acquired greater wisdom and moved beyond 'having-ness' back towards 'being-ness'. I've summarised how I see this in an age-scale diagram below (Figure 11). I personally feel we should ensure that both young people and elders are more involved in important decision-making processes that affect us all and that it is essential for young and old to have experiences in nature in order to retain a connection with her.

We come to the planet as 'human beings' with open hearts and minds.

Between 6-18 years we slowly become 'human havings'; we may lose some of our trust and sense of wonderment and come to operate more out of fear and a desire to control, possess and 'own' things.

This can continue into adulthood and through middle age but as we grow older we may gradually mellow and may start to return to a state of 'human being-ness' where material possessions, control and so on have less importance.

Alas, so many decision-making bodies in the world, such as governments, companies and other organisations, seem to be dominated by the 'human havings'; they have the vote and wield the external power.

It might be better to incorporate both sides of the scale (as depicted below), taking more account of the voices and opinions of the young and of elders, and thereby empowering the 'human beings' while limiting, or transforming, the power of the 'human havings'.

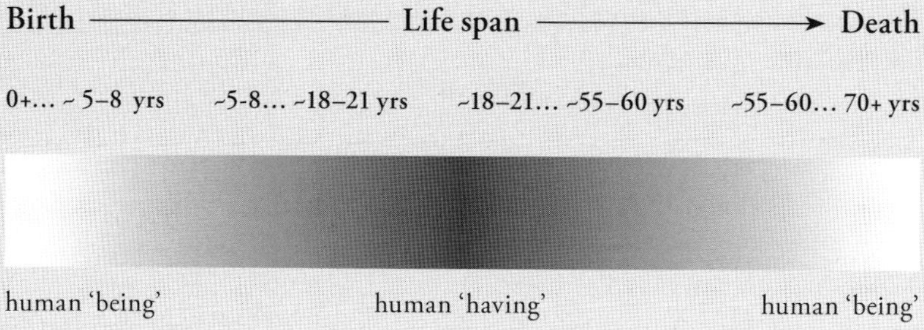

Birth ————————— Life span ————————→ Death

| 0+... ~ 5–8 yrs | ~5-8... ~18–21 yrs | ~18–21... ~55–60 yrs | ~55–60... 70+ yrs |

human 'being'   human 'having'   human 'being'

Figure 11. Age Scale and 'Being-ness' in Western Society

We all share what I call, 'response-Ability' to bring back into the natural cycle those elements that have been taken out of their natural context for human purposes. If we can develop increased awareness of both our collective and individual responsibilities for the full effects of our use of natural resources, then we may be able to correct and prevent our dysfunctional culture of nature, which is creating such problems today[11]. By using our free will in a functional way, we could develop a culture that is in harmony with the Natural Law of Cyclical, Evolutionary Creation.

Authentic Power and Self-Development

When we act in the world, we bring into play our own power. Yet what power do we, one amongst the billions of people, really have? How can we use our power authentically and appropriately? And what is power in reality? The term 'power' is so often used and misused but seldom clearly examined or defined. It is often understood in terms of the power of one person, or a group of people, to dominate other individuals or groups, such as in terms of military might or sports prowess. As a reflection of our collective belief systems, often reflected in the laws of a country, many of us have given our individual power away to our leaders. In order to maintain their power and control over people these leaders sometimes foster fear and anxiety as an instrument with which to manipulate their followers or the masses. In turn, people can buy into that fear and anxiety when they have not yet learned to develop and rely on their own inner power.

Yet, seen from an understanding of the Natural Law of Cyclical, Evolutionary Creation, the only authentic power in the finite is the functional use of the free will that each of us has. So I would define power as the force that comes through each living being, from the Infinite, rather than coming from the finite universe around us. It is the power we can discover through following Divine Law, as discussed earlier. Let's consider some further examples of power to explore this idea in more detail.

In our daily lives we often see transfers of power, such as the huge energy transfers from supporters to their sports heroes. The supporters identify with their idols, try to imitate them and are focused on them winning. If the idol/team wins, or performs well, then the supporters are happy or sometimes even ecstatic. On the other hand if they lose then the supporters are downhearted and may even become angry and aggressive. We often see this with football fans in Europe at huge cost to the police and to society at large. While it is, of course, fine to be enthusiastic about a football match and to enjoy the sense of belonging that it brings, if the person's whole state of mind and well-being is dependent on the outcome of the match this can hardly be healthy.

---

11. A good book on this subject is *Cradle to Cradle: Re-making the way we make things* (Vintage Press, 2009) by Michael Braungart and William McDonough.

In relationships we may also allow others to exert power over us, such as the man or woman who allows their partner to dominate or control. These kinds of relationships hinder us from taking responsibility for our own lives since, in this process, we give our individual power away to others. These transfers of power are dysfunctional for both leaders and followers, sports idols and their supporters and partners in unequal relationships.

The way I see it is that, in essence, the need to control is based on fear. The need to be controlled is also based of fear of one's own authentic power. Yet, if this dysfunctional bond is broken on either side, then a change towards a more functional relationship between individuals and groups, and with oneself, can start. The process of leaving the apparent security and comfort of a dysfunctional relationship and standing on one's two feet can be painful and difficult but can ultimately be very worthwhile.

Developing an awareness of our individual, authentic power, and allowing that power to become stronger, is, for me, an example of real, functional power. This type of power is the God-given power that resides in each of us, expressed as the functional use of our free will. Such power exerts no force or dominance over others and does not seek to manipulate or control. Rather I see it as a process of successful self-development that leads to calm self-assurance and inner strength, while at the same time retaining vulnerability. This power can be connected to the source of all power, the Infinite, yet is also gentle, humble and pure. If we respect this power in its essence, then I do not think it can be misused; instead it can be used externally with wisdom and restraint. In this sense the path towards authentic power could be described as 'development' (rather than 'envelopment'), and this unfolding is, in my opinion, the same as evolution.

Vulnerability, which is an aspect of the 'female' principle, is often confused with weakness and thus labelled dysfunctional. Yet, we forget that out of this vulnerability comes the manifestation of authentic power; for example, an acorn falls on the earth and is vulnerable to moisture, temperature, nutrients in the soil and so on and yet, with the right conditions, it can grow into a mighty oak. I feel that the power of vulnerability can be tremendous and it is often underestimated. For example, with the sense of touch, caressing someone gently can have a much more powerful effect on their being than being pushed forcefully.

Physical strength itself, which is an aspect of the 'male' principle, can be either functional or dysfunctional. When it is used to enable our bodies to work or to exert force in the construction of buildings, bridges, roads, for transportation and so on, this is functional whereas if it is used for an assault this is dysfunctional. Therefore the key is how we chose to use physical power.

When our mental clarity is undisturbed we can make clear, functional decisions with ease and use our power to carry them through effortlessly. At the same time, we can experience the power of vulnerability without being weak.

In our present-day situation we can see that the traditional power structure of leaders and followers has led to some productive outcomes; magnificent projects have been initiated, progress has been made in many aspects of society and inspiration has been provided for future generations. On the other hand this power structure has also cost humanity and the planet a great deal; everywhere we see human suffering and environmental damage. I feel this is because people allow themselves to be manipulated and kept in ignorance about the true nature of reality. Thus we all suffer the consequences of the greed and selfish interests of certain political and business leaders, or other organisations—for example in the form of monopolies or oligarchies.

In the original edition of this book I gave the examples of the American company, Enron and the Italian company Parmalat; these companies kept their respective shareholders and the public in ignorance about the true state of their financial affairs in order to maintain their (false) position in the marketplace. This deception was eventually discovered and led to criminal charges and convictions against some members of these companies.

More recently, as we all know, there has been a major financial and economic crisis worldwide, unmatched in recent history. Much of the blame for this has been related to complex and inappropriate financial control systems as well as greed and mis-management by players in national and international finance.

Such examples of the misuse of power on a grand scale have been well publicised, but we can also see many lesser examples, involving manipulation of individuals or the environment, in everyday life.

The dangers of dysfunctional use of power are the reason why, in essence, I don't believe in the principle of leaders and followers. As I see it, leaders can take away power from their followers while followers can give away their power to their leaders; it is a co-dependent relationship.

In our society, we have created many power structures based on a belief in this kind of power transfer, while not recognising the power of the Infinite working through each of us. If only we would all use more of the real, functional power that we have within us, then we might be less willing to step into these roles of followers and leaders.

In my experience those who have a deeper understanding of authentic, functional power act more as guides, inspirers, or co-ordinators rather than taking on the role of dominant leaders for submissive followers. Their position is based on a sharing of experience and wisdom and reflects respect for the real, functional power in both themselves and the other person. An analogy for this might be the parent who nurtures and coaches their child but then, at a certain point, just like a bird pushes them out of the nest so that they can learn to fly.

Of course, I realise that it is not possible, realistic, or even desirable to change societal structures overnight; this is usually a gradual process allowing people to adjust. Yet, I do believe that facilitating changes in the inner attitudes of those who we call leaders or followers could gradually lead to a more functional society if the wish for change gathers sufficient momentum.

If we can work together to increase our awareness of these principles and develop real, functional power expressed through our free will for the benefit of all, then I believe we will be taking important steps towards transforming our world.

Synthesis

If we stand back for a moment and consider the wider question of the purpose of our presence here on earth, we see how these principles are vital for our development. From the human being's point of view, it could be said that we have been given this world, and beyond, as a teaching tool to develop our consciousness. In my view, the aim of this process of developing consciousness is to have an ever deeper and wider understanding of the functioning of the Natural Law of Cyclical, Evolutionary Creation, and to use our free will with the awareness that this understanding brings. To me, an understanding of this Law underlies a sense of spirituality. One does not need to follow a specific religion to have an appreciation and a sense of wonder about the Law or about the awesome, universal power that lies behind it.

To paraphrase the words from the mystical, *Book of Mirdad*:[12]

The power beyond birth, growth, degeneration, death and decay is itself not born nor grows, degenerates, dies or decays. This is the power of God.

I feel that this sentence describes the Infinite well. If we look at its meaning in terms of the evolution of human consciousness we can see that the source is the Infinite consciousness of our Creator. We could imagine this Infinite consciousness as a grid through which the infinite 'electricity' of consciousness flows. Our human consciousness is like a light bulb that is plugged into the grid for the duration of our lifetime. It may burn brightly or, for example when we are ill, it may just flicker. At the end of our lives this light is extinguished. Yet the electricity of

---

12. *The Book of Mirdad: The Strange Story of a Monastery Which Was Once Called the Ark,* Mikhail Naimy (Watkins Books, 1992).

Infinite consciousness flows on and will find other 'light bulbs' through which to shine. The question is how will each one of us use our time to shine? Infinite consciousness also expresses itself through animals, plants, minerals and all living beings and materials as well as all the planets and solar systems in the universe. All the different levels of consciousness in the finite universe have their source in the grid of Infinite consciousness.

Looking back on my exploration of free will and authentic power the key lessons that I have learnt are:

- Our inner nature is connected with outer nature and governed by the same Natural Law of Cyclical Evolutionary Creation.
- We can make ever more functional choices if we utilise our free will with greater consciousness.
- Authentic power resides in each one of us, rather than outside of ourselves, and it can be reclaimed.

6. Caring, Sharing and Connecting

Each of us has the potential to live our lives while being consciously and fully connected with the Infinite. If we strive for this then I believe the process of transformation can be set in motion. Indeed this process is happening right now for we are all a part of the cyclical, evolutionary processes that are an aspect of the Law of Creation, whether we know it or not. The point is that by making a conscious decision to embrace change, we go with the spiralling flow of cyclical evolution rather than remaining in a cycle without evolving. In an inner sense, the change can be immediate and profound. In an outer sense, it may take its own time to work through.

As a result of these changes our perception of the world becomes transformed. Physically, we may live in the same place, meet the same people, walk the same streets, and do some of the same things yet, from an inner perspective, everything is different. Perhaps we can facilitate this by focussing more on caring, sharing and connecting. Let's explore these ideas in more detail.

Comparing and Sharing

This process of transformation has wider implications, for as we change individually so does society. As we bring our sense of the Infinite into the outer world this challenges many of our belief systems and ways of working. As I have mentioned, a great deal of our societal structures today are based on the concepts of competition and exclusion, and of fears of scarcity, rather than belief in abundance. Yet on a global level, I would argue that there are enough resources for everyone. The issue is more about how we share these resources around the world.

If we cling to the belief that there is not enough to go around then each individual, group, or nation will continue to fight for what it can get at the expense of others, rather than realising that there is plenty for all to share. I have witnessed and been part of this competitiveness for decades in the corporate world where companies, including ours, compete to be the biggest, the best, and the most successful, fighting off competitors along the way.

Yet I have thought over the whole concept of competition for many years and I am now convinced that in the long run there is an alternative from which everyone can benefit, rather than a few benefitting at the expense of the many.

Economics, as it is taught, is based on the premise of scarcity, such as the scarcity of natural resources, resulting in the constant fighting for ownership or control of them. We can see this clearly demonstrated in ongoing disputes over offshore oil rights, mineral reserves including diamond and gold mining rights, fishing rights, and so on.

If only we could realise that we all exist together in time and space, all breathe the same air, are all subject to the same gravitational pull and share the commonality of our human birth, then maybe it would be easier for us to share our resources.

Scarcity, as a concept, functions on different levels. Besides the belief system implanted in our minds, from which the idea of competition grows, there is also a link between scarcity and consumption. I realise that currently in many parts of the world there are not enough resources to meet basic needs. At the same time in other parts of the world consumption goes beyond basic needs and so there is an imbalance. My core beliefs in this regard are:

- In essence, scarcity doesn't exist and the false belief in it leads to competitiveness.
- If we can change this belief system, then together we can open up to abundance.
- With a caring, comparing and sharing attitude no-one needs to go without.

An example is world nutrition and the production, supply, and consumption of food. We know that the average male and female needs approximately 2,200kcal and 1,800kcal respectively daily to meet their energy needs. However, many Westerners now consume calories far in excess of these amounts daily, leading to an epidemic of obesity and associated health risks, while in other parts of the world people suffer and starve. When viewed in terms of global availability of food, this over-consumption can be seen as parasitic, depleting global natural resources.

Other aspects of wasteful consumption are excessive and unnecessary packaging, throwing things away rather than reusing or recycling them and buying goods that we don't need. Unfair trade practices by wealthier countries can also work against a more equitable distribution of the earth's resources. On the other hand, the empowerment of small and local food producers, for example by forming co-operatives, can help to ensure a fair price for all.

Functional consumption, such as eating according to daily energy and nutritional needs for health and strength or avoiding excess packaging, is inspired action that contributes to abundance, since available resources can be spread more widely. With this awareness and, adding gratitude, the sum effect of these actions becomes greater than the individual outcome, since a contribution is made to global consciousness as well as to our physical nutrition and life balance.

Another issue is that of food choices. Globally, around one third of the world's cereal harvest is fed to farm animals, mainly cattle, and one fifth of the world's land area is used for livestock grazing, twice that given over to growing crops[13].

Meat-eating habits are therefore threatening food security as well as wilderness areas so choosing to eat less or no meat will, in the long-term, have a big impact on the overall supply of food worldwide. Similarly, over-fishing is depleting global stocks, so there are powerful arguments for a predominantly vegetarian diet.

There is also concern that the clearing of forests, grasslands, and peatlands to produce crops grown for fuel may result in major carbon emissions that outweigh the benefits of using such 'bio fuels' in place of fossil fuels. Many also believe that taking such crops out of the food chain could ultimately lead to food shortages[14].

In fact, nobody needs to go hungry or starve in this world. That there is starvation and hunger is a product of fear (in the form of greed, selfishness, and belief in scarcity) and the resulting dysfunctional economic policies. These also include overproduction of certain foodstuffs, destruction and wastage of 'Food Mountains' and national competitiveness over trade issues. If we can all take re-

---

13. Source: Food and Agriculture Organisation (FAO) of the United Nations.

14. From a study by The Nature Conservancy and the University of Minnesota published in *Science*, February 2008.

sponsibility for caring, comparing and sharing and for sustainable farming and permaculture, then we could contribute to the eradication of scarcity and help to ensure there is nutritious food for all. The same principle can also operate for other types of resources such as oil and gas, if we are willing to ask ourselves, "Do I really need to travel?" and "Can I do so with the lowest carbon footprint?" This is something I am still working on in my own life.

Of course, there are many places in the world that do have a real scarcity of water, food and other resources as well as funding, workforce, educational, and health care facilities at this time. Yet if we look at the planet as a whole, we can see that there is actually enough for these to be provided for all —it is just their distribution that is unbalanced.

Therefore, our challenge is to:

- Empower people to find ways of distributing resources more equally.
- Ask ourselves, when we are about to acquire or buy something, "Do I really need this?"
- Develop an attitude of caring and sharing on an individual, community, national, and global level to empower our fellow women, men, and children.

My thoughts about these challenges can be summed up in the phrase: "*Instead of competing why don't we compare with care in order to share?*" I also feel that we need to move away from over-consumption towards nurturing one another. I find it reassuring to find that philanthropy is coming back into fashion. In the last decade, many individuals have given over large sums of money and their time and attention to charitable activities. These include Bill and Melinda Gates, George Soros, Warren Buffet, Ted Turner, Tom Hunter and Anita and Gordon Roddick, amongst many others. Philanthropy on a small scale is also hugely effective and, with all the challenges of the recent global financial crisis, we can see many encouraging examples of individuals reaching out to share and care for each other even when their resources are increasingly limited.

Competition

Competition has produced many advantages for society at large. For example, it has helped to improve the quality of many products and keep prices low. Competition can also produce greater efficiency and it has helped many of us, especially in the West, live a more affluent life. Thus we live in a world where competition is held up as being indispensable for society to function but do we really always benefit from it in the long run? At present, much competition could be said to be counterproductive. We can see the dysfunctional aspects of the game of competition as it is played, by using the metaphor of tennis.

To me, tennis is a game in which the Natural Law of Cyclical, Evolutionary Creation can be well expressed. Apparently in the original game, people played co-operatively and tried to keep the ball in the game for as long as possible in order to help each other stretch and increase flexibility and in order to keep on playing. The game, as it was played then, reflected the Natural Law of Creation: serving one another in order to give and receive as part of the evolution of play, by keeping the ball 'in the loop'.

Nowadays, however, the game has become competitive so that one plays in such a way that the other person cannot return the ball, i.e. each player deliberately tries to break the game's cycle of continuity. Not only does the person break the cycle, but s/he is also rewarded for doing so by gaining points and finally the one with the most points is termed 'the winner'. If there are 'winners' then there must also be 'losers'. Yet this is really just an illusion, for there are no actual 'winners' or 'losers', just two or more people playing a game together, reflecting the cycle of life in different time-and-space zones.

Similarly, in business, and in the culture of the celebrity, many people aspire to be the big boss, the top celebrity, the most popular recording artist, or the greatest leader. By encouraging such aspirations we encourage people to want to be better, faster, richer, more beautiful or more powerful than others. Yet, in these examples and according to this way of thinking, only one person can attain these positions at any one time and so large numbers of others are left with feelings of dissatisfaction, disappointment and even worthlessness.

When we expend so much energy on being better than somebody else, or when we lose so much energy by worrying that we are not as good as others, a lot of energy is wasted in the process.

Language can also reflect these attitudes and actions. It is fascinating to note how much corporate language is couched in terms of winning, losing and profit, rather than there being much mention of care, compassion, or virtue. This has been dramatically illustrated in a chart that I came across over a decade ago (see Figure 12). As far as I know it came from the *Wall Street Journal* but its exact source is uncertain. However, I am including it here as I think the message it conveys is important.

Perhaps this language is now changing in the twenty-first century as it becomes more fashionable for companies to have a caring face, showing concern for the environment and so on. Certainly many companies are now demonstrating their eco-credentials and openly supporting charitable initiatives, even though these actions may have been stimulated by consumer concerns and demands externally rather than internally.

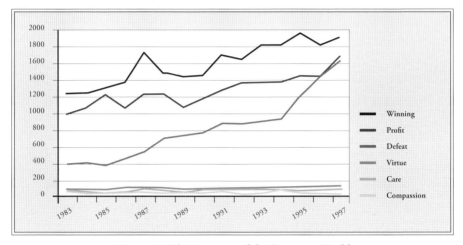

Figure 12. The Language of the Corporate World

From all this it might seem that I am against all competition. If this were the case I might be asked to answer how businesses, including mine, could survive without it. Actually I believe there is nothing wrong with the functional, comparing aspects of competition as long as these can stimulate creativity, innovation and efficiency with a caring and sharing attitude. The reality is that we are all born into this world and we all partake of its abundance, so we could enjoy the playful and interactive aspects of competition without becoming attached to it or fully identifying with it. The constant, natural cycle of creation, destruction, and recreation replenishes the planet and ensures that there is enough for all. We could put a ceiling on our individual or national wants and share with others, even those with whom we are not directly connected.

It is also interesting to consider how the earth happens to have been created as a globe, or ball, rather than say a more rigid structure such as a cube with ends and sharp corners. Its spherical structure is therefore, in itself, a symbol of a never-ending cycle. We could go round and round the globe and never reach an end point; so I also view our planet as an expression of the Infinite. It is also a reminder that we, as one human family, share the same planet in the solar system, with all other forms of creation; how great would our power be if we could all cooperate together rather than compete?

Instead of competing against each other we could use self-comparison instead. Let me give an example of this in terms of a children's race at a school sports day. In such a competition children are usually encouraged to race against one another and some come out winners and others losers. Instead, using self-comparison, each child would be encouraged to assess their own performance by comparing it with previous ones. In other words each child would be encouraged to try and get their best performance, according to their own ability, when they race. The children would still put in maximum effort but the comparison would be with themselves—with their own personal goals and individual progress—rather than them competing against each other.

In this way a child who might have come low down in the ranks of the race might instead compare his current race time with his previous ones and find that he was a winner as he had improved and beaten his own record. If children were introduced to this approach from an early age, then they would learn to emphasise self-growth rather than competing to get the better of others.

To sum this up from my perspective, the process of competition excludes while the process of comparing includes. So I suggest we can resolve this issue and create a functional model for our own lives by focussing on comparison and mutual caring and sharing, rather than competing at the expense of others.

To explore this further, you may like to think about situations in your own life where you are competitive. I find it is sometimes when I am queuing in a shop, or accelerating away from traffic lights against other vehicles. How might your attitude and behaviour be different if, instead of competing for things, you focused on comparing and sharing; what would the outcomes of this approach be? If you are a businessman or woman what would the effect be if you went and talked to your competitor and explored ways in which you might co-operate and share ideas for mutual benefit? It could open up a whole new way of doing business and, more importantly, of being in the world. Of course, this is already happening with many people worldwide who are already working together in co-operatives but still more could be done.

Practising this comparing, caring, and sharing attitude also means that we would feel less pressured and have less stress in our lives, helping to bring about a healthier, happier, society. These principles can also be extended to business workforces. If we see our colleagues as valued fellow human beings, we can create a more functional organisation where everybody benefits. Rather than constantly trying to push the workforce harder, we could support them in their own self-development to achieve a good work/life balance which is, in the end, in everyone's interest. For example, greater flexibility with work hours, including time set aside for personal development, would produce a happier and more functional workforce. It would also be possible to gradually reduce hours of work as people reached retirement age, which would make it easier for those who wished to carry on in a part-time role to do so. So much experience and wisdom are lost when the older members of work teams are let go.

An abrupt change from full-time work to retirement can also leave people feeling disorientated and lost. They can easily deteriorate physically and mentally at great cost to themselves and those around them as well as society at large. If we can see people as a whole, rather than trying to exploit just the parts that seem of immediate usefulness to a company, then unexpected benefits may be found from the person's continued working with the company. There are many examples of this holistic approach in various businesses today, not least in my own country, the Netherlands.

Staying Connected and Living in the Present

The way I see it, living a life fully connected with the Infinite is not about floating in some dreamland but about being fully present each moment of the day. We can bring the Infinite into our daily lives (or if you prefer, allow the Infinite to work through us) in order to transform ourselves and the world in which we live. Maintaining this connection will help ensure that the 'being' aspect of our human being is alive and well and integrated with our 'human' side. This sense of connection can extend to all areas of our lives; it can include connecting with our inner nature as well as with outer nature (the natural world).

For me, connecting with our inner nature involves:

- Connecting with our whole being.
- Connecting with our sense of playfulness and joy.
- Connecting with our heart

We also need to connect with outer nature by:

- Connecting with the natural world

Let's consider each of these one by one.

Connecting with our Whole Being

In 1991, I took a course at the Schumacher College in Devon in the UK, given by Matthew Fox[15] and Satish Kumar[16]. I liked the teachings of both these men, who have the courage of their convictions and are good at communicating them. One Sunday, Matthew gave a public lecture in Dartington Hall with a few hundred people present. After half an hour of speaking he stopped and said, "You are all looking rather tired of listening to me—so let's do some exercises!" He then had everyone standing up and doing some exercises, and I was interested to see how it changed the whole atmosphere in the room.

I had never before experienced a lecturer doing exercises with the audience in the middle of a lecture. Yet I could see that it had a good effect, as everyone was laughing, smiling and energised by what he had done. Matthew's exercises illustrated to me the important connection between mind, heart and body and how we need to integrate and balance these to stay healthy and alert. Earlier I explained how, in my opinion, thoughts and feelings need to come together. I also believe that our actions can work out best when both our minds and hearts are both engaged.

In modern society it is quite a challenge to stay connected with our whole selves in this way as well as with each other and our planet. Yet, in my view, feeling disconnected from ourselves and our fellow human beings can be at the root of anti-social behaviour, such as stealing or violence. Damaging our bodies by filling them with narcotics or excessive amounts of alcohol can be another way of disconnecting ourselves from our feelings as well as the world around us.

Fortunately, we have the freedom to make functional choices and to choose self-development instead. We can nurture our bodies and our minds by eating healthy food, drinking lots of water and listening to music that relaxes and uplifts us and stimulates healthy brainwave patterns. We can limit our exposure to external noise and information overload and instead be aware in meditation or quiet reflection of our inner selves and the beauty around us. By letting go of our fears we can also learn to live lovingly in the here and now and be in tune once more with the Infinite.

---

15. Matthew Fox was formerly a Catholic priest but went on to explore courageously, and somewhat controversially, the tenets and practice of Catholicism to determine his own truth that went beyond religious dogma. For Matthew's story in his own words please see his contribution on page 238. I kept in touch with Matthew and later supported the founding of his original Centre for Creation Spirituality in Oakland, California and shared a week of teaching with him there in 2001.

16. Satish Kumar is the Founder/Director of Programmes at the internationally renowned Schumacher College (*www.schumachercollege.org.uk*), a nuclear disarmament advocate and the Editor of Resurgence magazine.

This reminds me of an image I once saw of a Buddhist monk meditating in the middle of a busy traffic junction in the USA. The traffic was roaring all around and all the sights, sounds and smells could have overloaded his senses, yet he was sitting, apparently totally calmly. He had filtered out all these stimulants and was relying on inner information, the connection of his whole self with the Infinite, enabling him to access an internal sensation of total calm and peace. I believe that we can all have access to this state of wholeness.

Connecting with our Sense of Playfulness and Joy

It is important to remember that all our self-development can be put into the context of playfulness and joy. I am a great believer in having fun, joking and laughing, qualities that I probably inherited from my parents. Throughout my life I have enjoyed sharing and receiving playfulness and joyful activities with children and adults in all kinds of settings. Even complete strangers can enjoy sharing a joke together. So joy and humour in any activity can lift the spirits and transform.

Humour can be deeply healing, too. A friend once told me about an American who had been diagnosed with terminal cancer. He decided to banish all misery and sadness from his hospital room and said that anyone visiting him had to come with smiles, jokes, funny stories, humorous videos and so on. His friends and relatives all did as he asked and the room was constantly filled with uproarious laughter. Everyone wanted to visit and join in the fun, whereas normally people feel more inclined to avoid visiting places of serious illness. Some time later it was discovered that the man's cancer had totally disappeared, to the utter amazement of his doctors. They could only explain his miraculous recovery as a spontaneous remission but we now know that laughter actually does precipitate the release of 'feel-good' chemicals in the body. So perhaps all the joy and good humour that he shared with his friends somehow changed his body chemistry and healed him.

The essential point I want to make is that, regardless of how he was cured of his cancer, his new attitude to life healed something within himself and those around him. We are all in the cycle of life and death. It is the attitude with which we choose to live and die that is the issue.

My friend Patch Adams is also renowned for his use of clowning and humour in his medical work and healing (see page 231) and many healers around the world have also been inspired by him and his work. My own love of fun gave me the idea of founding the Twinkling Eyes Club (see page 112 for details). I have had lots of fun spreading 'miles of smiles' and 'sprinkles of twinkles' around the globe. I hope you too will become a member of the club in the course of reading this book. I am sure you must also have lots of your own ideas for spreading fun and laughter and I hope you put them into practice regularly.

Connecting with our Heart

I often remind myself of the phrase that popped into my head one day in my office that I talked about earlier: "The chaos in the en-vironment is a reflection of the disorder in our minds and hearts ('in-vironment')." I believe that it is through reconnecting our hearts with our minds (our 'in-vironment'), via our feelings, that we can handle the chaos around us (in our en-vironment)—including damaged relationships with other people and nations, global pollution, energy crises, global warming, financial crises and so on— and restore balance.

As I described above, I think it would help if we could stop competing and taking advantage of each other so much and basing our actions principally on our intellect. Instead, if we could be more in touch with our hearts, allowing them to influence our thoughts and actions, we would then be more likely to be in tune with the Natural Law of Cyclical, Evolutionary Creation. I am sure that this, in turn, could help make our world a place of balance, dynamic harmony, inspiration, and peace.

Connecting With Nature

Connecting with nature is, for me a key element in our relationship with the Infinite. Yet, so often, our business and political leaders, and we ourselves in the developed world, live in urban environments divorced from nature and her inspirational power.

Offices and urban environments can act like an anthropocentric screen standing between our inner and outer nature. Think, for example, of how many governmental buildings, companies, office and even schools in different countries contain little natural light or natural air as well as few plants or animals and are dominated by office equipment, computer screens and so on. Urban architecture is often concrete and dominated by unnatural right angles rather than the more natural curves and spiral forms found in nature, such as in shells, fruit, trees, and even our own bodies.

In such environments people often end up tired or depressed and cut off from their feelings, suffering from what has been termed 'sick-building syndrome', whereas in nature we often feel tremendous vitality and invigoration.

When leaders are not connected with their own inner nature, or their authentic power, their decisions can reflect their numbed feelings and overpowered intellects. Yet they may make decisions about our natural world that can have devastating implications while even sometimes keeping people in ignorance about these. We may accept this as normal conduct since we ourselves often lack awareness and a close connection with nature. For example we all go through education systems where we learn lots of facts but engaging with the natural world is not often a very great part of the curriculum

In my view, it is often sad to see how decision-makers have created their own urban prisons. I spend a lot of time in such 'prisons' myself. I remember one international summit on the environment that I attended in 1993 where I was in a room full of influential people discussing nature and environmental issues. I observed that we were sitting in a room where the only aspect of nature was a single, wilted plant in the corner. So we were, in fact, totally divorced from the issues that we were discussing. I pointed this out and suggested that we reconvene the meeting outside, where we would be surrounded by nature. While some people got the point of what I was saying, nobody took it seriously and the meeting simply continued in its 'dead' environment. So, although there were people present who did care about environmental issues, the voice of nature was not really present or heard.

To me, this meeting was quite symbolic, and it kindled my strong desire to facilitate greater contact with, and awareness of, the environment and to stimulate dialogue on this issue. I do believe that having experiences in the natural world is vital for everybody, including young people, to stimulate an understanding and appreciation of nature. For this reason I have been inspired to initiate and contribute to projects that take people, especially children, out into nature and even on wilderness expeditions. The Sacred Land Foundation, which was established in the early 1990s under the auspices of our Foundation for Environmental Awareness has helped many primary schoolchildren to experience nature in this way.

I also joined forces with Ria Lubbers,[17] who had a real interest in the environment and social welfare, to facilitate the creation of an environmental booklet under the auspices of one of my foundations. It was offered to all secondary schools in the Netherlands in 1989 and aimed to stimulate discussions and raise

---

17. For twelve years Ria was an active volunteer and board member of The Sunflower, a Dutch association supporting people with physical disabilities. In 2000 she was awarded the Frekie Prize by the Netherlands Organisation for the Welfare of the Disabled in recognition of her work. She is the wife of the former Prime Minister of the Netherlands, Ruud Lubbers.

environmental awareness amongst children and their families. It also encouraged environmentally-friendly actions such as recycling. The booklet also contained a specially commissioned musical score and tape with an environmental message. Six hundred schools participated, and I attended one of the delightful and inspiring performances at the school of one of my daughters.

Many inspirational people have also spread the environmental message. One is my friend, Jane Goodall, who encourages young and old to become more aware of conservation and the environment. Another is Irene van Lippe-Biesterfeld, who comes from an aristocratic background and yet has followed her heart to write, teach and inspire others about nature.[18]

Fortunately, people are becoming much more aware of, and thus concerned about, environmental issues nowadays. Films such as Al Gore's, *An Inconvenient Truth* and the environmental school programme based on it, continue to raise awareness and promote debate as well.

However, it still strikes me how sometimes awareness programmes and environmental discussions may focus on intellectual aspects, while the participants are still divorced from nature, including their own inner nature (which is waiting to be rediscovered). I would love to see men, women, elders and children all together in nature and taking time to reflect on the environmental situation. This would not be to focus on what has gone wrong or to blame one another but to talk together, to see if we can recreate our present and future and bring our lives and environments back into greater harmony with the Natural Law of Cyclical, Evolutionary Creation.

Going Beyond Conventional Beliefs

In developing my philosophy I have been inspired by people who have had the courage to go beyond the conventional mindset, or to think how we have each been challenged to do this in our own lives. I can think of many marvellous people who, for me, demonstrate this in action. Several have already been written about in this book but here I would also like to mention two other people who helped me challenge my ways of thinking about the body and ageing.

---

18. Irene van Lippe-Biesterfeld, Princess of the Netherlands, is a social reformer, honorary member of the international think-tank, The Club of Budapest and founder/president of the Lippe-Biesterfeld Nature College Foundation. She manages a nature reserve in South Africa and is the author of *Dialogue with Nature* (Findhorn Press, 1997) and *Science, Soul and the Spirit of Nature: Leading Thinkers on the Restoration of Man and Creation* (Bear & Company, 2005).

One was the late Norwegian adventurer and ethnographer, Thor Heyerdahl, whose courageous Kon Tiki expedition, amongst others, and his discovery of pyramids in Guimar in Gran Canaria challenged our conventional understanding of history. I had the pleasure of meeting him through Mikhail Gorbachev's Green Cross Foundation and we became good friends, spending long periods of time together on several occasions.

Thor did not believe in conventional concepts about ageing and deterioration and took great care of himself. He retained great physical and mental fitness right into old age and when we went on walks together I remember having difficulty keeping up with him, even though he was about thirty years older than me.

Enjoying Thor Heyerdahl's company

His attitude towards health and fitness changed my beliefs and expectations about ageing and this led me to develop my ideas on the ageing process itself. To me, ageing is natural, just like breathing in and breathing out. I think that the actual process of ageing is not as important as the way in which we relate to it. Some people invest vast sums of money into retaining a youthful appearance and the beauty industry promotes this. Yet I believe that the ageing process can help us develop mentally, emotionally, and spiritually. If we allow this process to happen and go with the flow maybe we can cope with the physical changes better and in the end have an easier transition.

Another person who taught me an important lesson about the physical and spirituality is a Dutch lady, Debby Noordhoff, whom I met through Jerry Jampolsky. When I first met her, she was very frail and had a range of physical challenges. She suffers from a muscle disease called polymyositis and needed help from her female companion, Darby, to climb the stairs. She also had difficulty swallowing, problems with her vision, and had to spend a lot of time in bed. Yet I was struck by her wonderful spirit and great sensitivity; she seemed so in tune with everything that was going on around her. I felt uplifted by her presence and we have become great friends. To me, Debby is an example of how human consciousness and Divine connection is far greater than any physical limitations of the body. She has also written a wonderful contribution for this book (see page 268).

So, amongst others, Thor showed me that you can keep yourself in great physical shape and maintain sharp mental faculties right through to old age while Debby showed me that you can go beyond any physical challenges when you develop a strong spiritual connection. Overall I feel that if we put our trust and faith in the divine, connecting with our consciousness and allowing the Natural Law of Cyclical, Evolutionary Creation to work through us, then all will be well and we can live a loving and inspiring life.

Synthesis

Gradually I have come to understand that each of us, and all other forms of life on this planet, are expressions of unconditional love. Our lives in the finite universe are not only bound by time and space but also by the most fragile of ecosystems in which we live. We operate within a band of breathable air only a few miles wide. We can only function within a certain range of temperatures. Even our sense of smell has limits—a sufficiently concentrated amount of manure can actually make people faint! Our planet itself orbits at just the right distance from the sun—making it neither too hot nor too cold and giving us a suitable amount of sunshine. The physical forces that govern the universe, such as gravity and electromagnetism, are so finely tuned that even a miniscule change in any of them would fundamentally alter the cosmos and make life as we know it impossible. All the conditions that make life possible exist in a delicate balance and we are actually so vulnerable. Truly our lives are a miracle. When I reflect on the balance of all these factors that support life, I am filled with a sense of gratitude for this Divine gift. Yet isn't it extraordinary that, given this vulnerability, we seem to focus more on creating weapons of destruction and on fighting each other than on working together to support life?

I respect this sacred gift of life—mine, other people's, life in all its forms—and want to make use of it as much as I can according to Divine Law. Learning to co-exist with all other expressions of life is part of that process. Awakening to our connection with all creation as part of the Infinite is another. Finally, bringing our sense of the Infinite into the finite is a wonderful creative opportunity for us all. We can not only co-create with our fellow human beings but also, in allowing the Infinite to work through us, become co-Creators too.

So some of the lessons I have learnt about caring, sharing and connecting with the Infinite in a finite universe are:

- Comparing, caring, and sharing can replace competing.
- Playing joyfully expresses the Infinite in our lives.
- Rediscovering our hearts can help heal ourselves, each other and our world.

7. Are We Ready to Be the Change?

I am keenly aware that initiating and accepting change is not always easy and so the implementation of the principles I have been discussing in this part of the book can be, for any of us—including myself—difficult. Perhaps the difficulties that we have relates to the ways in which we have been educated and to the types of belief systems that we have adopted. We may have been encouraged to think in a limited way rather than to believe in our ability to change and in abundance.

Yet, I do believe we can all connect with the Infinite. In my experience, such a connection can be life-transforming. It can make us more peaceful, more loving and joyful and it can help us to make this world a better place to live for all its current inhabitants, as well as for future generations of all living beings. So the vital question to ask ourselves now is, "Am I ready to be the change?"

In my view the most important thing is having the courage to realise that human systems based on having, on power and control and on separation and exclusion do not work anymore. With open hearts and minds and with courage we can now explore the creation of new systems based on an understanding of the need for empowerment and 'self-response-Ability' for all human beings. I know I am just one human being, like you dear reader, who cares about our planet but I do believe that if we can join forces we can make a difference for the good of all.

So I would like to invite us all to 'be the change' and to cooperate in develop-ing a more functional society here on earth. Perhaps the key principles I have outlined in this the book and also the wonderful shared visions of the contributors that follow, may support you.

Please turn to Part III and be inspired!

Glossary of Terms Used in Part II

Anthropocentrism—The egoism of the human species that regards humans as the centre of the universe.

Culture—The taking of elements from nature out of their natural context by humans, and then re-combining and utilising them in new contexts and new ways to suit human purposes. Functional culture is the utilisation of elements from nature according to the Natural Law of Cyclical Evolutionary Creation. Dysfunctional culture operates against this Law.

Cyclical, Evolutionary Creation—See under 'the Natural Law of Cyclical, Evolutionary Creation

De-velopment—The process of opening ourselves to an ever higher consciousness, and deepening our understanding and experience of the Natural Law of Cyclical, Evolutionary Creation. The opposite is 'envelopment', which is the closing off of consciousness.

Egoism—Selfishness and not harmonising with the interests of others and nature: the product of losing contact with our sense of connection with the universe and God.

Emotion—Emotion is sensation based on past experiences or expectations that block our true feelings.

En-vironment—All matter, whether subtle or dense, that exists outside of our own bodies (see also 'in-vironment').

Evolution—See 'De-velopment'.

Feeling—Experiencing fully in the present, and connecting with the inner experience yet being detached.

Finite, The—The physical universe in which we live. It is bounded by time and space and each person, animal, plant, mineral element, or speck of matter occupies its own point in space-time.

Free Will—God-given power of discernment to make choices that are functional rather than dysfunctional; that is, not distracted by judgements or emotions.

Functional choices—A choice, or decision, that is in line with the will of God as expressed in the Natural Law of Cyclical, Evolutionary Creation.

God—The Divine source of creation, or Infinite Being, also expressed in the finite (see also The Infinite). God has both 'male' and 'female' qualities and yet transcends them both and thus is neither 'female' nor 'male'.

Infinite, The—That which is beyond the finite and yet also encompasses it. The creative source of the universe, which is God.

Information—'In-formation', that which is in a form in matter and which may be both subtle or dense,

In-vironment—The 'inner world' of thoughts, feelings and emotions.

Loving detachment—Being able to use our hearts, minds and feelings with clarity and without the blocks of fear, emotional attachment or judgements.

'Male' and 'Female' Principles— A range of interconnected qualities or aspects as in the ancient Chinese philosophical concepts of '*yin*' and '*yang*'. '*Yang*' is linked to 'male' qualities of hardness and action and with the mind and the intellect; '*yin*' is associated with 'female' qualities of softness and receptivity as well as with feelings, intuition and the heart.

Natural Law of Cyclical, Evolutionary Creation, The—The Divine Law by which all creation evolves through a series of cycles. This Law works at the level of the individual or group, the evolution of nature and the entire universe.

Resistance—The dynamic, natural forces of push and pull or attracting and repelling by which the finite universe exists and is maintained.

Response-Ability—Experiencing fully in the present, and having the ability and willingness to interact with the world around us with awareness that we are all part of the Infinite. Being accountable for our actions.

Transcendental—Beyond the limitations of the finite universe.

Under-standing—Used to refer to 'standing-under God', that is, having a greater realisation and awareness of the true nature of reality and of Divine Will.

Universe—The entire finite.

PART III

Contributions—'Visions of Change'

PART III

Contributions – 'Visions of Change'

In this part of the book I have invited friends and acquaintances from all walks of life—men, women and children, both well-known and unknown and drawn from the worlds of business, politics, health, arts, schools, youth groups and so on—to share their visions and dreams for creating a better, more functional, world and future for us all.[1] There are many others whom I would have loved to invite to contribute but there just was not the space or time to do so.

Each invited contributor was asked to consider the following questions:

- What are your visions/dreams for the future of the planet?
- How can you/we make these visions/dreams happen?
- What particular experiences in your life shaped your vision?

Some people chose to answer each question briefly while others were inspired to write more. All contributions were written especially for this book and are truly individual. Some common themes also emerge.

I am grateful for all these contributions, which I have found truly inspiring and uplifting and a joy to read. I hope you will enjoy reading them too and will feel inspired to create your own visions for change, along with the will to put them into practice for the benefit of all. Our shared visions shape our society now and in the future.

THE CONTRIBUTORS ARE:

1. Hafsat Abiola-Costello (Nigeria)—Democracy Activist, Founder KIND (Kudirat Initiative for Democracy)
2. Sipho Abram Nkosi (South Africa)—Orphan and Student at Nkosi's Haven
3. Dr. Patch Adams (USA)— Doctor, Clown, Performer, Social Activist and Founder/Director of The Gesundheit! Institute
4. Roman Bumbi (The Ukraine/Netherlands)—Student
5. Antony Burgmans (Netherlands)—Former Chair of Unilever LV and PLC

---

1. These contributions were all written for this book's original publication in July 2008.

6. Jan Ebeltjes (Netherlands)—Aid Worker/Project Co-ordinator for the Fred Foundation (Ukraine)
7. Matthew Fox (USA)—Educator, Author, Co-initiator of the YELLAWE Programme in Oakland, California and Scholar-in-Residence with the Academy for the Love of Learning, Santa Fe, New Mexico
8. Dr. Jane Goodall (UK)—Founder of the Jane Goodall Institute and UN Messenger of Peace
9. Azra Huzanovic (Bosnia-Herzegovina)—Student and Former Worker at the Peace Flame House, Tuzla
10. Dr. Gerald G. Jampolsky (USA)—Doctor, Author and Founder of The International Centre for Attitudinal Healing, Sausalito, California
11. Vandy Kanyako Jr. (Sierra Leone)—Student
12. Rola Khoury (Italy)—Media Director and Public Relations Consultant
13. Craig Kielburger (Canada)—Founder and Chair, Free The Children
14. Nsaa-Iya Kihunrwa (Tanzania)—Member, Robert Swan's Inspire Antarctic Expedition 1996 and Worker on Dr. Jane Goodall's global humanitarian and environmental programme
15. Marc de Klerk (Netherlands/Bosnia-Herzegovina)—Entrepreneur, (NGO) Project Developer and Freelance Consultant in the Western Balkans
16. Olesya Koba (The Ukraine)— Worker and Translator for Fred Foundation (The Ukraine)
17. Indra Kumari Khattri Tamang (Nepal)—Housewife
18. Ervin Laszlo (Italy/Hungary/USA)—Author, President of the Club of Budapest
19. Irene van Lippe-Biesterfeld (Netherlands)—HRH Princess of the Netherlands, Chair of The Lippe-Biesterfeld Nature College Foundation
20. Ruslan Lokotosh (The Ukraine)—Ukrainian Orphan
21. Prof. Ruud Lubbers (Netherlands)—Prime Minister of the Netherlands 1982–94 and UN High Commissioner for Refugees 2001–5
22. Chris Matser (Netherlands)—Housewife
23. Dr. Hiroshi Motoyama (Japan)—Scientist, Author, Psychic and Shinto Priest
24. Caroline Myss (USA)—Author, Teacher, Medical Intuitive
25. Debby M. Noordhoff (Netherlands)—Retired Person
26. Thomas van Nouhuys (Netherlands)—School Student
27. Rev. Alex L. Orbito (Philippines)—Spiritual Healer
28. Matthew Parrish LaCasse (USA)—Student
29. Jasmina Redzepagic-Avdagic (Bosnia-Herzegovina)—Volunteer and Trauma Therapist, Manager of the Peace Flame House, Tuzla

30. Floris Rost van Tonningen (Netherlands)—Entrepreneur
31. Marika Verheijen (Spain)—International Co-ordinator
32. Ernest Volosin (The Ukraine)—Ukrainian Orphan
33. Herman Wijffels (USA/Netherlands)—Executive Director of the World Bank, Former Chief Executive Officer of the Rabobank, Netherlands
34. David R. Woollcombe (UK)—Founder and President, Peace Child International
35. Glynda Yoder (USA)—Friend and Spiritual Teacher
36. Michael Young (UK)—School Student

Afterword by Dr. Deepak Chopra

1. Hafsat Abiola-Costello (Nigeria)—
Democracy Activist Founder, KIND
(Kudirat Initiative for Democracy)

What are your visions/dreams for the future of the planet?

My current vision for the creation of a more functional society is one founded on the principles of solidarity. Among the South Africans are the Zulus who speak of '*ubuntu*'. It translates roughly as 'humanity towards others' and is the spiritual foundation of African societies that involves a belief in a universal bond of sharing that connects all of humanity. I would like to see a world where the mechanisms are in place to support fellow-feeling among humankind, a world where the mechanisms and incentives encourage people to share so that no child or adult goes hungry, dies from preventable diseases, becomes a victim of violence, or feels other forms of human suffering.

What particular experiences in your life shaped your vision?

I was raised in a family by parents with a strong sense of responsibility to their community. Although in his adulthood my father became materially wealthy, his measure of well-being was whether he was making a positive difference in the lives of vulnerable people. Among my ethnic group in Nigeria, called the Yoruba, there is a proverb that encouraged my parents to adopt the values that they held. It says 'people are the clothes I wear'. The proverb affirms the belief that clothes (material well-being) are not important; paramount is one's standing among his or her fellow people. My parents' values and commitment led them to participate in my country's democracy movement. Their efforts cost them their lives but the manner of their living shapes my vision today.

2. Sipho Abram Nkosi (South Africa)—
Orphan and Student at Nkosi's Haven

What are your visions/dreams for the future of the planet?

My dreams for the future of the planet are to see a high reduction of poverty in the world. I want to see a world where everyone should have enough to eat. I would like to see a world with equal distribution of world economy in my lifetime.

How can you/we make these dreams happen?

I am fortunate to belong to a group called the Teleios Korban Organisation. In this group, we have already started to make a difference through the arts. In our plays, we highlight the problem of poverty, especially among children, and we perform them to the various departments and bodies that matter to the community. Secondly, everyone comes from a community. It's high time we opened our eyes to see people who are truly suffering from malnutrition and severe poverty and donated food to them. If all the food that goes into dustbins everyday is properly managed, hunger could be greatly reduced.

What particular experiences in your life shaped your vision?

I came from a family where I experienced what it means to go for the day without food or to depend on luck to survive. This happened even more after I lost my mother and my dad was not available. I can't really imagine how life would have been if I hadn't encountered Mr. Isidore Martins Duruji, who introduced me to the group. It was through the help of this group that I met great people and especially those with Kidsright. That brought about a turning point in my life and the life of my family. Many may not be as fortunate as I am. Many have died from hunger, especially here in Africa, because they never met an important person who changed their life around.

3. Dr. Patch Adams (USA)—
Doctor, Clown, Performer, Social Activist and
Founder/Director of The Gesundheit! Institute

What are your visions/dreams for the future of the planet?

My goals for planetary transformation are peace, justice and care for all people everywhere, at all times, and to live in harmony with the rest of nature as simply one of the members.

What particular experiences in your life shaped your vision?

The most significant pivotal experience of my life was at my birth. I had a fabulous mother who lived by loving others in every way. I never saw her otherwise. Being loved by her gave me self-esteem. So any time in my life that I have decided to do something, I was sure I could do it and did. As a schoolteacher, she filled me with a lifetime of exuberance, wonder and curiosity. I never saw her unkind, derogatory or rejecting in any way to other human beings, so I grew up loving people. All people. She embodied care in every moment. I recognised many years later that I am simply a reflection of her gifts of love to me.

My father being a professional soldier led to another pivotal moment. When I was sixteen, he died as a soldier. It broke my heart. We moved back to the United States in 1961, to the southern States, which was in the throes of fighting racism.

I immediately joined the Civil Rights Movement. I was frequently beaten up. These two events crushed my spirit and three times, when I was eighteen, I was hospitalised because I wanted to die. I did not want to live in a world of violence and injustice.

In the last hospitalisation, on a locked ward of a mental hospital, I realised that instead of escape, I could choose to be a political activist. I changed overnight. I made two decisions that changed me forever. I chose to serve humanity in medicine and have now been a free doctor for thirty-five years. I also chose, as a political act, to never have another bad day. I have lived a joyful life every day since, which has also manifested in my becoming a clown.

Another choice I made at that time was to pursue a thoughtful life, seeking out thinking people and their works. This led me to read many thousands of great works and to cultivate intelligence in everything I do. In this fertile soil ideas blossom and solutions are forged for whatever question or dilemma comes. A life in sensitivity has eliminated the possibility of burnout or discouragement.

One final pivotal choice that was so important was the decision to live communally, to be part of a tribe. Friendship is my spiritual path. I get my strength from the sweet embrace of friends. My two artistic creations, a free hospital and taking clowns (love) to places of horror (poverty, refugee camps war, etc.) have been easy because they are done by a group of committed friends. Tribe feels like the nest of our most ancient selves.

How can you/we make these dreams happen?

I think capitalism is the worst thing that ever happened in history. We could have chosen love, compassion and generosity as a value system. Instead, men have historically chosen money and power as their value system. As women more often choose the values of compassion and generosity, I would put them in charge of everything. Not the man-woman types such as, in my opinion, Margaret Thatcher or Condoleezza Rice, but women like those I've seen all over the world in orphanages and refugee camps, and teachers and nurses who exude love. I would take all personal and corporate wealth (except that which is donated) to middle-class levels and use the funds to build this loving world. And I'd clean up our disasters to people and the environment. I would make our schools into temples of culture and our teachers into society's heroes (quadrupling their salaries until wages equalise). I would only use the TV for education and to help create a loving world for all people. Loving would be taught in schools every day, just like mathematics is. Children would become excited to serve their society, like they are excited by sports now.

The internal combustion engine must go. As capitalism disappears and living and harmony become important for all, the pace of today would change. I see roads mostly returned to nature and, over time, people loving to live nearer to each other—interdependently—and cities as flourishing garden cities, with much land returned to nature and (communal) family farming. There would be no more than fifty weeks of 'work' each year. People would have time to travel the world by bicycle, sailing ships and maybe even a trans-continental slide. As we get safe with each other we could stay in houses along the way and help out whilst there. Manufacturing would decentralise to local crafts and people would be 'living-oriented' rather than 'thing-oriented'. Celebrity would disappear and ideas would become interesting.

Yum!

Let's do it.

Patch

P.S. This is an inadequate report on what methods we can use to transform the world, because an accurate answer by anyone who has thought about it for years would fill volumes, so this is just a teaser.

For more, see: *www.patchadams.org.*

4. Roman Bumbi (The Ukraine/Netherlands)—
Student

What are your visions/dreams for the future of the planet?

My dream is that every child and every human has a family. Also, that there is no poverty any more, because the rich share their wealth with the poor. Then peace will come.

How can you/we make these dreams happen?

God is an example for all of us. When everyone is an example for others, there will be no poverty and sadness anymore.

What particular experiences in your life shaped your vision?

I was raised in an orphanage in the Ukraine. Six years ago, I came to Holland. I was and still am very ill. In Holland, I was blessed to experience the warmth and love of a foster father and a family. I have learned a lot from that love. It has enabled me to deal with my illness.

5. Antony Burgmans (Netherlands)—
Former Chair of Unilever NV and PLC

What are your visions/dreams for the future of the planet?

The world needs more solidarity, a sense of mutual/global responsibility; it lacks a communal sense. An example of this is the fact that, at the time of writing this, the USA—responsible for 25% of the total global CO_2 expulsion—has not yet fully ratified the Kyoto Protocol. There should be a better balance between individual energy and global energy. This should replace the indifferent, anti-social and egotistical behaviour that seems to flourish nowadays. Indifference on a lower level creates an intolerable society.

The ultimate aim is to include society in its totality as well as to create space for individual and personal development.

The main task of any government is to create the right conditions for society and to keep it habitable. It is too easy to constantly blame the government. According to the democratic principles we ourselves agreed upon, everybody is to blame and thus responsible for solving the problems that we all created.

People perceive nature as something outside of themselves, and as something of which they are not a part. Some global problems, such as global warming, for example, are frustrating because they seem to be irreversible and uncontrollable. What we need is a mature discussion between all parties, representing all different interests, and to combine our forces in order to get them aligned.

Very important in the creation of a more functional society is:
1. investment in education
2. enhancement of respect for each other and nature
3. more focus on non-material things (we are numbed by luxury)
4. creation of true (world) leaders

Our world today desperately needs authentic and profound leadership. Leaders who give perspective, who are able to think from different points of view (instead of only from a materialistic or one-dimensional point of view) and who are capable of creating a communal sense/solidarity (thus overcoming individual or personal interests).

People should be taught to ask themselves: "Who am I in relation to my fellow human being, to nature, to the previous generation and in relation to culture?"

For me, Nelson Mandela is a very good example of a great leader. He has shown the world the importance of communal sense and has always promoted this, instead of focusing his interest on taking revenge on the people who locked him away for over twenty-five years.

Communal sense/solidarity can sometimes come about as a result of the course of history. Europe is a good example of a continent, once hopelessly divided by wars, that has managed to overcome separation according to different (border) interests and create a communal sense. It is very unfortunate, however, that Europe needed two World Wars and the Holocaust to establish this. Yet often, in the vacuum left by a disastrous event, the greatest opportunities and higher forms of consciousness can develop. So this could be a hopeful example for the rest of the world.

What particular experiences in your life have shaped your vision?
A trip I made to the continent of Africa. This trip brought tremendous enrichment and awareness; the feeling of going back to one's roots. It showed me how essential nature is for our own and for society's development. Most people in powerful positions live 'outside' nature and thus are infected with too much 'urbanity'.

6. Jan Ebeltjes (Netherlands)—
Aid Worker/Project Co-ordinator
for the Fred Foundation (Ukraine)

For many years, the questions kept going round in my head: "What am I doing here?", "For what purpose have I been put on this earth?" I thought I would be able to find the answer in a successful business career, but I found it did not satisfy me. The more I strove for success the more I saw this effort and its result as forms of individualism and egotism. This insight often made me quite depressed. But what should I do? And how?

The answer came in 1992. I met some Polish youngsters and spent a few days with them. This led to strong ties between us, an overwhelming kind of friendship that I had never experienced before. I made time to visit my friends in Poland. I was aghast at the poverty in that country and felt I had to do something about it. Together with my Polish friends, we organised a number of aid expeditions for mentally handicapped children, who were living in an institution in the Polish village of Izdebnik. I was deeply touched by the gratitude of the children and the workers in the institution. All this rather complicated my life. My world had been one of production and profit-making, but my experiences in Poland had opened a whole new world to me. How could I combine these two worlds? I found a solution by spending all my free time on aid to Poland. With great difficulty I was able to live in both worlds at the same time.

In April 1994, I visited a children's home in Cinadiewo in the Ukraine. It is difficult to describe what I found there: 135 malnourished children, who were ill because of the human faeces that were everywhere, who were psychologically scarred by the lack of (parental) love and suffering from maltreatment by drunken personnel. A little boy of six came up to me, looked at me inquisitively and whispered: "Are you my father?"

Completely thrown by this I returned to the Netherlands, horrified by the injustice and suffering of these children. Every day I heard the little boy's question in my mind and I longed to be able to do something for these children. But how? I created a Foundation and brought the plight of the Ukraine to the attention of people around me. Gradually, schoolchildren started to become involved and churches and other organisations contributed to the work in the Ukraine. This involvement got me even more fired up. My employer gave me the opportunity to work a six-day week, which enabled me to save time in between for my work in the Ukraine. I gained the trust of the people in the children's home and, more than once, I smuggled sick children out for hospital treatment in the nearby town of Mukachewo.

In 1996, I made contact with 320 orphans who had been housed in a home in Perechyn. I found out that the majority of these children had been abandoned by their parents. Conditions in the home were appalling; there was a serious shortage of food and the lack of hygiene was abominable. The mental suffering of these children was immeasurable. Over and over the children asked me if I knew where their parents were and whether I could perhaps search for them. I tried as hard as I could to become the answer to the little six year old's question: "Are you my father?" Meanwhile, the foundation to help the Ukraine grew and opportunities arose to improve the living conditions of these children. As a result, we were able to achieve some good improvements in their health care.

The increasing work for the Ukraine created an imbalance between my two worlds. My work with my employer came under pressure and I no longer felt at home in the world of commerce, but resigning wasn't an option—after all, I had to make a living, didn't I? However, in January 1998 I did resign and chose to become an interim manager for an agency. I did temporary work for a number of companies and between each job I would be found in the Ukraine. In conjunction with Ukrainian organisations, I worked towards short-term solutions for the problems in the children's homes. And with everything I did, the question from the six-year-old boy kept ringing in my ears.

In 1999, I took two terminally ill children with me to the Netherlands for medical treatment. Volodymir underwent three operations and after a little over a year he returned to the Ukraine a healthy boy. Roman was said to be incurable but, against medical advice, I continued to care for him in the Netherlands. The boys' stay in the Netherlands created a lot of media interest and this contributed to the development of a plan to bring Ukranian children to stay with Dutch families during their three-month summer holidays. Every year, around seventy children come to the Netherlands to become part of a family and, although it is only for three months, to have an honorary father and a mother.

I enjoyed my job as an interim manager particularly, as, between jobs, I was able to devote myself to helping children in the Ukraine. However, this arrangement became untenable as I did not earn anything during my visits to the Ukraine. Finally, in 2001, I was forced to look for permanent work again. This was a hard decision: my work in the Ukraine would suffer if I resumed full-time work but I could see no other way out.

During that time I had an invitation from Fred Matser to tell him something about my activities in the Ukraine. He was extremely interested and I was impressed by the way he communicated his attitude to things, and his understanding. When I had finished talking, Fred indicated that he wanted to support my work in the Ukraine and a few days later he donated funds sufficient to renovate a children's home.

A few weeks after that, I was offered a job as an office manager, but on the day that I was due to sign the contract, the phone rang. It was Fred Matser again. He asked if I would like to work for the Fred Foundation that he had recently set up. I was amazed. How was it possible that Fred, with this question, had unknowingly brought my uncertainties to an end by enabling me to unite my two worlds? With enormous gratitude I accepted his offer.

The Fred Foundation gave me full scope to further develop the work in the Ukraine. We started up the Fred Foundation (Ukraine) and decided to begin by concentrating on around forty youths who had been locked up for years in a stable. They ate food that was intended for cows and pigs. They had no shoes or underwear. In short: they needed everything. We developed a living and working plan for them. The Fred Foundation bought dwellings and apartments and, in consultation with the Ukrainian authorities, work was found for them. Now, a few years on, most of them are happily married and almost all of them have found their place in Ukrainian society.

The Fred Foundation (Ukraine) also set up a Crisis Centre in Uzhgorod and a Shelter in Vingradov for child addicts. Contacts were made with two psychiatric institutions where hundreds of people were housed. Renovations have been, and are being, carried out and hygiene is being improved. Every year, holiday camps are organised for children from problem families and aid is transported to homes in the Vinogradov region.

The Fred Foundation (Ukraine) also gives a great deal of individual support. We remain in contact with our original target groups, the forty youngsters in Perregrestya and the hundreds of people who are being cared for in psychiatric institutions. Help also means being able to listen, give encouragement and offer a pat on the back.

We are concerned with street children, children who have become involved in prostitution, single teenage mothers and young people in prison. I often ask myself how I have come to be doing this work, but I am so grateful to be able to do it and I always keep in my mind the question of the little six-year-old boy. He is now eighteen and attending university in Uzhgorod. Whenever I see him he calls me 'father' and his faith in me gives me the strength to continue this work for children who are so unfortunate.

I have now adopted Roman, one of the two children I brought to the Netherlands in 1999, as my son. We were so grateful when he was able to have a successful liver transplant. Roman is now eighteen and in his opinion people ought to work together more in order to tackle the problems of the world. "Together we are capable of so much more and when everyone works together there will be peace," says Roman. Is it possible to think of anything more beautiful?

7. Matthew Fox (USA)—
Educator, Author, Co-initiator of the YELLAWE [2] Programme in Oakland, California and Scholar-in-Residence with the Academy for the Love of Learning, Santa Fe, New Mexico

Transformation: my Visions and Experiences Yesterday and Today
When I look back on pivotal moments in my life that awakened me to issues of global transformation, there are many. Much of this is due to the generation of which I am a part and the times in which I came of age. I was twenty years old when John F. Kennedy was elected President and challenged my generation to "ask not what your country can do for you but what you can do for your country." I was twenty-two years old when the beautiful Pope John XXIII wrote his amaz-

ing encyclical, Pacem in Terris, in which he called on all people of good will to make peace happen. It was the same year in which Dr. Martin Luther King called for racial justice by filling the jails of Birmingham, Alabama and encouraging young and old alike to return violence with non-violence, hatred with love.

I was twenty-three years old when a family friend who was a graduate of West Point was captured in Vietnam by the Viet Cong and was killed in captivity—but who, just before he was captured, had sent a letter to the Maryknoll congregation saying he wanted to quit the military and become a priest missionary in Vietnam because he had fallen in love with the people.

Whist studying for my doctorate in Paris from 1967 to 1970, years that included the events of 1968, such as the student riots that brought down the de Gaulle government among other things, I had the privilege of encountering my mentor, the Dominican theologian Fr. Marie Dominic Chenu. Father Chenu was a 'worker priest' theologian who worked closely with unions, and the Marxists in them, in France after the war. He thereby developed a methodology for listening to the poor that would later be basic to the methodology of liberation theology.

For his efforts on behalf of bridging Christianity and the alienated blue-collar workers of France, Pope Pius XII forbade him to publish for twelve years. But, under Pope John XXIII, and the Vatican Council that he launched in 1963 to 'open the windows' of the Catholic Church, Fr. Chenu was rehabilitated and indeed it was he, more than any other theologian or 'peritus' at the Council who was most responsible for its most radical document, The Church in the Modern World. This essentially told believers to get into the professions and into history and make a difference according to the Gospel values of justice and compassion.

It was Fr. Chenu who named the 'creation spirituality' tradition for me in my studies with him in Paris—a tradition that combines mysticism, art and social justice. It was he who, during our last visit when he was about eighty-eight years old, put his arm around me and said: "Never forget, the greatest tragedy in theology of the last 300 years has been the divorce of the theologian from the artist, the potter, the poet, the musician, the dancer, the film maker." Chenu died aged ninety-five years—the very day Nelson Mandela was released from prison. Chenu was the effective 'grandfather' of liberation theology. The first book on liberation theology, published by the Peruvian theologian Gustavo Guttieriez, cites Chenu many times.

Those heroic people in Latin America, who stood up to decades if not centuries of injustice and oppression by founding base communities and listening to

---

2. Youth and Elder Learning Laboratory for Ancestral Wisdom

one another's efforts to interpret the message of justice found in the Gospel—were my heroes in my own efforts to tackle the injustices in US society. Among these injustices in the 1970s was the issue of sexism highlighted by the rise of the women's movement (I taught for four years at an all-women's college near Chicago and learned much of what women had been going through). The gay and lesbian liberation movement and the environmental movement were also integral to my growing awareness and education in issues of global transformation.

What am I currently involved in and what have I learned from these decades of interest in global transformation?

1. With the passage of my sixty-fifth birthday, I looked forward to stepping out of administration of an academic institution, but I do not use the word 're-tirement'. I prefer the term 'Re-Firement'. I think elders have a grave obligation not to spend their lives on golf courses but rather to refire and rekindle their hearts and minds. Never in history has there been such a deep need for elders working with and serving the youngest generation. Never before has more than 50% of the human race been under sixteen years of age. We cannot afford elders looking only to their own security and pleasure and financial investments. We elders must give back and do so creatively. Giving our time, our wisdom, our creativity, our ideas and—if we are so blessed—our money or connections to places of power. So that marks one of my current interests: awakening my 'boomer' generation to our possibilities and responsibilities as elders, especially as to how we are serving the young.

2. A second passion of mine, closely related to the first, is to contribute to reinventing education. The Dalai Lama has wisely observed that "education is in crisis the world over". He is correct. Education is in crisis because our species is in crisis (and one reason our species is in crisis is because education is in crisis). For too many centuries we have been satisfied with educating people from the neck up; Descartes defined truth as "clear and distinct ideas" and Western academia bought this nonsense hook, line and sinker and called it 'education'. Now, with the destruction of the planet ("most of it at the hands of people with PhD's", according to Dr. Thomas Berry), the chicken is coming home to roost.

   We must unite heart and head again in our education. This would mean we train people for wisdom and not merely for knowledge. A Native American teacher has said: "Only a mad man thinks with his head." Well, Western culture has been turning out mad men for centuries because the form or system of education has been trained too exclusively on the rational, on the heady, on the left hemisphere of the brain.

This can be turned around—I know this from years of experience. Thirty years ago I designed a model of education for adults (master's and later a doctoral programme) that integrates right and left hemispheres of the brain, the intellectual/analytic and the heart/intuitive/mystical parts of the brain. It necessarily involves the whole body and all its chakras (the heart resides in the body after all). And it works!

It is energising, serious, fun and joyful. Learning can be fun and joyful—indeed learning is one of the greatest pleasures humans can enjoy. The key to this education is the recovery of Awe and of Creativity and of our place in the Cosmos. I remain fully committed to reinventing forms and models of education and am currently completing a book on this topic called *The A.W.E. Project*.

3. Another passion of mine that I have been actively involved in for the past twelve years is the reinvention of ritual. Melidome Some, the African spiritual teacher, says "there is no community without ritual". Clearly our species has to rediscover community as a primary value. Indigenous peoples have a wealth of experience to teach us about that. Modern physics, with its teaching that the universe and the earth and our bodies are machines and that atoms are rugged individuals, not interpenetrating, took the rug out from under our awareness of community. Today's post-modern physics has a different story to tell. Atoms link up with other atoms and form molecules; molecules link up with other molecules and form cells; cells link up and form organisms that in turn link up and form societies or communities. Contemporary science's rediscovery of the habit of 'interconnectivity' in eco-systems, cosmic systems and microcosmic systems all set the stage for a revival of community.

But humans have to celebrate their interconnectivity: our shared joy and our shared grief. There is so much to grieve about in the world today—the loss of tens of thousands of species per year, war, poverty, abuse of many kinds—all this begs for rituals that gather communities together to honour their beauty and to grieve over their suffering; to bring out the artists and creative ritual-makers and to make ritual-making one of the great 'industries' of our time, where true community is always participatory.

With this in mind, I have been working with teams of others to reinvent Western liturgy and to move it from sitting in benches and pews and being read to and reading to dancing and using the image-making potentials of the post-modern language of computers, fractal-making, djing, vjing, rap and other new languages to help us explore our hearts together. We call our worship experience the 'Cosmic Mass' and we borrow much of the language from pre-modern sources and from rave, which is a kind of a global celebratory model that youth the world over are experiencing.

Drugs do not have a place in our gatherings (unlike many rave happenings), and they do not have to be if you connect valid forms of worship with ancient liturgical traditions. One gets very high without drugs. Canadian Television filmed a recent Cosmic Mass and that fourteen-minute DVD is available on our website at *www.thecosmicmass.org*.

I believe that when we dance again as a species and as communities, we will return to our lower chakras and reject the rational madness in our heads that justifies wars and religious and imperial propaganda. This puts us in touch with the sacredness of existence and of the earth. The survival of our planet as we know it and the marvellous species that share the planet with us requires we do so.

4. Another direction for global transformation that calls me today is the issue of moving from Religion to Spirituality. We all need spirituality—that is, we need to calm that reptilian brain that is over 400 million years old and that is destroying the earth and one another through its overdeveloped sense of action/reaction response. This crocodile brain can be calmed by meditation. That is what meditation does: it calms the reptilian brain. Then our mammal brain—the compassionate brain of kinship, family and compassion (the Hebrew and the Arabic words for compassion both derive from the word for 'womb')—can rise. Our third brain, our creative and intellectual brain, must be connected more profoundly to our mammal brain and be less occupied with reptilian responses.

Because I am a Westerner, my particular responsibility is to challenge Western religion, which today is at an all-time low as regards credibility, energy and spirit. Protestantism has practically lost its capacity for protest and, in the USA, has pretty much rolled over and played dead for versions of fundamentalist and re-constructionist Christianity, which dominate the air waves, television and politics itself. Coming from a Roman Catholic tradition, I must blow the whistle on the emperor (or pope) who also has no clothes. The paedophile scandals in Catholicism represent just the tip of the iceberg of a tradition that has sadly invested so much in keeping its hierarchy all-male and all-celibate (or claiming to be such) and all-ignorant (the current pope dismissed and silenced over 107 theologians during his previous office, thus effectively closing down thinking in the Catholic Church). In fact the hierarchy was totally dumbed down during the previous papacy. Dumbed down leadership opens the door to folly.

To wake up both wings of Western Christianity, at Pentecost in 2005, I went to Wittenburg in Germany to pound ninety-five theses at the doors where Martin Luther began his Reformation 500 years ago. We need a new Reformation in religion in the West. One that moves us from religion to spirituality, from patriarchy to gender-justice, from anthropocentrism to love of all creation, from preoccupation with sexual morality to preoccupation with ecological, economic racial, gender and gender-preference issues of justice. We have no time to waste. For more on the New Reformation, you can go to the website *www.matthewfox.org* or, if you speak German, to *www.publikforum.de*. You can also look at my book, *A New Reformation!*, available through my website.

I am, of course, very much interested in Interfaith or what I call 'Deep Ecumenism' which is the subject of another of my books, *One River, Many Wells: Wisdom Springing from Global Faiths*. I agree with the Dalai Lama that the number- one obstacle to Interfaith is a bad relationship with one's own faith tradition.

Most Christian Westerners, for example, do not even know their own mystical tradition—great souls such as Meister Eckhart, Hildegard of Bingen, Nicolas of Cusa, the Celtic tradition, Jesus as Mystic, the Cosmic Christ, Thomas Aquinas as mystic. I have published books on all these subjects in order to awaken us Westerners to our own in-depth heritage so that we can join forces with Buddhists, Taoists, Hindus, Jews, Native Peoples, goddess worshippers and modern science to see a true renaissance emerge in our species. A renaissance is a rebirth of civilisation based on a spiritual initiative. We need that today.

Many are the hands, heads and hearts contributing to the same. My friend Fred Matser, who has gathered together the contributors for this book, is such a person, as are all the contributors to this volume. May the work continue!

8. Jane Goodall, PhD, DBE (UK)—
Founder of the Jane Goodall Institute and UN Messenger of Peace

What are your visions/dreams for the future of the planet?
In the world of my dreams all people have the opportunity to raise themselves from poverty and ignorance; spiritual growth is valued above the acquisition of material wealth; all children enjoy true childhood; no end can ever justify cruel or unjust means; people understand the interdependency of all life, and respect not only each other, but also animals and the natural world—and realise, too, that the heart is as important as the head in determining how we behave.

In this world, there is much laughter and singing and a sense of the Divine and there is hope for lasting peace based on tolerance, compassion and love.

How can you/we make these dreams happen?

The world today seems to lie under a dark shadow of violence and war, cruelty, injustice, human greed and lust for power. Millions of people are living in fear or suffering from depression, apathy, or bitterness and anger. Millions have lost hope. Indeed, the problems to be solved are daunting. How can we end mushrooming human population growth, raise the standard of living of the poor, and curb the unsustainable lifestyles of the wealthy? The answers lie with each one of us: for the collective power of 'we, the people' is potentially unlimited.

We must stop leaving all the decision making to greedy, weak or corrupted corporate leaders and politicians. We must realise that each of us makes an impact on the world around us every day: all the little choices we make as to what we buy, eat and so on, affect people, animals, the environment—and the future of our children. We must support companies with sound ethical values and practices. Refuse to buy anything produced by exploiting children, the poor, and animals. Buy into the growing and eating of organic foods, adopt a mainly vegetarian diet. We must listen to our hearts, not only our heads.

We must also recognise the tremendous importance of early childhood experience, the need for wise parenting and a nurturing family. Nothing should be more important or worth spending more money on than the preparation of the citizens of tomorrow.

Roots and Shoots, an education programme that I established, now has some 8,000 groups in over ninety countries, and is growing. It emphasises the value of each individual. It enables young people from pre-school to university and beyond, to chose and perform activities that will make the world a better place for people, animals and the environment, and helps to break down the barriers that we have built between people of different cultures and religions, and between us and the natural world. By partnering with other organisations that share our philosophy, we move towards creating a critical mass of young people—the next teachers, scientists, lawyers, businesspeople, politicians, parents and so on—who understand that they will not find meaning in their lives through simply acquiring money and possessions but that caring about and helping others makes the heart sing and that doing all this in a group is fun. They understand, too, that violence seldom provides lasting solutions to disputes.

What particular experiences in your life shaped your vision?

During years alone in the forest I became increasingly in awe of the mystery and beauty of that world, increasingly aware of the Great Spiritual Power that we call God, Allah, Tao, the Creator and so on. I occasionally had almost mystical experiences that left me feeling that I knew, deep within, more than I understood about the nature of God and human existence on earth. At the same time, the human population in the surrounding hills grew, refugees arrived who were fleeing conflicts in neighbouring countries and suddenly I found that, beyond the boundaries of the tiny, national park, virtually all the trees had gone. Desperate people, needing firewood and meat, were jeopardising the sanctity of the park. In the villages I saw at first hand the terrible results of poverty, overpopulation and a lack of opportunity to create change. We developed a programme (TACARE) that includes reforestation, new farming techniques, primary health care, micro-credit and information about family planning, HIV-Aids and soil and water conservation. I witnessed the dramatic change when people, especially women, received the opportunity to improve their lives. Now we are replicating the programme in other places. (For more see: *www.janegoodall.org*).

9. Azra Husanovic (Bosnia-Herzegovina)—
Student and Former Worker at
the Peace Flame House, Tuzla

What are your visions/dreams for the future of the planet?
Well, I am hoping for something big to happen that will change the whole quality of life that exists today. The established social order of things is such that the true virtues such as humility, kindness, loyalty, etc. aren't recognised, causing real friendships and deep human relationships to be rare and short lasting. Put it like this—the most important things are put in the last place in the consciousness of the masses—and this has to do with the sort of life that is being promoted by the dominant societies (i.e. Western society). There are too many lies around us.

What particular experiences in your life shaped your vision?
I cannot think of any one particular experience. Rather, this is my view of the world after all that I have been through during my twenty years of life. It is also one of my favourite topics of conversation with friends.

How can you/we make these dreams happen?
Everybody has to be aware of these problems. It is something that cannot be changed quickly. We have to find a way to teach all of us, and ourselves, what is

good and what is bad, what is moral and what is not. The change has to start from the bottom, from the people… and then somehow I hope that the capitalistic and destroying mechanisms around us will start to change.

10. Dr. Gerald G. Jampolsky (USA)—
Doctor, Author and Founder of The International Centre for Attitudinal Healing, Sausalito, California

What are your visions/ dreams for the future of the planet?
My vision would be that each of us would begin to live as if the future and the present were one and the same and that we would live each moment as if it were an eternal never- ending moment filled with unconditional love. It would be for each of us to take responsibility for our own happiness and let go of the belief that the past was going to predict the future. It would be a moment where Love would be our only reality, and that we would live in harmony with each other and the planet we live on.

It is my vision that, as each of us heals our split mind, the world we see begins to change. The world we used to see begins to disappear and we enter a world of no time, no space and only Peace and Love.

How can you/we make these visions/dreams happen?
Each of us can make this happen by making forgiveness as important as breathing. We can make a difference by seeing our purpose as loving, caring, serving and helping others and experiencing and demonstrating Oneness. In other words, it is letting go of the illusion of any kind of separateness in the universe.

What particular experiences in your life have shaped your vision?
In 1975 I was introduced to some, then unpublished, writings called *A Course In Miracles*. On reading just one page I heard an inner voice for the first time in my life stating "Physician heal thyself. This is your way home". I then had an experience that I have never adequately been able to put in words. I was an atheist at the time but what I experienced was the Peace of God and inner knowing that my life was going to be one of service where God's Will and mine would be the same. Today I am still a student of this Course, which shows us ways of letting go of the blocks that interfere with our experience of unconditional love. I continue to be a work in progress and do my best to make decisions based on love rather than fear.

For more see: *www.attitudinalhealing.org*

11. Vandy Kanyako Jr. (Sierra Leone)—
Student

What are your visions/dreams for the future of the planet?
I dream of a future for the planet without the ravages of wars and environmental degradation. I dream of a world where people live in harmony with one another and with nature, a world circumscribed by respect for diversity and cultural tolerance, a world where the beauty and nurturing care of mother nature is revered by the present generation and preserved for future generations.

I dream of a future in which the ever-widening gulf between the haves and the have-nots is addressed, to make it possible for those plagued by hunger, malnutrition and preventable diseases to be able to meet their basic dietary needs and have affordable, quality health care. I dream of a world where a sizeable proportion of the global poor are not forced to live on less than a dollar a day while governments spends billions of dollars on arms. I dream of a planet where the world's massive technological advancements can be put to proper and effective use to eradicate famine, malaria, HIV/Aids and so on. I dream of a future where the poor and the disempowered take control of their own destiny, a world where they choose their leaders freely and fairly. I dream of a future where people are judged by their ability rather than by their national origin, race, gender or sexual orientation. I dream of a future in which nations and communities resolve their differences peacefully rather than resort to the use of violence, which more often than not only begets more violence. I dream of a world in which the twenty-first century becomes more peaceful than the preceding century which by all accounts was the bloodiest in the history of humankind.

What particular experiences in your life shaped your vision?
The civil war in my native Sierra Leone (1991-2000) shaped my outlook on life in general. The conflict brought out the worst as well as the best in humankind. The rather senseless war claimed over 15,000 lives, left countless others maimed and scarred for life and the country's infrastructure in ruins. The social fabric of the society was torn apart as people's lives were disrupted and in some cases consumed by the carnage. Family members, friends, neighbours and colleagues whom I knew to be loving and caring in peace time, suddenly found themselves armed, on different warring sides.

The consequences were disastrous. I witnessed the radical transformation of once-peaceful communities as they degenerated into chaos and anarchy. The war also brought out the best in people, for, side by side with the ravages and brutality of the conflict, went the sacrifice, dedication and resilience of some individuals and groups (both local and international) to change the situation for the better. Some, such as the peacekeepers and humanitarian aid workers, put their lives on the line to end the human suffering. Others used their time, energy, expertise and resources to bring succour to the traumatised and war-weary population.

The bravery, commitment and dedication of such groups and individuals was critical in saving thousands of lives, including mine, and was no doubt a source of inspiration to those of us who have since decided to dedicate our lives to working for peace. Without such interventions and proactive stance, countless more would have died.

How can you/we make these dreams happen?

I have been a peace and human rights activist for most of my working life. This job has taught me several important lessons. One is that we all have the potential, as well as the responsibility, to make the world a better place. Indeed, both war and peace begins and ends in the minds of the individual. Being aware of the impact of our actions and decisions on the lives of others, both near (acquaintances) and far (strangers), will go a long way to creating a more peaceful world.

The second lesson is that we can indeed make dreams a reality by being true to ourselves and to our individual philosophies. We can do this by putting into practice what we preach, especially as we live in a world where a huge gulf exists between rhetoric and practice. This vocation offered me the opportunity to use my talent, skills and experience on behalf of the marginalised and the disempowered.

We have to bridge the economic divide by levelling the playing field at all levels of society: internationally, nationally, and in our local communities. Creating opportunities for young people is critical to achieving this goal. Some of the most unstable regions in the world, including mine, are those that lack opportunities for young people.

Finally, we have to see the world we live in as a truly global village and to think of ourselves as global citizens. The latter sees humanity first before anything else.

12. Rola Khoury (Italy)—
Media Director and Public Relations Consultant

What are your visions/dreams for the future of the planet?

I don't really rely on the future as much as on the moment, as my future will come in the form of this moment called NOW, and what I hope is only that I have my heart fulfilled in this moment and each human being, like me, will aspire to this most noble gesture, to pursue his, or her, heart fulfilment, now.

How can you/we make these happen?

KNOW THYSELF!! No two people are alike, each person's needs are different and our hearts know our own truth. If I get to know myself and this becomes my goal, then I'm in charge and I can be responsible for making things happen, and thus express myself and be fulfilled. When I know myself and connect to the knowledge I am born with, I experience an intimate field of joy and peace that is immeasurable… if each of us concentrates on such fulfilment then we can ALL make it.

If you are not a lighted candle, you cannot pretend to light others, or inspire others to become lit, yet one bulb can illuminate a stadium. If each of us cultivates our own light, then we can light the whole world.

Experience is something the heart feels. Some are beyond words or manuals; they simply are.

What particular experiences in your life have shaped your vision?

Every breath that comes to me, and that is not wasted, is an experience full of joy and happiness. This life is a miracle and each breath is proof that life is worth living. I don't wait or rely on circumstance and conditions outside of myself to determine how fortunate I am. BEING is already the biggest gift and miracle that is happening now.

13. Craig Kielburger (Canada)—
Founder and Chair, Free the Children

What are your visions/dreams for the future of the planet?

My dreams for the future are rooted in one goal: that this be a world in which every child receives an education.

About 121 million children around the world between the ages of six and eleven have never stepped foot in a classroom. Two-thirds of these are girls. And yet education is the solution to everything: child labour, AIDS, poverty, gender inequality.

An education means people can read health awareness posters and women and men can get vital AIDS education and prevention. Education is the key to women's empowerment so that they know about their basic and inalienable rights. An education means parents are not putting thumb prints at the bottom of contracts they can't read, giving away their assets, their rights, even their children. Education allows democracy to thrive. It means a child can break out of the cycle of poverty.

Education means a child has a future.

How can you/we make these dreams happen?

Children must be at the forefront of making these dreams happen. They must challenge the adults of the world to take action.

Through Free The Children, more than 100,000 young people from around the world have raised millions of dollars to build more than 400 primary schools in developing countries, providing education to more than 35,000 children every day.

Children have collected more than 200,000 backpacks full of school supplies and created entire support programmes, such as mid-day meal programmes, which allow their peers to receive an education.

Youth have been at the heart of raising awareness and funds for clean water programmes so that girls don't have to walk long distances to fetch water. Young people have built health clinics, so that students can be healthy as they learn, and funded alternative co-operatives for women, so that they can afford to send their children to school instead of sending their children to work.

Through Free The Children, young people around the world are helping to fulfil that dream of making education possible for every child.

What particular experiences in your life shaped your vision?

Through my travels to more than forty countries, I've spent time with thousands of children in the many slums, shantytowns and jails of this world. And whether it was a girl cutting sugar canes in the fields of Brazil, a boy pouring molten metal without any protective gear in a factory in India or young girls and boys fighting as child soldiers in Africa, they all shared the same dream with me: to one day receive an education.

Mary Smart was nine years old when her family was killed by rebels in Sierra Leone, a country still recovering from a brutal eleven-year civil war in which more than 30,000 children fought as child soldiers. Mary lived in the bush for months, always moving on so that the rebels wouldn't capture her. She realised her only dream when she began attending a Free The Children school. Education gave her the chance to build a future while also giving her a safe environment in which to cope with the trauma of war and loss. We nicknamed her 'Very Smart' because she graduated at the top of her class, becoming the first female in her village to go to high school.

For Mary, education is hope for a brighter future.

For more see: *www.freethechildren.com*

14. Nsaa-Iya Kihunrwa (Tanzania)—
*Member, Robert Swan's Inspire Antarctic Expedition 1996
and Worker on Dr. Jane Goodall's Global Humanitarian
and Environmental Programme*

What are your visions/dreams for the future of the planet?

Currently the world's leading nations are bad examples of serious cases of systemic repression, human rights violation, acute injustice and inequitable and unfair economic treatment to poor nations. My dream for the future is for a more peaceful planet. I dream of well-accepted global ethics that will bring a lost vision for peace.

I dream that there will be a significant reduction in global conflicts, increased tolerance and understanding among nations and individuals, sustainable population growth, reduction in diseases and poverty, sustainable exploitation and use of resources, less greed and competition among nations and individuals on available resources.

What particular experiences in your life shaped your vision?

Conflicts and Crises

My dreams are very much influenced by past and current personal experiences. Although conflicts and crises are part of life, wrong solutions have deliberately been applied in solving conflicts due to mediators' self interests. Be it in Africa, or elsewhere on the planet, I believe that personal interests, dogmatism and stereotypes of mediators are detrimental barriers to arriving at effective and sustainable conflict resolutions.

Greed forces nations to support conflicts in other places if they will benefit. These conflicts create inequity among societies, which establishes competition. The world still has hatred and suspicion of ethnicity, religion, politics and class, which is arguably the result of mishandled conflicts. Unresolved conflicts and crises have resulted in a loss of vision towards peace. The justification of military force following a particular political circumstance and the approval of pre-emptive strikes accelerates fear and jeopardises global peace initiatives tremendously.

Democracy

As a Tanzanian and a true citizen of the world, I question the existence of an effective, honest democratic election process. The recent elections in my country have left me with a big question. Will we ever have a 100% democratically elected government whereby citizens obtain a leader agreed by all to be freely and fairly elected? I am not yet convinced. Losers have the right to complain when they are dissatisfied with the result. We may be said to have a culture of complaining but in some cases complainants may have valid reasons. Yet their appeal gets nowhere in a bureaucratic appeals process that is not independent. I wonder if elections that are said to be free and fair have final results that are actually genuine. Have the losers truly lost? I have lost faith.

Injustice and Human Rights

Is there justice? Thieves on the streets are killed or burnt to death by mob justice because of a lack of confidence in the law-enforcing agencies. Participants in petty corruption are punished severely if found guilty, while those who engage in white-collar crime and people who engage in grand corruption walk away scot free. The poor are made poorer by the rich through various tricks.

Overpopulation, Poverty and Diseases

At almost seven billion, the world is unbalanced and overpopulated. My dream is to have a sustainable population growth that is equitably distributed for our own benefit. The past fifteen years, in which I have been working for Dr. Jane Goodall's global humanitarian and environmental programme, has exposed me to environmental issues, especially those of habitat destruction. I have witnessed thick forests turned into eroded bare land due to the development of settlements and the clearing of fields for agriculture. Hunting for scarce food has resulted in animals' extinction while overpopulation has lead to outbreaks of uncontrolled diseases. Since animals cannot talk for themselves, they continue to be brought to the brink of extinction day after day.

Our resource requirements at six billion plus people have increased dramatically. Overpopulation in Tanzania has brought about an increased consumption of resources and production of waste. The government is concerned, with its limited capacity to provide basic services. Under-capacity has accelerated ignorance, resulting in poverty and diseases. With inevitable globalisation, poor nations become weaker and will eventually fall prey if not harmonised well.

Understanding, Tolerance and Accommodation

In 1996-7, I was very fortunate to visit the Antarctic when participating in an adventure of a lifetime to celebrate fifty years of UNESCO. I was sponsored by Fred Matser's Twinkling Eyes Club and was among thirty-five young people from twenty-five different countries.

Among the many lessons learned was the way the Gentoo penguins living at Port-Lockroy (British Antarctic Survey Base) accommodated us. When a penguin is walking to, or from, the shore and encounters a stranger—as long as it is not a leopard seal—they will stop and wait for the stranger to move off before continuing with their journey; a unique demonstration of accommodation.

The Antarctic, being very quiet, pure and peaceful, is a great place to learn about the interaction of animals. If only all humans could have such tolerance and understanding and live with their neighbours in this co-operative way, then nations and all individuals would have a guaranteed peace for life. I oppose authoritarian rule, where an individual or nation thinks they know best, and forces others to adopt their way.

How can you/we make these visions/dreams happen?
My dreams are lofty but they have a sound basis in ethics. We can gradually attain our dreams by following these simple rules:

- Focusing on attaining sustainable peace by avoiding conflicts and effectively resolving current conflicts
- Having more understanding and tolerance and being more accommodating of others
- Treasuring and living by sincere, commonly accepted and sound ethics
- Finding a way of establishing sustainable population control and of safeguarding and distributing scarce resources
- Being less selfish, more considerate and sharing resources fairly
- Not practicing acts of power that favour greed for wealth accumulation

We can all agree that the benefits of having peace surpass the benefits of having wealth and power. Treating each other with justice and questioning our moral ethics are prerequisites to attaining long-lasting peace. We should all work towards restoring a common standard of ethics and justice and building equity. Equitable societies have no reason to compete. There is no hope for the future unless we come to terms with this and change the dogmatic perceptions and motives of others for our own, collective higher good.

15. Marc de Klerk (Netherlands/Bosnia-Herzegovina)—
Entrepreneur, (NGO) Project Developer ansd Freelance Consultant in the Western Balkans [3]

What are your visions/dreams for the future of the planet?

I don't dream realistic things. I dream of beautiful people and love and high endurance sports and of flying and of surfing. I love to dream, but it's not really realistic.

I also cry, sometimes out loud and many times in private. I cry mostly out of happiness. This happiness is something different from feeling happy—this happiness is a realisation of the truth. This is the most beautiful thing I know: the truth. This is a layer on top of whatever you want: love, friendship, family, romance, sex, work, politics, economics, psychiatry, everything! Unfortunately this layer is not used very much around the world.

When I notice that someone has forgotten to put the layer of truth on top, I get disappointed but that doesn't affect me that much. I have decided to sit and watch when something disappoints me, unless it is within my power to change it. When I notice the layer of truth, I cry because of that happiness and I feel truly connected to myself, the world and my spiritual environment. I rarely dream about that. I often notice or feel the possibility of it, though, and I hope that this layer will be used by people more often, because it is so beautiful.

What particular experiences in your life shaped your vision?

Many! There were many special experiences in my life. Death is one of the most apparent ones. I have often wondered why we seem to get so sad about death and I think it's because we notice the truth—there is nothing we can do about it—death has an intrinsic layer of truth. And the beauty of the truth makes us cry. It's too bad that death has such a negative connotation in our culture, because it blinds us to see this layer. Another experience is music, also complete and intrinsically true—except for bad music, and the way to realise that music is bad is to notice that it doesn't affect our emotions. Listening to real music makes me cry as well for the exact same reason.

How can you/we make these visions/dreams happen?

We have to concentrate on our environment: colleagues, friends and family, home, culture and the city and nature. All this is supposed to be layered with the truth and that would make it truly beautiful, healthy and peaceful. Secondly,

---

3. Marc worked as a Peace Flame Project Developer 2003-4, was with MDK Development 2005-6 and has worked with Vision EDG since 2007.

we have to concentrate on ourselves and make sure we dress ourselves with this layer of truth: in our love, spirit, hope, friendship, work and other daily activities (including the most simple ones) and all these other aspects that make life interesting (nothing in life is uninteresting). These two strategies will make us live life in truth and this beauty will make us cry more—cries of happiness!

16. Olesya Koba (The Ukraine)—
Worker and Translator for Fred Foundation (Ukraine)

The destiny of a person, their way of life, is marked by their birth. It's not only a matter of which lucky or unlucky star we are born under but more a case of which family, or genealogical tree we are born into.

My mother was born into a large, friendly family, where nobody was indifferent to the life of others. On holidays, the whole family gathered at the table and we cooked together. It was often crowded but always very joyful and interesting, too. If something bad happened, then the whole family came together to help each other, too. When my grandmother, died my mother was only twenty. At that time, my mother was dating my father, but the whole family felt sorry for her, as she was the youngest child to be without a mother.

From early childhood, I've received much care and parental love. My father carried me everywhere until the moment that my younger brother, Vasyl was born. From that moment, he replaced me in my father's arms. But my father's love and care was enough for both of us.

Fifteen years ago, my father became the director of an orphanage. One day my father took me to the school. There I saw little children who only knew the words 'mother' and 'father' from books. Nobody helped those children to go to bed in the evening; nobody said "good night" to them. No mother woke them in the morning. They called my father, 'father' as they did not have their own fathers. These little children knew that every child must have a mother so whenever a new woman came to the school they asked, "Are you my mother?" This struck me the most and stayed in my memory.

When I see such children now I am always reminded of this moment. My brother and I studied in a normal school and our parents both worked. My father brought home the sorrow and pain of these children and so their life paralleled my own. We learned about everything that was going on in the boarding school and in this way my father taught us to think of those in a worse situation than our own.

I remember one of my birthday parties very well. I was sixteen and it was New Year's Day. We invited many people and my father should have been the first to congratulate me, but he had to go to the boarding school. There were troubles with the heating system and he did not come back until the following morning, wet and tired. I was very sad and angry because he had been with the children at the orphanage and not with me. But these thoughts were soon replaced with another; these children needed him most that night. Slowly they came into my life in this way and these 'grains of goodness' became embedded in our minds by my parents. Later, we met Jan Ebeltjes, who was the first person I encountered, other than my father, who cared about these suffering children.

I was a student when I got to know about Jan. My father told me how much he helped Ukrainian orphans, especially those in boarding schools in Perechyn and Chynadiyevo. He put so much effort, energy and time into helping them that I used to ask myself what would have happened without him. I also asked myself why he did it. It was difficult for him to win the trust of local and regional government officials. People were unfamiliar with the idea of 'charity' and wondered what he hoped to gain from these activities.

In 2002, we met another good person, Fred Matser. He is one of the most inspiring people that I know and made me think about my own choices in my life. He invited Jan to work for the Fred Foundation (Ukraine) and Jan asked my father for help in finding a place that really needed their aid. My father suggested Perekhrestya.

Once male orphans became too old for their various orphanages they were re-homed in Perekhrestya. Dozens lived together there in one big room that was really just a hut; there was no heating, water or furniture, apart from beds and they had no shoes, underwear or soap. Most had no jobs and no income for their survival. Nobody cared about them. Just a few of them were working in a local village for food.

When my father heard about their situation, he was very upset. He wanted to do something to help, but no-one was interested. I went there with Jan and was really shocked by what I saw; it was even worse than we had expected. It's impossible to describe how bad the conditions were. You would need to experience it for yourself. Fortunately, Jan and the Fred Foundation decided to help these young people.

I cried all night after what I had seen and, from that day, I realised my life had changed forever. When we had spoken with the youngsters in Perekhrestya they had told us: "We want to be like normal people; to have a normal life, a family and a home." This had made me realise that I wanted to use my life to help. Jan asked my father about this, suggesting that I was perhaps still too young to be involved, as the work would be difficult and demanding. But my father answered calmly and clearly, saying: "The time is ripe for her to choose her future life." And so I did.

Thanks to the Fred Foundation, many of the youngsters from Perekhrestya now have their own homes and families. One of my greatest joys has been when one of them calls me to say things are going well or that they have a new baby.

Unfortunately, our work continues to grow as the situation in the Ukraine has worsened. Plenty more orphans and homeless people are coming our way and it is not possible for us to take all their sorrow and pain away or solve all their problems. But at least I have the possibility of doing something to help and I have come to I realise that to give is more joyful than to receive.

A lot of Ukrainian people thank God that they had the possibility to meet Fred and Jan and I am grateful to God that I met them as well.

May God help you in all that you do too.

17. Indra Kumari Khattri Tamang (Nepal)—
Housewife

What are your visions/dreams for the future of the planet?
Our planet is beautiful. Its beauty should be maintained. I dream our planet may be healthy, friendly, secure and spiritually linked between human beings, animals and plants. The active players on our planet are human beings. Our main concern has been to maintain a friendly environment for human beings. Yet, in my view, a whole ecosystem approach will help our planet to be healthy. Our planet provides food, shelter, energy, and other necessities to all forms of life. People can live happy, healthy and secure lives and enjoy our planet if they can love one another.

What particular experiences in your life shaped your vision?
I would like to share one experience which I consider a major event in my life. When I was about ten years old, I experienced an accident that totally changed my life. I fell into an open fire and burnt most of the left side of my face. Due to that accident, I also lost one of my eyes. I was unconscious for two days. I was treated for over a month at a local health post, but due to a lack of proper medicine and training of the health workers, I did not recover fully. My brother then helped me to travel to Kathmandu, the capital of Nepal, where I was operated on several times. My burnt face was healing, but I was left with ugly scars.

Someone suggested that I visit a German nurse who had been working locally as a volunteer for several years. Seeing my condition, she told me that she would do everything that she could to help me, saying that she regarded seeing me as her Christmas gift from God. Due to her kindness, I was put in touch with Fred Matser, who has such a compassionate heart. He invited my brother, Man Bahadur, and I to come and visit him in Hilversum, in the Netherlands, and arranged for some treatment for me there. This made me realise that we can work together to help each other make the planet healthy.

In rural areas, nature may be healthy but that does not imply that the whole planet is healthy. Environmental issues have become complex, and I feel we no longer know how to respect nature. We expect to use nature for our own benefit, but nature has its own law, and what I would call 'nature spirits'. We humans have our own spirits, too, and I think it is important to start to think of both as natural. Spirituality is natural. The planet is also a part of spirituality and nature plays a large part in that. A healthy planet helps us develop a good spirituality, which is good for people, animals and plants. From the time of my accident, I have been helped by various people in the Netherlands, Germany, Norway and Nepal, and this gave me the feeling that the spirit of nature and goodness exists in human beings. It may exist in different forms in different places, and may be due to 'God' or a 'supreme spirit', but it does exist.

How can you/we make these visions/dreams happen?
I am just one woman. Our planet has billions of people like me yet each with our own individuality and individual life process. The important thing is to use our individual capacities for the good of the whole planet. In Nepal, we have a saying that if one person spits, it dries up rapidly, but if hundreds spit, then it will turn into a river. Similarly, I believe that my warm, good or positive spirit can contribute to the healthy spirit of our beautiful planet. I ask from my heart that the billions people on our planet join hand in hand to help make our planet healthy and to link with heavenly spirit.

18. Ervin Laszlo (Italy, Hungary, USA)—
Author, President, The Club of Budapest

Global transformation—how I came to be involved with it, and what my involvement has taught me:
There was not a single pivotal experience that has led to my involvement with the problems and possibilities of global transformation, but a whole series of events that 'drove' me in this direction—without my conscious will (but not against it). The series began with a seemingly innocent phone-call from Professor Richard ('Dick') Falk of Princeton University's Centre of International Studies. This was in 1972, if I remember correctly. I was teaching at the time in the Philosophy Department of the State University of New York at Geneseo, in the quiet rural regions of Upstate New York. I was deeply immersed in systems theory, attempting

to elucidate the philosophical implications of thinking in terms of systems that are integral wholes rather than in terms of isolated or semi-isolated entities that are, at best, fragments of more inclusive systems. I had just begun to develop the evolutionary implications of what I called 'Systems Philosophy', moving towards what later came to be known as 'General Evolution Theory' (that is, a general theory of evolution as it applies to physical systems, living systems, consciousness, and even to the universe as a whole system).

The call from Dick Falk was unexpected: while I had known of him and his work in the context of a project called World Order Models Project, I knew nothing about what the models were, how successful they were, and what problems they encountered. I explained this to him, yet Dick was not to be deterred and asked me to come to Princeton to give a series of seminars on the 'world system.' He said that it would be sufficient that I present my conception of complex evolving systems; he and other members of the Centre's faculty would see what could be made of them in regard to the world system. I was dubious, but the challenge was intriguing, and I accepted. This was the first, and as it turned out fateful, step on the way to my involvement with questions of global transformation.

The other steps can be summarised more briefly. Out of my seminars at Princeton came a book, *A Strategy for the Future: The Systems Approach to World Order*' It was read by Aurelio Peccei, the visionary founder, and at the time President, of the Club of Rome, who was just then thinking about how to state the more human implications of the Club's first report, the legendary, *Limits to Growth*. Aurelio asked me to set up a project to look at what aspirations people and societies have in regard to the future, and whether these aspirations could be fulfilled on a small and finite planet. Within six months, I pulled together a small but enthusiastic team of young scholars and budding activists. We developed a project; Aurelio as well as Alex King, the co-Founder of the Club of Rome, liked it, and I set about implementing it.

Since this required vast international contacts (and there was no e-mail and internet at the time), Aurelio asked the Executive Director of the UN's 'think tank,' the Institute for Training and Research (UNITAR) to invite me to work at the Institute as a Special Fellow. I moved to the city, brought the core team with me, and we began to work. The Club of Rome Report was completed in about a year and was published first in English and then in various other languages under the title, *Goals for Mankind: The New Horizons of Global Community*. I returned to my quiet, upstate campus and that, I thought, was the end of my involvement with global issues.

But another phone call came a few weeks later, this time from Dr. Davidson Nicol, the Executive Director of UNITAR. He asked me to represent the Institute at the founding of the United Nations University in Tokyo. I could not say, "No" and one thing then led to another. First I was asked to head the research on the New International Economic Order, which was to be adopted at the UN General Assembly at a special session in the autumn of 1980. When it came to voting at that session, the USA, the UK, and Western Germany, three major economic powers, announced that they would 'not participate': the entire NIEO project was forthwith dropped.

The UN Secretary-General Kurt Waldheim asked what other ideas I might have to re-launch the dialogue between North and South, and I suggested a systemic concept. Let's not attempt to move from the nation-state level directly to the North and South level, but prepare the ground by helping the South to be an economically more equal partner. This meant creating integration, organisations among groups of developing countries, following the model pioneered by the European Community. The project 'Regional and Interregional Cooperation among Developing Countries' was adopted by UNITAR and a high-level 'Panel of Eminent Persons' was created to present the conclusions to the Secretary-General.

This took another four years of intense effort. At its conclusion, I decided to spend a year at our Tuscan farmhouse, returning to my concerns with systems and evolutionary theory. I did not have a whole year, however, since first the Vice-Chancellor of the UN University Prof. Kinhide Mushakoji, and then the newly elected Director-General of UNESCO, Prof. Federico Mayor, called on me to collaborate and advise.

In the meantime, I recalled the promise I had made to Aurelio Peccei on the occasion of the ten-year anniversary meeting of the Club of Rome: to try to create a sister-club made up of artists, writers, and spiritual leaders. The rationale for this was the recognition that addressing leaders in politics and business is not sufficient to move beyond lip-service to new ideas and strategies: we must also mobilise the thinking, the imagination, and the creativity of people in civil society.

When I presented this concept at the Third World Congress of Hungarians in Budapest, Jozsef Antal, the Prime Minister of Hungary, who was present at the event, called on me to set up such a club in the city of Budapest. I accepted gratefully, and suggested that we should call it 'The Club of Budapest'.

As this brief account indicates, my involvement with global problems and transformation came about as a series of challenges that both surprised and intrigued me. They ended by involving me intellectually as well as emotionally. For the insight that dawned on me—and it is time that I get to this point—was that we live in critical times.

The critical nature of our times is not just that they harbour dangers, but that they offer unprecedented opportunities for change. And, above all, that the chance to seize the opportunities for positive change is not limited to a few who have the power and the wealth: it is in the hands of everyone. For fundamental change, I realised, does not come about by throwing technology or even money at the problems, nor by attempting to cover them up by political rhetoric or mitigate them with cosmetic solutions. It only comes about by a deep-seated transformation that is nothing less than a shift in the dominant civilisation.

A civilisation is the expression of the culture shared by people, whatever their place in society. Culture, in turn, is the expression of the thinking, the feeling, the priorities and perceptions of individuals: in one word, of their consciousness. Thus to renew our crisis-prone civilisation we need to evolve our consciousness. This is a realistic project, because our consciousness is not an isolated entity, limited to our body and brain. It is a powerful emitter that is constantly in communication with the world at large, including the consciousness of our fellows in society.

The evolved consciousness of one individual can spread and grow and if it resonates with the thinking of an entirely new culture, it can shift the nature of the whole civilisation. This must be a global shift, for the dominant civilisation—the mechanistic, manipulative, and fragmented civilisation of the industrial age—is already global. However, the new civilisation, unlike the current one, need not and must not be monolithic. It can be organic and 'systemic', nurturing diversity and at the same time seeking unity. These are the principal insights on which the Club of Budapest was founded. Its twin mottos express and illustrate them: "You Can Change the World" and "Toward a Planetary Civilisation."

For more see: *www.clubofbudapest.org*

19. Irene van Lippe-Biesterfeld (Netherlands)—
HRH Princess of the Netherlands,
Chair of The Lippe-Biesterfeld Nature College Foundation

What are your visions/dreams for the future of the planet?
If we could learn to listen to each other, the effect could be quite dramatic. Often we are afraid to be open to other ways of thinking and we react according to our own cultural background or our own little sub-culture. To open up and listen to others might bring about new views and that might bring change. It seems we prefer to stick to our old ways, even when they are uncomfortable or even painful, rather than to step into the unknown. This fear of change and the unknown makes us judgmental and too often intolerant. This makes it almost impossible to really listen and hear.

How can you/we make these visions/dreams happen?

I have discovered through my work, bringing people in contact with nature and opening up to the oneness of all that lives, that nature is a place that makes no difference between cultures, or species. It is a non-judgmental surrounding, all and everything can be just as it is, open. This makes it a place of healing and bonding, also to our own inner nature.

Being in nature can help us humans to listen to who we really are, to open up to what binds us and what we can learn from our differences. And we can learn much, not only from our fellow humans, but also from all life forms around us. This creates far greater results than being enclosed in our well-known and seemingly safe ways, or 'little boxes'. The non-human part of nature can teach us and help us to open our hearts and get to know our inner nature.

What particular experiences in your life shaped your vision?

Through my trans-cultural work, I have learned to listen to other ways, thoughts and starting points than my own cultural background; it has brought me new insights and broadened my views. Through listening and being open to the ways of non-human life forms, I have learned that, in effect, we are part of the web of life. The illusion of separateness has only brought pain and endless suffering. This divide from nature is what needs to be healed in all of us humans. Being acutely aware of the oneness of all life brings us to acknowledge the wonders of synchronicity. A whole new world opens up, and this can bring a continuous joy and gentle compassion for life. If we would make the oneness of life our starting point, we would take care that all our decisions would be non-detrimental to life around us, because we are in fact one.

20. Ruslan Lokotosh (The Ukraine)—
Ukrainian Orphan

I don't know my parents, I have never met them. When I look at myself then I know that my parents must have been gypsies, because I'm dark-skinned and have black hair. I've never tried to find my parents, because a lot of Gypsy people have the name Lokotosh, so it would be very difficult to find them. Besides, I'm not interested in them; they were not interested in me. They abandoned me after my birth.

I spent the first six years of my life in an orphanage in the village of Cinadiewo. After that they brought me to a boarding school in Chaslivtsi. It was terrible. No-one loved me and nobody was interested in me. A few times I ran away from the school and I lived in the streets of Uzhgorod. But the police always brought me back to the school. I was always afraid about the future because I had no place to go, no family at all.

I knew that, in time, when I became seventeen I would have to leave the school. And I wondered, "What then?" When I was in the last class at school I was offered a job and a place to live in the village Perregrestya. Other boys in my class also planned to go there, so I agreed.

The first weeks in Perregrestya I just cried. It was so difficult for me. There was no job and the promised living conditions were actually extremely bad. We had no food, no clothes and no one took care of us. We were settled in a stable and we ate the same food that was given to the pigs. Escaping was not possible as our passports were taken from us and anyway where would we go?

We had no idea about the world around us; we just had our own (terrible) world. I always thought that, although I am living in a terrible world, there must also be a 'normal' world for 'normal' people but that this world was not open to me. I now view my life in Perregrestya as a really traumatic experience. In the group, there were ranks and I had one of the lowest. I was often beaten by others and several times I planned to kill myself. After a few years in Perregrestya a Dutch man, Jan Ebeltjes, appeared one day. He came with a very pretty girl called Olesya Koba, who was translating for him. Jan spoke with us and took an interest in us. He bought us a lot of food and clothes and for the first time in my life someone was taking care of me.

I didn't know what was going on, but Jan and Olesya had never-ending discussions with a lot of important people. One day Jan told us that the stable where we lived was going to be closed and that the Fred Foundation was going to buy apartments for us. I couldn't believe it and started laughing. Jan asked us to be patient, but he and the Foundation kept their promise and gradually our new homes were purchased. Finally, the day came when I moved out of the stable. I will never forget that day. The Fred Foundation bought a house in the village of Irshava, far in the mountains. The house was big, so Jan asked me if I would like to live there with some of the others from the group. I said that I would like to live with my friend Roman. We have now lived in Irshava for two years. Roman is married and I have a girlfriend. We are very happy; we have work and very good contact with our neighbours.

Often, in the morning I wake up and listen to the birds singing. Then I think about my life back in Perregrestya and remember the screaming and fighting in the group. Then I remind myself that now I am free and independent and a member of the normal world.

I am very, very thankful.

21. Prof. Ruud Lubbers (Netherlands)—
Prime Minister of the Netherlands 1982–1994 and United Nations High Commissioner for Refugees 2001–2005

What are your visions/dreams for the future of the planet?
"We are the times" has become known as one of the most famous sayings of Augustinus. There are two important dimensions to this saying. Firstly, it underlines the responsibility of us, human beings. We cannot afford to be fatalistic. Although people are the word in God's story, in the fulfilment of history we cannot hide away behind God as the mover behind everything. We cannot just complain about 'the times' that we have to endure. We had better respond to the challenges. There is a thin line between the 'hubris' of humankind wanting to build a tower of Babel to reach heaven and humankind leaving it all to God. Augustinus, a man of faith, considered it useful to point to human responsibility. Secondly, this saying underlines the importance of 'we', rather than 'me' or 'I'. 'We' is about society and in order to make it possible for everybody to belong to 'we', this begins with the understanding that everyone is important and should be seen and treated as relevant and co-responsible. There was, and is always, a tendency to exploit people (and nature), but 'we', in its very essence, means that we have to celebrate life: all human beings and the diversity of life, including nature.

How can you/we make these visions/dreams happen?
At the beginning of this third millennium there are new opportunities to be aware of the inter-generational dimensions of humankind: 'we' includes the generations before us and the generations to come. Also, we have become more aware that the diversity of life includes us, human beings; inviting us not to exploit, but to celebrate life.

Half a millennium ago, we enjoyed Enlightenment; a very positive word, which liberated human beings as actors or drivers of history. But at the very same time, it introduced the exaggeration of 'the economy' as well as systematic exploitation. Enlightenment also brought us the concept of democratic states.

Today we have become aware that politics is only one dimension of life. Business and not-for-profit initiatives are just as important. Therefore the magic of 'good society' or of 'health and harmony' is inclusive thinking which complements different avenues of life.

The potential of our times, the beginning of the third millennium, is even more challenging because, living in relation with generations to come and living really together, has to be practised in a globally interconnected world.

This is not so much a question of good governance or a managerial fix; it begins with mutual respect. Not respect for power but for the diversity of cultures and life itself. Erasmus of Rotterdam[4] was rightly considered a great humanist. But this same Erasmus, when asked to what purpose he was living, simply responded: "to honour and serve God and in doing so to find happiness". The churchman Augustinus[5] was a philosopher and theologian and a key figure in the development of Western Christianity.) invited us to take responsibility by using the term 'we', and the humanist, Erasmus, calling on individual responsibility, conveyed the same message. It is now up to us, half a millennium later, to move the world by and to harmony.

What particular experiences in your life shaped your vision?

During my walk through life I have been privileged to have so many experiences that enriched me; too many to tell.

However, it has been especially gratifying to help overcome violence where people, by frustration, have turned to violence. I remember in particular the Moluccan people in the Netherlands, who seemed to change once they sensed that there was some respect for their history.

It was also so gratifying to contribute to the 'mastering' of the arms race in the times of Reagan, Bush and Gorbachev and, in so doing, to overcome a fundamental rift in Dutch society. It was all about not giving in to cynicism and instead investing in projects such as the 'Hoffnung Project', which sought to promote understanding between people in different countries in Eastern Europe and to support the development of new social structures.

It has also been so gratifying for me, in my role as the UN Commissioner for Refugees, to work with and to start to understand the realities of refugees, especially refugee-women/mothers. I especially tried to promote this role in the refugee camps and communities and they told me they were touched by this support. They also said "If only it would only be possible to continue our role when we return to our home villages" and so I tried to encourage this as well.

Finally, it was also so gratifying to be able to contribute to the Earth Charter Initiative. The Earth Charter is about the way forward for humanity. It is about values and action. It is about 'do's' and 'don'ts' as well as the celebration of life. It reflects the need to do justice to democratic politics without interfering in, or being dominated by, religion.

---

4. A Dutch humanist and theologian who lived in the fifteenth and sixteenth centuries.

5. Augustine of Hippo (354-430AD) was a philosopher and theologian and a key figure in the development of Western Christianity.

The charter is ecumenical, as it invites people of all religions, or no religion at all, to co-operate in the spirit of mutual respect. It is about living up to generations to come in a more and more interconnected world. It is about giving direction to all institutions: political, national as well as international and supranational, business, not for profit and from local all the way to global. It is also about the complementarity of law and ethics.

The inception of the Earth Charter is very much related to our phase in history where we began to become aware of how we need to overcome:

- the weaknesses of capitalism and socialism
- the cold war, the arms race and the politics of 'domination'
- the era of colonialism and apartheid
- the exclusion of women in institutions
- the exploitation of natural resources, exhausting them without respect for nature
- the clash of civilisations

22. Chris Matser (Netherlands)—
Housewife

What are my dreams for the future of the planet?
I find it challenging to move beyond the grim news of global warming, terrorist attacks and wars that are currently happening around the world. I can feel overwhelmed by extreme poverty, suffering, injustice and polarisation of religions and borders. So this question helps make me aware that maybe I need a dream for a better planet. Not because I know how the future should be, but to realise that I have a choice to open or contract to the future. Martin Luther King's words, "I had a dream…" penetrated many hearts and minds and reminded us that the seed of change often starts with a dream.

My dream for the future is grand and simple. It would be that all hearts unite. Free from barriers we would be ONE, united in kindness and love.

How do you/we make this happen?
Seeing beyond our independence to accept our interconnectedness.

What particular experiences in my life shaped my vision?
Being in the presence of innocent babies and playful small children remind me that we were all born with pure hearts!

23. Hiroshi Motoyama Ph.D, Ph.D (Japan)—
Scientist, Author, Psychic and Shinto Priest;
President of the Motoyama Institute for Life Physics (Tokyo, Japan) and
the California Institute for Human Sciences (CIHS)[6]

Coexistence with Nature

From childhood I was brought up to chant holy *sutras*[7] and practice asceticism[8] including waterfall asceticism[9] in mountains. Through such strict practices, I was able to realise that not only the universe, but also micro-entities, such as atoms and quanta[10] are filled with God's love, wisdom and creative power. This enables all things to co-exist in a certain order within a given time space. In the present age, humans use and deal with nature just according to their life needs and selfish purposes. They have no idea how to respect nature as phenomena filled with, and supported by, God's love and creative power. Unless humans become aware that nature is holy, and that we too are manifestations of God's creative power, we will not be able to survive, for we cannot live here on this planet without nature. We need to return to the old and wise human ways of co-existing with nature and respecting nature as God's creation.

24. Caroline Myss (USA)—
Author, Teacher, Medical Intuitive

What are your visions/dreams for the future of the planet?

My hopes and dreams for the planet are rooted in a vision of co-operation, a vision that I know we of this generation will never see come to pass. Nor will the next generation or many to follow. The people of this planet have yet to learn co-operation, sharing, forgiveness, and respect for one another's religion, traditions, and cultures. We have now entered the cycle of shortages and we are now fighting wars as to who will control the last of the resources on this planet.

---

6. *www.cihs.edu*, Encinitas, USA.

7. Holy verses in Buddhism and Hinduism based on the sermons of the Buddha.

8. Practices involving self-denial, abstinence and austerity in order to facilitate the attainment of a high spiritual and moral state.

9. A Japanese practice involving standing underneath a cold, powerful mountain waterfall for a brief time while chanting prayers. It is regarded as an aid to purification and spiritual development.

10. In physics a quantum (*plural: quanta*) is an indivisible entity of energy. For instance, a photon, being a unit of light is a 'light quantum'.

First, we are fighting over oil; next, water. My hope is that somehow, in some way, the truth that fighting resolves nothing and that hoarding and greed are the true cancers on this earth will finally penetrate into the politics of humanity.

How can you/we make these happen?

The only way anyone can make this happen is by example and by confronting the magnitude of the crises we face. We cannot afford to believe that someone other than ourselves will make problems vanish or that the problems facing us are 'really not that bad'.

People in our contemporary spiritual culture prefer to only see the positive, blinding themselves to the depth of negativity in this world. While we must have faith and be agents for positive change, we must also be mature agents for change, which means we must be educated about what is taking place in our world and we must invest our life energy into activities of purpose.

What particular experiences in your life shaped your vision?

All of my many experiences, combined with my religious background, combined with my wonderful family and friends and my personal spiritual life—these are the ingredients that motivated me to think about these things. What else is there to think about?

25. Debby M. Noordhoff (Netherlands)—
Retired Person

What are your visions/dreams for the future of the planet?

That is not an easy question to answer, for one's first thought would automatically be to ask for peace and harmony, mutual love and understanding, provisions for the hungry, better education for our children, awareness and compassion of our earth's wounds, and the list goes on. . . . I have come to notice, however, that, during my entire life, I have had the tendency to focus on the underdog—the ones who're easily overlooked or even forgotten.

And so I share with you that my heart goes out to our troubled children who're wasting their precious lives away in un-safe schools and communities or in juvenile prisons, where spirits are often crushed and mangled, offering them little or no hope for a better, healthier and more self-fulfilling life, which every child so deserves. So my dream for the future of our planet is that we become aware, not only as individual nations, but throughout the world, that our children ARE our future and that the time has arrived for us to take better care of them.

How can you/ we make these happen?

I believe that this may be achieved if we can help these children restore hope and success in their lives and if we can re-establish communities based on mutual support, giving and receiving and founded on the basis of the key principles of respect, co-operation and shared responsibility.

What particular experiences in your life shaped your vision?

Oh yes! My sister Alice and her daughter Sara both work in a certain school district in the USA. We correspond on a regular basis and all too often I am confronted with letters that describe shootings, gang-related issues, fights, wounded students and parents who are worse than their children and incapable of communicating on a decent level. Here's an excerpt from one of her letters:

> "Things are hairy around this neighbourhood the past few weeks.
> Another shooting two nights ago. One of our expelled students again.
> This one was killed at sixteen. There is racial tension building up. The
> campus is crackling with it. We have had fights every day for the past
> four school days."

My heart wants to cry out to everyone to include these ill-fated children in our dreams of a better earth, for their often vacant (or very, very angry) eyes have witnessed more pain and frustration than many of us experience during a lifetime. Why punish them relentlessly for who they were? Can we not instead teach them WHO they truly are?

26. Thomas van Nouhuys (Netherlands)—
Schoolboy

What are your visions/dreams for the future of the planet?

That there is less poverty in the world. Because now, millions of people are dying for nothing. And I want to help these people in the future when I am older and wiser.

I also think that racism has to disappear because some people are not treated the way that they should be. I think that people have to know themselves better instead of looking at each other and blaming others. People are blaming other people a lot and they are not looking at themselves. If people looked at themselves more, then I think we would have a more functional society.

What particular experiences in your life shaped your vision?

I saw these kinds of things in the news and it makes me sick to see people without any water or food. It makes me feel that I have to do something, but unfortunately I am not really in a position to do so right now. Also, I see a lot of people in my school looking at others and talking about them and sometimes I do it too. It's quite tough at our age, but in the future I want to learn to look at myself more and have more self-knowledge.

How can you/ we make these dreams happen?

I want to start some projects in Africa or South America to do something for those people that haven't got anything. Kind of the same job that Fred is doing.

27. Rev. Alex L. Orbito (Phillipines)—
Spiritual Healer

What are your visions/dreams for the future of the planet?

That there will be a new Light of Life, filled with Love for each other, where violence has no more room. That we allow ourselves to be guided more by the heart and less by the mind. The heart unites, the mind separates.

How can you/ we make these happen?

Through our unity in desire, prayer and meditation to God, our dreams and heartfelt wishes will manifest. The key is to believe in our power to create and to eliminate all doubt.

What particular experiences in your life shaped your vision?

As a spiritual healer, almost all my life these visions have come to me in my dreams. The healing I do is only possible when I fully trust and believe in the divine healing power to cure, thus eliminating all doubt.

28. Matthew Parrish LaCasse (USA)—
Student

What are your visions/dreams for the future of the planet?

I dream that one day the end of extreme nationalism will lead to an all-accepting world.

What particular experiences in your life shaped your vision?
My travels made me realise this. I saw that though many people have many things in common, there is not one trait that everyone shares. That infers that in order to obtain peace, everyone must learn to accept the ideas and beliefs of others.

How can you/we make these dreams happen?
Share this idea with everyone. Everyone should be able to have their own beliefs, but no one should have the right to force their beliefs on others.

29. Jasmina Redzepagic-Avdagic (Bosnia-Herzegovina)—
Volunteer and Trauma Therapist,
Manager of the Peace Flame House, Tuzla

I am twenty-nine years old and live in Tuzla, in Bosnia-Herzegovina. I was born in Yugoslavia, and lived to see this country fall apart.

Due to the war, my parents had no work, and although I was the youngest of my family, I started working when I was sixteen years old in a theatre group. After high school, I started working in the NGO sector, where I am still active. Though working, I was also studying, successfully finishing pre-school teaching and psychology. Besides this, I have trained to work as a therapist with people who have experienced trauma, and am one of eight trainers of Creative Expression through Painting in my country.

During the summer of 2003 I volunteered to help paint the colourful walls of the Peace Flame House that was being built in my town, initiated and founded by Mr. Fred Matser. Today, this House is a beautiful socio-cultural centre for the citizens of Tuzla. Together with a group of other people I have contributed with my work since the House opened.

Through my work here, I had the pleasure of meeting Mr. Fred Matser and learned more about his different initiatives. I feel honoured to be a part of this one.

30. Floris Rost van Tonningen (The Netherlands)—
Entrepreneur

What are your visions/dreams for the future of the planet?
Picasso once said: "Every child is an artist. It's a challenge to remain an artist when you grow up." My dream for the future of the planet is that people revisit the wonder of childhood and get in touch with their inner child more often. With the

mind of a child, we can see the world in a fresh, joyful and unconditioned way.

The mind of a child is the key to escape from the mental prison that restricts us from living the passionate life of which we dream. I like to compare this with the physical phenomenon called gravity. All objects on earth are 'stuck' to earth because of the force of gravity. However, if an object reaches a certain escape velocity, it can break out of its gravitational field and enter into a freefall in space. Sometimes, people, too, are unwillingly stuck in such a field of inertia and have difficulties in breaking away. There are dreams, passions and ideas of which they are not always aware. But at the same time, there are constraining beliefs and preconceptions that keep them inert. Wouldn't it be nice if we could all make a freefall once in a while and start a new adventurous journey, just as one would if one had the mind of a child?

What particular experiences in your life shaped your vision?
I had my first freefall experience at the age of twenty-one. I had accumulated the escape velocity to leave my gravitational field and make a freefall into the unknown. Although it was a scary thought at first, the experience itself was liberating. I had just decided to quit my education at the university and start an internet company. At the time, the internet had just made its presence known and the possibilities were unprecedented. There was an opportunity, a strong passion to start an adventurous journey and enough support from the people closest to me to escape the field of gravity. This energy enabled me to overcome the forces that were keeping me from making this journey.

How can you/we make these vision/dreams happen?
Most journeys require a creative stimulus that inspires us to walk the talk and let energy find its destiny. If we are lucky, our friends and family already serve as the impetus for our adventures. But if we seek to leave our gravitational base, this stimulus might not always be found in our direct environment and new networks should therefore be consulted.

Still, there are quite a few barriers to overcome in finding a new source of inspiration. Where do you find these people and how do you get in touch with them? For some, this barrier is too high and inertia prevails.

With this in mind, I foresee an important role for technology. In some respect, globalisation has flattened the world and diminished the variety of several unique cultures and traditions.

On the other hand, technology, as one of the drivers of globalisation, has made the world smaller and yet a bigger place for a lot of people. It facilitates the exchange of ideas and unique stories all over the world, with almost no barriers.

Technology can help people break out of their patterns and get them to embrace fresh stimuli, perspectives, ideas and experiences. In a place where so many different people can interact, some interesting creative surprises are bound to happen and a technology-based inspiration network might come into existence!

31. Marika Verheijen (Spain)—
International Co-ordinator

What are your visions/dreams for the future of the planet?
That all people are able to realise the dreams and vision of their souls, so we can allow ourselves to fully live our passion and purpose in life.

How can you/we make these happen?
By uniting people, skills, talents and resources from across the world to inspire, empower and stimulate each other: *www.unitingpeople.com*, the civil empowerment platform can make our dreams come true!

What particular experiences in your life shaped your vision?
As a people's coordinator, I have always been amazed to witness the human empowerment and inspiration that comes from working together for a higher (soul-related) goal.

32. Ernest Volosin (The Ukraine)—
Ukrainian Orphan

My name is Ernest Volosin. I am twenty-four years old and this is my story. My parents left me after I was born. They saw that I had some mental problems. I grew up in several orphanages and boarding schools.

Besides a lot of bad moments, there were also good ones, but to grow up without the love of parents is very, very difficult. After a few terrible years in a boarding school in Chaslivtsi (for mentally ill children), it was time for me to find work, a place in society. But it was impossible, as no-one was interested in me and no-one would take care of me. A lot of my schoolmates disappeared; they tried to find a place in the streets of cities like Kiev and L'vov. I didn't. I was too afraid.

Then a man came to our school and he offered us a job and a home in a village called Perregrestya. He took me away and before I knew it I was locked up in a stable, together with thirty-five other young men with similar problems to mine.

There was not enough space; every metre of space was used. The only privacy I had was a mattress, and sometimes I had to share it with others in the group. Years passed. Sometimes we did not have enough food; we ate pig fodder and used snow to wash ourselves. We didn't have any underwear and they even took our shoes to make it impossible for us to escape. Sometimes one of us became ill and then they took him away and we would never see him again. After a few years, they brought a few girls to our place; girls with the same mental troubles that we had. The situation became very critical, because most of the boys were 'interested' in the girls. I fell in love with one of the girls called Lesya. But what could I do? I was one of the weakest of the group. How happy I was when Lesya told me that she loved me, too! After that, I shared my mattress with her. I was thankful to God that the other boys respected our relationship. Some of the other girls became pregnant and were sent away to other places. And so we lived our life, day by day, year by year...

Then in 2001 a car stopped near our stable. A man and a girl got out and started to speak with us. The man introduced himself as Jan and said he was working for the Fred Foundation. He spoke with us, he listened and gave advice. He brought a lot of goods, food and clothes. The most important thing for us was that he was interested in us, that he took care of us. To us he was like a father. Jan came often and went everywhere, trying to find a solution to our problems.

To cut a long story short, I am married to Lesya now.

We've got a nice apartment from the Fred Foundation and we are very happy. We have two little sons, Christian and Augustin. Lesya is a very good mother and I think that I'm a good father. We love our children very, very much, so we are different to our own parents. . . I have a job and we have a lot of friends. Sometimes Jan comes over to see how we are doing or to give us some advice. I think that Lesya and I are the happiest people in this world.

33. Herman Wijffels (USA/Netherlands)—
Executive Director of the World Bank; Former Chief Executive Officer, Rabobank, Netherlands.

What are your visions/dreams for the future of the planet?
Humankind has arrived at a crucial phase of its existence. We have become so numerous and the technologies that we apply so loaded for the earth as a living environment, that life itself is being threatened.

To continue with our present manner of life, a life of producing and consuming leads into a dead end and is therefore no option. I do not consider this understanding, shared by an ever- growing number of people, to be a condemnation of the phase in social development which is the result of the Enlightenment. I look at it as a logical and necessary step towards the development of the human consciousness. But at a certain moment, ideas that have functioned as carriers for a development stage have done their work. Holding on to those ideas too long leads to perverse effects. That is where we are right now, certainly in the Western world: at a point where the ideas on which our current way of life is based have a perverse effect.

The task that evolves from this insight is both clear and radical. We will have to acquire new understandings and ideas in order to get back on a maintainable path of development. Maintainable in the sense of not threatening for life as such and as in shaping the next phase of evolution. In other words: what is necessary is a next step—or is it a leap?—in human consciousness. Enlightened thinkers and scientists have already provided us with what would be an essential aspect of that: the understanding that everything, the earth with all forms of life on it and the entire cosmos, is one connected, interdependent whole. The consequences of that understanding for our way of life is far-reaching. Seen from a connection point of view, we wrong ourselves if we wrong others or, on a larger scale, if we eradicate other kinds.

Our present social and economic order is mainly based on rivalry and competition, on one living at the cost of the other, on the principle of survival of the fittest. If unity and connection become the starting point of view, everything will start to evolve around working together for the greater good, co-operation, sharing as in multiplying, surviving together. That would be a very radical, let alone revolutionary change, a change that will evoke a lot of resistance from vested interests, but at least one that is necessary for humankind to continue its evolutionary path.

How did these insights and understandings become my own?

The core answer is: by living with an open and receiving mind and by taking the signals of an ever-developing human consciousness seriously. Two circumstances in particular have helped me a great deal with that. The first is to have married a woman with a profound sense of purity and essence based on a spiritual attitude towards life. The other is that I have been given the opportunity for a long period of time to take responsibility at the highest level in several large and socially relevant organisations. Both circumstances have always given me the opportunity to reflect carefully on nature, on the purpose of life in general and on my own personal role in that. That has definitely contributed towards my development of consciousness.

34. David R. Woollcombe (UK)—
Founder and President, Peace Child International

What are your visions/dreams for the future of the planet?

My dreams are relentlessly optimistic: they have to be—I work with young people who will be alive in fifty years' time, when I will not. I have to think that the world will be happy, prosperous, peaceful and secure—with everyone living in a sustainable way in an inter-connected, richly diverse global village.

However, the media reminds me daily of the nightmare future—a world spiralling into ever-more-vicious resource wars, out-of-control population growth, environmental destruction, the rich getting richer, the poor poorer—and the whole world heading for a seemingly inevitable nuclear or ecological death.

The only way to retain the dream of the positive future is through faith—faith in the power of the spirit—God, if you like; and for me, faith in the endless inventiveness and good will—and love—inherent in the make-up of every human being. I see that most strongly in the eyes of young people—in almost all of whom shines the light of hope, the energy of love and the willingness to help and serve.

How can you/we make these happen?

The energy of love and hope in young people is what will make the positive world come about. Young people are demonstrably better at uniting nations than the adult so-called professionals; most of them are less greedy and more willing to make sacrifices for the sake of others (especially those yet unborn). That is why we call on adults to 'Give youth a chance to make poverty history. . .'—yet currently they don't: we need to change the attitude where adults see youth as something of a threat. They are a threat, of course: their youth, strength, beauty, sexuality, charm, sense of fun are all qualities that people lose as they get older.

But older people have experience, powers of reflection, judgment, technical skills and human contacts that are invaluable to young people. Therefore the answer to 'making my positive dream happen' is a real partnership—an equal, loving and respectful partnership—between youth and elders. An inter-generational embrace, which I call 'co-management'—which delivers harmony between age groups and thence between ethnicities, nationalities, and—ultimately—between the poor and the prosperous, the oppressed and the oppressor.

What particular experiences in your life shaped your vision?

Sitting in the Cathedral of St John the Divine, in New York, one day I found myself without money (as usual) to put in the collecting pot. In prayer, I considered my general uselessness—but I had just started Peace Child and it came to me, as though in a word from God—"Don't worry about the money you might have put in the pot. You are giving your life to Me through your work for Peace Child…" I reflected on that for a moment: to give a life is a pretty big donation. In giving mine—I had the right to ask others to give a little of theirs, especially young people.

Governments throughout history have required young people to give their lives in warfare. They are still doing so today: my realisation at that point is that we should be requiring young people to be giving their lives to the regeneration of the planet—to creating peace, an end to poverty, sustainable lifestyles, etc. The detail on the ways to do that follow from that initial commitment. Many other moments have reminded me of that initial gift: rewards such as seeing Russian and American children embrace in real love during performances of Peace Child in Moscow—spelling the end of the Cold War with more certainty than any Presidential Treaty; also, seeing the pride on the faces of young people as they turn the pages of a Peace Child book they have had a hand in creating. St Francis said it so many years ago: "For it is in giving that we receive; in loving that we are loved." I have received more than I could possibly have expected in my life through my initial donation; I have been loved more than I have any right to be!

35. Glynda Yoder (USA)—
Spiritual Teacher and Friend

What are your dreams for the future?
My dreams are for when we have prepared in this time to navigate through the transition period ahead from our dysfunctional societies into societies that express all the Divine Goodness life has to offer. It is not a circling back to the past but rather a spiralling surge upward that has not yet been seen upon the earth.

How do we make this happen?
It will not happen by intending or wishing alone. There must be intent combined with very practical actions. Today, now, we must develop and refine technologies and interpersonal relating that will allow us to live well without the social, economic, and political structures of today. Those who have the innate instinct to seek a more conscious approach to life must honour such. If there is something that is yours to do, you must do it!

People must begin to connect with each other so that there is strength among them. When pushed, many will fall away. There does not need to be a majority. Throughout history the strength of the few has covered for the many.

What personal experiences contributed to these positions?

My personal awareness of such things began twenty-five years ago with visions and teachings. They were presented in lovingness so that I might have a larger perspective about what I would see in my world. They were given so that when there were catastrophic events, and what seemed to be utter chaos, I would know in my core that nothing was out of control; that the Creator/Loving One, and those aligned with Him in the unseen, kept the effects of man's actions in check, and aided the earth in righting herself. The teachings were to create comfort that nothing would occur that was not known in advance.

It was to know that the Creator/Loving One would seed the earth with His people who would hear and be conscious. And that these persons would act like individual drops of white paint dropped into coloured paint, affecting the tone of the world in which they had been born. They would be the source of change and hope. Success would depend upon humans. Divine Law requires the vote of humans. With this vote the God Force could combine so that both sides of reality, the seen and the unseen, could co-operate towards a positive outcome. The course of mankind would be charted by the vote of all humans under the Law of Cause and Effect[11].

The chartings are being adjusted daily by our choices on a collective basis. Of crucial importance are those individuals who do not act as victims but rather claim their right to choose from strength according to their conscience. We each cast our vote by our thoughts, emotions, and how we choose to live our lives. This is not a casual issue in pivotal times. Our Destiny will depend upon it.

36. Michael Young (UK)—
School Student

What are your visions/dreams for the future of the planet?

My dream is that poverty, war and cruelty will end and the world will be free of unfairness. Right now the world is sad and corrupt and many people are oblivious to how well off they are.

How can you/we make these happen?

By all working together and by thinking of others; by doing all we can and by changing our ways; by following good principles; by taking from the rich and giving to the poor and by putting our mind, body and soul into making a better world.

---

11. Described as the Law of Karma in Indian philosophy.

What particular experiences in your life shaped your vision?

I have been with my mother to medical camps in India and seen how some people live. The only way to know what it is really like is to see it for yourself, otherwise most posters, pictures, etc. only just lightly affect you. If you go and see the people who need our help then you can't help but feel bad that you are living in a nice, warm house with heating, a car, food and water. Then you realise the truth and that action must be taken.

Photo © Jeremiah Sullivan

Afterword

As human beings we are in a very critical phase of our evolution. Throughout the world human beings have managed to desecrate the environment, flounder, pillage, murder, go to war, cause the extinction of other species and risk their own extinction. We are the only animal on this planet that is capable of racism, bigotry, prejudice, and torture. We kill our own kind most frequently in the name of God. On the other hand, we are also the only creature that asks ourselves:

- Who am I?
- What is the meaning and purpose of my existence?
- Where do I come from?
- What happens to me after I die?
- Do I have a soul?
- Does God exist? If God exists, does God care about us?

We are capable of self-awareness and we can consciously participate in our own evolution. At this critical moment, it seems nature is asking us to make a choice. Continue to behave in the old manner and destroy ourselves and our beautiful planet or, through conscious evolution, participate in the next quantum leap in the creative elements and forces of the universe.

The universe has chosen to become self-conscious through the human nervous system. It is our privilege and responsibility to nurture this great gift. The eminent physician and researcher, Dr. Jonas Salk[12] has said the next phase of hu-

---

12. Jonas Edward Salk (1914-1995) an American physician and researcher known for his development of the polio vaccine.

man evolution will be 'metabiological evolution'. 'Meta' means beyond. Therefore, metabiological evolution is the evolution of consciousness and ultimately, the evolution of the consciousness of consciousness.

Dr. Salk also said, "Survival of the fittest will be replaced by survival of the wisest". Wisdom is that knowledge which nurtures well-being: well-being of life, well-being of nature, well-being of the environment, and well-being of civilisation. This well-being cannot come about through material means. It can only come about when critical masses of people in the world become true visionaries and leaders by actualising their full potential and helping others to actualise their full potential as well. Four fundamental human traits must be activated in order to accomplish this:

1. The art of being
2. The art of feeling
3. Clarity of thinking
4. Service and action without selfish motivation

In his book, Fred Matser goes through important key principles that can help activate these four fundamental human capacities. Of particular fascination to me are the sections that deal with information being accessed transcendentally, functional choice-making, self-empowerment, and the Natural Law of Cyclical, Evolutionary Creation. However, what is more important to me is that Fred has not just spoken about these principles but that he has lived them. I will not go over his numerous accomplishments and achievements and the humanitarian causes to which he has contributed. None other than the former President of the USSR Mikhail Gorbachev has eloquently described these in his Foreword to this book. All I can say is that the strongest message that can be given to the world is our own life. Mahatma Gandhi once said, "My life is my message." How many of us can actually say that with confidence? Fred may be too modest to talk about his own accomplishments and contributions, but it is my distinct privilege to say to Fred, "If there were a few more people like you then the world would be transformed." Margaret Mead once said, "Never doubt that a small group of thoughtful, committed citizens can change the world. Indeed, it is the only thing that ever has." With Fred's help and with the help of others like him, we are creating an Alliance for a New Humanity with that goal.

Dr. Deepak Chopra,
President, Alliance for a New Humanity
www.anhglobal.org

Combine *your* TIME with this SPACE to express your own Visions for Change and INFINITE INSPIRATION here.

———

You may also like to consider the three questions answered by the contributors:

- What are your visions/dreams for the future of the planet?

- How can you/we make these visions/dreams happen?

- What particular experiences in your life shaped your vision?

Combine *your* TIME **with this SPACE to express**
your INFINITE INSPIRATION here…

Combine *your* TIME with this SPACE to express your INFINITE INSPIRATION here…

Combine *your* TIME with this SPACE to express your INFINITE INSPIRATION here…

Combine *your* TIME with this SPACE to express
your INFINITE INSPIRATION here...

Combine *your* TIME with this SPACE to express
your INFINITE INSPIRATION here…

Combine *your* **TIME with this SPACE to express your INFINITE INSPIRATION here…**